Contents

BEFORE YOU START READING, DOWNLOAD YOUR FREE DIGITAL ASSETS!

 **Advanced Rental Income Analyzer**

 **Advanced Fix & Flip Property Analyzer**

 **Due Diligence Checklist**

 **Wholesaling Deal Analyzer**

TWO WAYS TO ACCESS YOUR FREE DIGITAL ASSETS

Use the camera app on your mobile phone to scan the QR code or visit the link below and instantly access your digital assets.

or

www.clydebankmedia.com/rei-assets

 SCAN ME

 VISIT URL

Introduction

I've created this book for the pre-investor, the individual who knows little to nothing about real estate investing but wants to know if such a pursuit is right for them. Given the way that popular media portrays real estate investing, I want to dispel the misconceptions and expose you to the truths of real estate. I want to show you how you can go from merely surface-level knowledge on the topic to an in-depth understanding of real estate as a way to make money and grow your wealth. More than that, I want to show you what to do, when to do it, and how to take each step along the way.

My Story

I received degrees in computer engineering and economics from UC Irvine. Figuring that two degrees were not enough, I went on to earn my MBA from Stanford. I began my real estate journey when I was hired out of school to work on commercial real estate acquisitions at a private equity firm without having any prior real estate background. Talk about getting thrown into the deep end. I was taught by "immersion" about the ins and outs of commercial real estate. I oversaw deals across a wide range of asset classes, geographies, and sizes. I mastered the tools used by institutional investors to evaluate investments. Ultimately, I helped the firm evaluate, acquire, stabilize, or exit from investments that were worth at least $500 million upon exit. From there, I went on to become a global mergers and acquisitions manager for Ingram Micro, a Fortune 80 company. I then landed a role as the head of marketing analytics for Panda Restaurant Group, the parent company for Panda Express, Panda Inn, and Hibachi-San.

Working at Panda, I was supporting the real estate team using the knowledge I had acquired in my previous professional roles. Taking notice of my acumen for real estate, some of my colleagues began discussing the possibility of forming an investors club, a means of pooling our money to make investments. We ended up moving forward with this idea and calling it "the Weekend Fund," because everyone involved had full-time jobs. With my knowledge and experience, I put together a framework for how we should proceed. Before long I was the group's go-to analyst. The other group members trusted my judgment when it came to crunching the numbers, assessing potential risk, profits, etc. They would often run a potential deal by me, and I would work through the details, deciding if it was worth our time to take it further. Ultimately, any deals pursued by the Weekend Fund committee required unanimous consent from the membership. But unless a proposed deal could pass my analytical scrutiny, it would not be considered.

In our first two years, the Weekend Fund acquired and stabilized rental properties exclusively in Nevada and Arizona, during a period where home prices in those markets were at a lull. Later, we expanded our portfolio and our reach, looking at rental units in Texas and California. At one point, we managed over thirty rental properties.

My work as the "group analyst" of the Weekend Fund began to attract some outside attention. I was asked to advise a man who had inherited a retail property from his aunt. After looking over his figures, I was able to help him sell off the property and pocket $360,000 more than he'd anticipated. Good times! I had another high-net-worth client in Asia who needed some options for parking his wealth. I laid out several ideas for real estate acquisitions, such as the flagship store and headquarters for a Hispanic grocery chain in Orange County, which, per my analysis, would provide the best overall returns. But this investor was more interested in the prestige of the acquisition than an absolute return on investment (***ROI***). He elected for option B, to invest in several properties currently under lease by BJ's Restaurants, a swanky American restaurant chain based in Huntington Beach, known for its famous Pizookie® desserts and selection of craft beers. In another consulting gig, I advised a residential developer on the inclusion of various select features in his homes. I showed him how adding $55,000 worth of add-ons could boost his resale value by $200,000.

As I spent more time analyzing real estate investments from many different angles, I became more keenly aware of some of the dynamic factors affecting real estate investing. I decided to pursue an in-depth study of the new phenomenon of short-term rentals—think Airbnb, Vrbo, or FlipKey— from an investor's perspective. I currently run one of the oldest and most popular blogs on short-term rentals, www.learnbnb.com. I also co-authored *Airbnb for Dummies* for investors who want to learn more about this exciting new dimension of real estate investing.

In addition to the investing I did through our Weekend Fund collective, I began to build out my own personal portfolio. At the time of this writing, I am still an investor in over 150 real estate investment properties. Though many of my plays in real estate are traditional, direct investments, the majority of my holdings are through syndicates. This approach has helped me achieve my goal of securing a comfortable ***passive income*** while building wealth at the same time through appreciation of my assets.

Before I tell you about my ongoing endeavors as a coach and mentor for aspiring real estate investors, I want to share my motivations for teaching this entrepreneurial art form. One of my students knew nothing about real estate investing six years ago, but after taking my course, he interviewed for a job out here in California, my neck of the woods. He moved here from Atlanta and has now become one of the youngest VPs at a major development firm. Another student, also with no real estate experience, took my course. He then moved into several analyst roles and has just been tapped to run his own private equity firm.

As exciting as investing has been for me, I discovered two important truths that showed how I could give back and inspire others. The first truth was that the knowledge surrounding investing was for everyone. I noticed that sophisticated investors would use a certain set of common tools and methods to analyze their large-scale investments. I found that these tools and methods could be easily learned by private, individual investors as well. In other words, the same techniques used to assess massive multimillion-dollar projects could be applied to the single-family rental home down the block.

The second truth I discovered was that the desire for knowledge about real estate investing is incredibly widespread. I realized this when I found myself regularly fielding questions on the topic. At first, the questions came from the office. Colleagues would stop me and ask about a rental property they were looking into. A coworker would ask me to look at some figures for a potential commercial property investment. Before long the questions were coming in not just at work, but from friends, family, and neighbors as well; it seemed everybody who knew I was involved with real estate investing had a question they wanted me to answer. And the questions were often the same:

- » "I'm looking at a rental property. Do you think it's a good idea?"
- » "I want to find a rental, but where should I look?"
- » "How do I choose between these three properties I'm evaluating?"
- » "Is this a good deal or not?"

I wanted to provide an easy way to answer all those questions, so I created an online course that walked even the most inexperienced investor through the steps and tools they would need to make an investment. Rather than fielding thousands of calls and emails one by one, it seemed that the most efficient way for me to share what I'd learned was to create the course, which I actively moderate to this day. Over 300,000 students have taken my real estate courses across 179 countries; many of them had the exact same questions you probably have right now.

The Reality of Real Estate Investing

One of the problems with many of the real estate books out there is that they cater to a more experienced crowd. The terminology used is full of jargon and abbreviations. These books are brimming with "inside baseball" words that only make sense to knowledgeable investors. While they might technically answer the questions you have, they don't do so in a way that's easy to understand. I do not plan on dumbing anything down in this book, but I will not make your eyes glaze over, either. I truly believe that real estate investing is for everyone, and in order to fulfill my goal of teaching you the essential principles, I've chosen to write this book in a way that makes it accessible to every reader, experienced or not.

So You're Telling Me I Can Actually Do This?

I'm not going to claim that everyone is ready to become an investor, but I do believe that investors can come from anywhere. There are very few prerequisites to success as an investor. In fact, I can only think of three off the top of my head.

First, you need time. Simply looking for an investment takes hours and hours of work. You need to dedicate nights and weekends to sorting through opportunities, visiting with agents, attending open houses, driving through neighborhoods, talking with locals, and much more just to find your first investment. I've found that some of my students aren't realistic about this, imagining that they'll stumble upon a suitable property within their first five minutes of browsing online.

If you work full time, then finding the time for real estate investing could pose a challenge. But it depends on your priorities. If you are committed to becoming a successful investor, then you don't just find time. You *make* time. You find those free moments in your day when you can plug a few numbers into a spreadsheet. You make a couple of calls to agents on the way home from work. You spend thirty minutes browsing the local listings to get to know what the **market** is like in your area. Nobody has more than twenty-four hours in a day, but we get to choose how we allocate them, making time for the things that matter to us. If becoming a successful real estate investor matters to you, then I have no doubt you'll make the time to do it right.

Second, you need money (or access to money). Although not every deal requires you to dig into your wallet (see chapter 3), it's going to take some *capital*, or some money you have set aside for this purpose, to make an investment. There are no benchmarks for the amount you need. With several options at your disposal, you can invest in real estate with a few hundred bucks or several hundred thousand dollars. It depends on your goals for investing. It also depends on the market where you buy. Property in San Francisco, Los Angeles, and New York is exceptionally expensive, but rural Texan towns and Midwestern cities can be much more affordable. The amount you spend on an apartment in downtown Manhattan can rival the price of an acre outside of Kansas City. I'm not putting a minimum figure on the amount you need to start, but you will need something.

The third prerequisite to becoming a real estate investor is commitment. Even for those of you who are laser-focused on building passive income assets, you should know that the path to attaining these assets is anything but passive. You need commitment. In my experience, the students who succeed in real estate investing are the ones who commit up front to seeing it through to the end. Frustration, delays, overruns, calamities, and difficult people can threaten your staying power, but if you commit right now to see it through, then you will overcome the obstacles that you encounter.

Historical Real Estate Returns

How much money you can expect to make directly correlates with the amount of risk you can tolerate. One question I'm often asked is whether real estate offers better returns than other investments, such as in businesses, funds, or stocks. Well, that's a tricky question.

The S&P 500 Index is the most widely accepted benchmark for measuring the performance of the stock market. This index, consisting of the five hundred largest publicly traded companies, has historically produced a 9.8 percent average return over the last ninety years (figure 1). If you invest in stocks, then you can reasonably expect a similar return on your money over a very long horizon of multiple decades. But in any given year, or decade, the total return can vary quite substantially—approximately once every five years (over the last ninety years) the S&P 500 actually returned minus 10 percent or worse!

GRAPH OF S&P 500

fig. 1

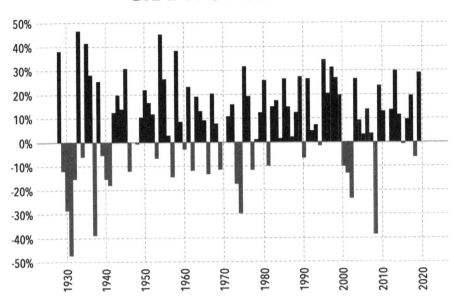

The S&P 500 year-to-year historical performance over the last 90 years (through 2019).

Over its ups and downs, the *equities* market shows a consistent return when you average it out over long periods of time. And when compared against the housing market, that long-term average does start to look better, and the purported superiority of equity returns seems to span much of the developed world (figure 2).

At first, it doesn't look like real estate is the right choice. In the United States alone, median housing prices have grown around 3.5 percent every year while equities have performed significantly better. It may seem as if you'll get better, faster returns on your money by choosing stocks over real estate. Not so fast. Real estate has a few advantages up its sleeve.

To begin with, the figure 2 chart does not account for one of the major benefits of real estate investing: cheap and accessible leverage. You can't easily borrow money from a lender, like a bank, to invest in the stock market. While online brokerages offer loans for stock traders, to allow for margin trading, those interest rates are often much higher than the interest on loans used for real estate investing. Better leverage allows real estate investors to control large capital investments without incurring massive expense.

GLOBAL HOUSING VS. EQUITY

fig. 2

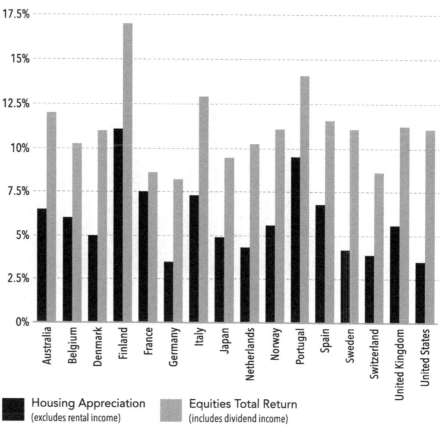

Source: Data from Jordà et al., "The Rate of Return on Everything" 1870–2015.

Comparison of total return from equities (or shares held in a company) to housing appreciation returns in 16 developed nations over the last 140 years.

Another advantage for the real estate investor is rental income. The chart in figure 2 only accounts for asset appreciation in the housing market. If you bought a home today strictly with cash and left it alone, you'd expect a 3.5 percent increase in its value, on average, over time. But let's take a look at what happens to the numbers when we add in expected rental income (figure 3). Remember, this is before we factor in the value of better leverage.

GLOBAL HOUSING VS. EQUITY

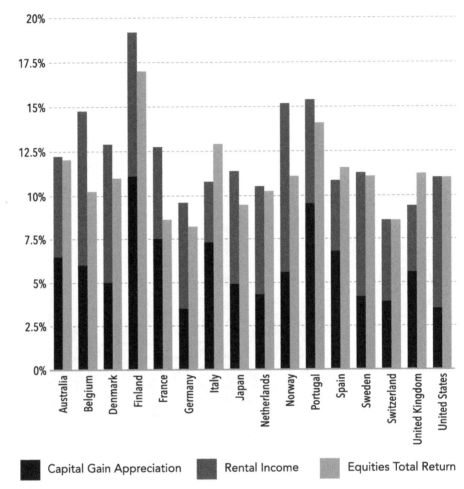

GRAPHIC

fig. 3

■ Capital Gain Appreciation　　■ Rental Income　　■ Equities Total Return

Source: Data from Jordà et al. "The Rate of Return on Everything" 1870–2015.

Given that the returns from real estate investments come from rental income and asset *appreciation*, both elements need to be included in our comparative analysis. The importance of rental income on returns cannot be overstated; it represents the bulk of our returns (figure 4).

Keep in mind too that the value of leverage and that of rental returns work hand in hand. The real estate investor's comparatively inexpensive access to leverage provides an opportunity to buy and control an asset with a higher total dollar value with the same amount of investment capital. And when used correctly, leverage lets investors earn a higher investment return for every dollar invested.

THE RATE OF RETURN ON HOUSING AND EQUITIES

	HOUSING		EQUITIES	
	Capital Gain Share of Total Return	Rental Income Share of Total Return	Capital Gain Share of Total Return	Dividend Income Share of Total Return
Australia	53.0%	47.0%	59.0%	41.0%
Belgium	40.4%	59.6%	62.3%	37.7%
Denmark	38.5%	61.5%	55.9%	44.1%
Finland	57.9%	42.1%	69.8%	30.2%
France	58.8%	41.2%	56.5%	43.5%
Germany	36.6%	63.4%	52.7%	47.3%
Italy	67.6%	32.4%	72.0%	28.0%
Japan	42.5%	57.5%	71.8%	28.2%
Netherlands	40.2%	59.8%	52.6%	47.4%
Norway	36.6%	63.4%	59.8%	40.2%
Portugal	61.6%	38.4%	80.4%	19.6%
Spain	62.3%	37.7%	57.6%	42.4%
Sweden	37.0%	63.0%	62.8%	37.2%
Switzerland	45.7%	54.3%	58.0%	42.0%
UK	58.6%	41.4%	58.2%	41.8%
USA	31.8%	68.2%	60.5%	39.5%

fig. 4

Source: Data from Jordà et al., 1870–2015.

Comparison between housing and equities across several markets, with *rental returns included.*

An investor has $100,000 to invest. If she puts all of her investable cash into a single property that generates $8,000 a year in rents after expenses, then her annual (yield) return will be 8%. Alternatively, she could use helping leverage and put her $100,0000 toward the purchase of two $100,000 residential rental units. The two units now generate $16,000 in rents after expenses. Even after taking $6,000 to pay the loan payments each year, she will still pocket $10,000, which gives her a 10% return on her $100,000 compared to the 8% she'd receive if she did not use leverage.

The third advantage of real estate is that you have the option—though not the obligation—to have more control over your investments. When you invest in a stock, you are placing your money (and your faith) in a company that you expect will make smart decisions in order to grow in the future. You have no control over those decisions as a shareholder (unless you own massive amounts of stock). But when you own property, you have the control to make decisions that affect the bottom line of your investment. You can make improvements to the property, add another bedroom, or even tear it down and build a better one in its place. This level of control, when wielded by a knowledgeable investor, can significantly improve the bottom line.

Some real estate investors, however, prefer the more passive approach. These investors make indirect investments in real estate through **REITs** (real estate investment trusts), which allows them to gain the benefits of real estate investing without having to deal with the typical downsides of directly owning and managing the properties. Although we will mainly focus on direct investing methods throughout this book, passive (or indirect) investments like REITs are worth a discussion.

We'll review the three real estate investment advantages throughout the book. The concept of leverage in particular merits a broader discussion and will be returned to frequently, beginning in chapter 1.

Personally, if I could only choose one asset class in which to invest, I would choose real estate every time. If you are willing to join me as we begin learning all about this exciting and highly attainable approach to wealth-building, then buckle up. What you are about to learn could change your life forever, and it all begins right now, with this first step. I've seen thousands of my students take this step and go on to do great things.

Let's get started!

Chapter by Chapter

» **PART I: Becoming a Real Estate Investor**

» Chapter 1, "Is Real Estate Investing for Me?," investigates the possibilities and realities of real estate. Before we get into the how-to's of later chapters, there are some foundational ideas that are key for investors to master. In this chapter you'll confront your appetite for risk, your expectations, and your goals as a real estate investor.

» Chapter 2, "The Vehicles of Real Estate Investing," will give you a bird's-eye view of real estate. You may be familiar with one or two approaches to real estate investing—fix and flip, single family rentals—but this chapter will open your eyes to the wider world of real estate investing techniques. You'll discover residential, commercial, and land investments.

» Chapter 3, "Investing Methods," will shift our conversation to the strategies that accompany specific investment types. You will be introduced to several different (sometimes vastly different) approaches to real estate investing. Although approximately 90 percent of this book covers direct investing, this chapter includes indirect methods like REITs to expose you to less aggressive means of investing.

» Chapter 4, "Recruiting the Dream Team," is an exciting chapter about some of the people you'll meet along the way. You'll need your "dream team" because no investor acts alone. We will cover who you need and what they can contribute to make your investment more successful.

» **PART II: Analyzing Your Investment**

» Chapter 5, "Finding Your First Deal," walks you through the process of searching for and discovering investment-worthy properties. This chapter will show you how to uncover and analyze local deals as well as those that originate well outside your neck of the woods.

» Chapter 6, "Deal or No Deal?," shows you how investors can evaluate potential investments, rejecting good deals in favor of great ones. You'll learn how to understand basic market cycles and discover crucial ways of measuring returns.

» Chapter 7, "The Deep(er) Dive Analysis," dives into the numbers of a specific property. This chapter will help you narrow down dozens of properties into a handful of potential investments worthy of more detailed analysis.

» **PART III: Day-to-Day Operations**

» Chapter 8, "Right On the Money: Financing" covers the money portion of your deal. We'll discuss the advantages of debt, typical loan options you can use, and what banks want to know before approving your loan.

» Chapter 9, "Landlording Essentials," works through how to successfully manage your investment as a landlord, including using professional property management and attracting the right tenants.

» Chapter 10, "Protecting Your Investment," explores the ways you can protect your assets using insurance and demonstrates the common risks investors shoulder and how they protect themselves.

» Chapter 11, "Adding Value," will introduce and expand on your options to add value to your property. Adding value is another unique and significant advantage of real estate investing. Using real-life case studies, I will show you practical methods for controlling your investment to generate larger returns.

» Chapter 12, "Planning Your Exit," deals with how to approach selling your real estate investment(s). This chapter will also introduce some analysis tools you can use to compare your investment's actual performance against its expected performance.

» **PART IV: Expanding Your Portfolio**

» Chapter 13, "Multifamily Real Estate," introduces the logical bridge for many investors between residential and commercial properties: the multifamily property. This investment can be a solid play, capable of generating large amounts of long-term income. This chapter will unveil some of the techniques investors use to operate these specialized properties.

» Chapter 14, "Commercial Real Estate," is an advanced chapter, meant to show you a potential next step in your investment journey. The concepts in this chapter will elaborate on the specific measures and tools used to evaluate and operate commercial property.

» Chapter 15, "Working with Partners," covers everything you need to know about investing with other people. It makes sense to join forces, but you need to do it the right way or you could get burned. This chapter talks about the benefits of partners and commonly used approaches to dividing up returns in an equal and fair fashion.

PART I

BECOMING A REAL ESTATE INVESTOR

| 1 |
Is Real Estate Investing for Me?

Chapter Overview
» Managing Your Expectations
» Learning the Benefits of Real Estate Investing
» Dealing with Risk

He is not a full man who does not own a piece of land.

– HEBREW PROVERB

As soon as I bring up the subject of investing in real estate, whoever I'm talking to pulls out that little file in their mind. It's where everyone stores their thoughts and stereotypes about the topic. Some think about the 2008 financial crash, not as just a news report or a talking point, but a scar for those who lost a lot of money and had homes that were upside down for years afterwards. Others will think of the most recent real-estate-themed TV show that they just watched where couples with little to no experience buy a home, renovate it, and make thousands of dollars, all in a convenient thirty minutes in TV land. Still others are intrigued to talk about the upsides and downsides of investing in real estate.

As you may have inferred by now, I am a big believer in the power of real estate investing. I also know that there are other ways to make money, and real estate investing may or may not be right for you. Many experts claim that there are only four real major investment *asset classes*: stocks, bonds, cash equivalents, and real estate. I want this book—and this chapter specifically—to focus less on my belief in the supremacy of real estate over other investment options and more on whether real estate investing is right for *you*. And to do that, I need to present a vision of real estate investing devoid of common stereotypes, both positive and negative.

The Polarizing Effect of Real Estate Investing

In 2008, it was all we as a nation could talk about as housing prices crashed and we were bombarded with images of people leaving their homes in droves. It was a scary time for investors. Today, there is a similar fervor around real estate investing, but now as a definitive investment tool. In the past, investments were primarily categorized as stocks, bonds, cash, and alternative investments. Today, real estate is widely considered by investors to have enough merit to be a primary category itself. Interest in real estate investment is peaking, with a surge of reality TV shows, online gurus, and "guaranteed" money-making programs fueling the fire. Crowdfunding sites like Fundrise, CrowdStreet, RealCrowd, and Patch of Land have opened up previously exclusive investment options to any investor.

From this polarized history of horror and hype, what's the underlying truth of the matter? That money can be made through real estate investing is self-evident, but how do you do it wisely and without exposing yourself to unnecessary losses? There are countless approaches to investing in real estate. While you may be familiar with one or two of those approaches by what's portrayed in the media, I want to expose some new ideas that might be perfect for you right now.

And even after you find a suitable approach with which to begin, your approach will surely change with time. Whether it's a long-term buy-and-hold strategy, a short-term fix and flip, or something in between, the key is to find what's right for you in this moment. Your experience in the field, your capital, your willingness to accept risk, and many other factors will come into play. You might begin with one strategy and progress to something else a little more advanced after gaining some experience. Not all forms fit everyone at all times. What works for the couple on the TV show might not work for you or in your area.

Experiential knowledge is the difference between reading about riding a bike and getting on the bike. Be sure you're prepared to take action, because that will be the best way to discover what works for you.

And though we will cover several strategies, ideas, and investing forms, I want to be sure you have the right frame of mind. I'm a firm believer that with the right information and the right tools at your disposal, you can cultivate a mentality that enables success.

Expectations and Plans

As previously noted, the term "real estate investing" is a loaded phrase and will take on various positive and negative connotations depending on the context. It is possible to think of real estate investing as both intimidating and conservative, both risky and smart, both frightening and sound. This same brand of nuance comes into play when considering returns on real estate investments. Will you become wealthy? Or will you become asset-rich and cash-poor? Will you be able to quit your job in twelve months? Or will your real estate investing prove only a hobby?

Guru Fatigue

Many real estate investing beginners are apt to encounter at least one or two real estate "gurus" early in their journey. I use the term "guru" somewhat pejoratively. I am specifically referring to those who aggressively market their programs and courses via hype and pie-in-the-sky promises. You will recognize this particular type of guru by their tendency to harp on a unique selling point, the "one thing" that you must know in order to be successful. These gurus don't like to acknowledge the complexity and nuance (that is, the reality) of real estate investing, because it doesn't sell well. While I'm not here to call out names or point fingers, I think they taint the real estate industry with unrealistic expectations. They show massive profits with little risk, but if you inspect the footnote or disclaimer in small text at the bottom of the screen, you'll always find the same four words: "Results are not typical."

I want you to be successful and I want you to be excited, but I also want to provide you with a sober and clear-eyed perspective on this topic. I believe that a reality-based approach ultimately leads to higher odds of success.

Setting Goals

Real estate investing can create quick cash, and it can set you up for a long-term gain. A lot depends on the strategy you choose and the risk tolerance you can accept. But it all begins with an actionable plan.

Goals are dreams with deadlines.

– DIANA SCHARF-HUNT

You might have a dream to quit your job, make your millions in real estate, and retire on a private yacht somewhere in the Caribbean. Though

I'm committed to keeping you grounded in reality, the last thing I want to do is tell you to dream smaller. Quite to the contrary, I want to help you set the goals that will bring your dreams into reality.

The best goal-setting approach is "SMART" goal setting (figure 5).

GRAPHIC

fig. 5

A simple mnemonic to create goals.

Let's take a moment and unpack each aspect of the SMART goal:

» **S is for Specific:** A bad example of a goal would be "I would like to make money investing in real estate." It's vague, ambiguous, and doesn't inspire action. A specific goal would be "I would like to earn four thousand dollars monthly from my single-family rental home investments." It's much clearer what you would need to do to achieve that goal. Even then, that four-thousand-dollar goal is a long-term goal. You can apply the same specificity to the short term, with a goal such as "I will evaluate five new leads each week."

» **M is for Measurable:** The old adage is true that you manage what you measure. Assign a number to your goal so you can track where you are and how far you have to go.

DIGITAL ASSETS

It's tough to know what figures you need to measure, so I've included a companion course online as a free bonus to help with this goal. Check it out by going to **www.clydebankmedia.com/rei-assets**.

» **A is for Achievable:** When you set a goal, make sure it's within the realm of possibility for you at your current level of experience. Making a million dollars on one's first investment is possible, but it's likely not achievable for the inexperienced beginner.

» **R is for Realistic**: If you set your goals too high, you will lose the momentum and motivation to pursue them. Make your goals realistic to inspire you to pursue them fervently.

» **T is for Timely**: Set a deadline on your goal, including a start date and an end date. Urgency is our friend, because urgency leads to action.

When determining your goals, it is important to delineate between short-term and long-term expectations. Short-term goals include those you seek to achieve in the next twelve to twenty-four months, whereas long-term goals may take three, ten, or even thirty years to achieve. Strategies such as wholesaling deals or rehabbing homes (what you might know as the fix and flip) allow real estate investors to make money within a shorter period, about twelve months. Examples of longer-term plays might include renting out properties you own to tenants on a long-term basis.

While I will cover both short- and long-term options in greater detail in an upcoming chapter, it's my opinion that the best strategy for investors with little experience is to focus on long-term gains while taking short-term actions. You can make thousands in the short term, but long-term gains can be measured in the tens or hundreds of thousands.

The Benefits of Investing in Real Estate

As discussed in the introduction, real estate investors have three advantages at their disposal: accessible leverage, rental income, and control over the investment. The choice to pursue real estate investing over other investment opportunities, however, is not always obvious. I've often heard so-called experts belittle real estate in favor of stocks or bonds. They make claims that annual returns from the stock market over the last fifty years average out to around 7 percent, whereas real estate returns average out to only 2 percent annually. How can this be?

In reality, even average real estate investors can often outperform the stock market's benchmark of 7 percent returns, but it's rare (or lucky) for even the most experienced hedge fund managers to beat the stock market consistently over the long run.

What the experts fail to appreciate in this side-by-side comparison is that real estate investing versus long-term stock investing is not an apples-to-apples comparison. If we compare the stock market's 7 percent average return to real estate's 2 percent, then we are assuming that the real estate investor is merely buying a residential property, sitting on it for forty years, and then selling it again. While asset appreciation over time can indeed help build wealth, there are a lot of other advantages to consider, many of which materialize on a faster timeline.

Financial Flexibility and Security Through Investment Income

By using rental properties, you can create a sustainable and predictable source of income. I hesitate to call it "passive" income because you still need to manage the properties (or hire someone to manage them for you) and actively monitor your properties' performance. Smart investors can create a positive, flexible cash flow, beginning with their very first investment. And once you expand your portfolio, it is possible that your investment returns will become your primary source of income, outpacing your salary or wages.

If you can maintain your day job while building and managing your real estate portfolio, then you may be able to see a significant increase in your disposable income. This level of robust, multifaceted wealth accumulation can provide a nice buffer to insulate you from unexpected life events and emergencies. Real estate investors who build strong positive cash flow enjoy a financial resilience that can sustain a more desirable lifestyle or provide added levels of financial security for many years. Think about what you would do if you had a debilitating injury, suffered a loss, or had some other major expense. How valuable would it be to you to have a strong, reliable second source of income to protect you? How hard would you be willing to work for it?

Leverage

Real estate investing has a significant advantage due to the value of debt financing, or *leverage*. There are two ways to think about using leverage: interest-only and fully amortized. In an interest-only loan, you can borrow a principal amount, pay only the interest over the *term* of the loan, and then repay the full borrowed principal in one balloon payment at the end of the term.

With a fully *amortized* loan, you pay off the *interest* in decreasing amounts and the *principal* in increasing amounts. The combined total of the payments (principal + interest) is the same throughout the term of the loan (figure 6). At the end of the term, your final payment completes the loan with no massive ***balloon payment***.

GRAPHIC

fig. 6

BORROWED PRINCIPAL

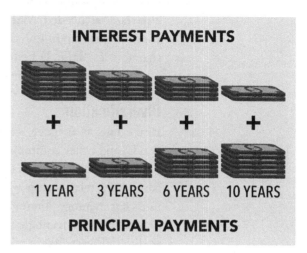

A fully amortized loan schedule visualized.

Why is leverage so important to real estate investing? Well, consider the power of debt to enhance returns from your investment.

EXAMPLE

> John's $100 investment nets him a $30 return every year. Brian has only $30 to invest, and to make the same investment as John, he borrows the remaining $70. He also makes a $30 return each year, but his loan repayments cost $15 a year (his net return is $15). Even with the expense of his loan repayment, Brian is making a return of 50 percent on his $30 investment, whereas John is making a return of only 30 percent.

Leverage, when properly applied, allows investors to make larger returns with each dollar invested while having to put fewer total dollars into any one investment.

Be careful of the risk here, because ***negative leverage*** can hurt your investment if the cost of the debt is more expensive than the return on the investment. For example, if Joe's repayment costs never exceed $21 (the point at which Joe would still earn a 30 percent return on his investment), he's doing well, but if loan costs were to become $25 without a substantial increase in his return, then his overall return would be reduced significantly.

Positive leverage allows for efficient use of your capital. You have limited funds to invest, but by using leveraged debt, you can have a greater impact on more projects. Using leverage also allows you to preserve more *liquidity*, meaning more cash can remain in your pocket ready to deploy elsewhere as needed. Without leverage, it is easy for you to get all of your cash tied up in the assets you purchase, leaving you less liquid, and therefore less agile. When you use leverage effectively, you can boost your returns, getting more money back for every dollar you invest.

Diversification

Real estate, as an asset, is a natural diversifier. Historically, when stocks, bonds, and other common investments have appreciated or depreciated, real estate hasn't followed suit. It follows its own trajectory and has a non-correlating relationship with other common investment types, at least in recent memory. Therefore, investing in real estate provides a built-in *diversification* advantage for an investor's overall portfolio that includes traditional assets like stocks and bonds.

The many investment options in the real estate universe are abundant, which makes it possible to pursue diversification within the confines of your real estate portfolio. If you are not planning on investing in assets other than real estate, you can still successfully diversify by making strategic investment selections within the real estate domain.

Building Equity and Hedging Against Inflation

There's always the risk that inflation will outpace your investment. When you invest in real estate, you build a constant *equity* in the asset, steadily creating a stronger portfolio over the long run. Therefore, it's important to understand how you build equity in your investment over time. Your equity share in an asset is the dollar value that accurately represents your claim of ownership in the asset. If the asset is worth $100 and you still owe $25 on the loan (principal) you used to buy the asset, then you have $75 in equity in that asset. As you pay down your debt, you gradually pay more on the principal and build more equity over time.

As the prices of goods and services go up, the rent you can charge your *tenants* will also increase. Historically, rents have kept pace with the rate of *inflation*, if not surpassing it over the long run. In constrained markets like San Francisco, where demand exceeds supply, rent outpaces inflation.

You will also build equity through the rent you charge. Those payments help pay down the principal of your loan. You can gain more equity when the market improves, causing the value of your property to appreciate. Let's say I owe $500 (in principal) on a loan I used to buy a property for $1,500. My equity is $1,000. However, if the property appreciates in value to $2,000, then I have $1,500 in equity in the property (assuming I still owe $500 on the loan). As the property appreciates, so does my equity. And here's the great news: appreciation is inherent in real estate. Although there are no guarantees, as long as you buy a property with strong fundamentals in a good market, your investment will have the best chance of success.

Appreciation of a real estate asset is a good example of the law of supply and demand. As the population of a given area increases, the demand for housing also increases. But supply is limited. Land is finite and the properties on the available land are restricted as well. And we know that as demand increases without a subsequent increase in supply, prices will inevitably rise.

GRAPHIC

fig. 7

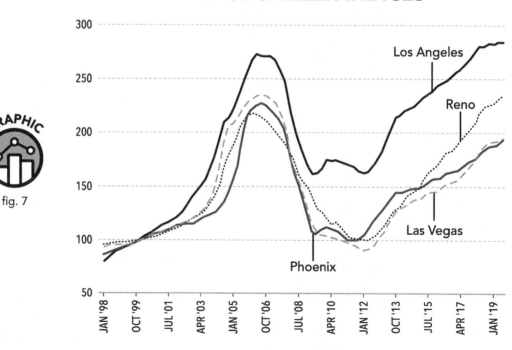

THE CASE-SHILLER INDICES

The **Case-Shiller Home Price Index** gives us good historical data to track housing values across time in the United States (figure 7). The index factors in the repeat sales of single-family homes over time to give an accurate understanding of house pricing trends in several markets around the country. It's one of the most widely accepted and respected indices used to track housing values. To give you an idea of what we've seen in the past, homes that cost $100,000 in the year 2000 would have sold for $160,000 in 2005, but that was in the boom years before the bubble burst in 2008. We can see that, over the long haul, housing prices have kept to a relatively steady trajectory upward, even when factoring in inflation and despite the massive crashes in the economy. The abundance of available data therefore suggests that real estate investing is a solid strategy for building equity.

A Healthy Relationship with Risk

Kevin O'Leary of *Shark Tank* and *Dragons' Den* fame said it best: "My money is my military, each dollar a soldier ... I send it to conquer and take currency prisoner and bring it back to me." There is no investment without an understanding and acceptance of risk. Some say that the riskiest behavior with money is to do nothing with it.

fig. 8

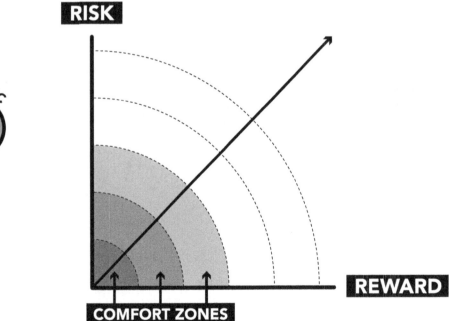

Where is your comfort level regarding risk?

I don't want to go too far in this book before touching on the subject of risk. But I also don't want to hit this topic too hard. I'd rather we take a bird's-eye view of risk, because I understand that everyone's risk tolerance is different. What's safe and easy for one person could be risky and difficult for another. For example, I have no experience in creating software, and to invest in a company that creates software would feel risky to me. But it would be natural and easy for someone like Bill Gates, if given the opportunity to invest in a software company, to consider the investment and put his money on the line, hoping to make a good return.

Higher risks attract higher rewards, just as lower risks attract lower rewards (figure 8). Consider the popular casino game roulette. If you put $10 on red, you'd have slightly less than a 50 percent chance of doubling it to $20. Not a bad return for a relatively low risk. But if you took that same $10 and put it on number 35, the risk is greater. Although you have just a 2.6 percent chance of winning, you stand to make $350 if the ball lands in your favor. Not a bad night out. The analogy for real estate investing isn't the same because, in the end, the house always wins at the roulette table. In real estate investing, both high-risk and low-risk strategies can yield long-term profits when you use sound investing principles.

Every time you ride in an automobile, train, or airplane, you risk your safety to get where you want to go. I think we forget that risk is just a part of our everyday lives. Similarly, risk and investing go hand in hand. We can even take it a step further and make the argument that all money represents some risk. Think about it. All money is in some sense a form of debt. The implied promise is that you can exchange your cash for something of value. Society owes you something for your money. And if all money is debt, and all debt comes with risk, then we can safely conclude that without risk, money would cease to exist.

It is also important to note that certain things may feel riskier than they are. We all know the statistics that tell us it's more likely that we'll die driving on the highway than flying in an airplane. Nevertheless, flying inherently *feels* riskier. I think investors must understand the risk tolerances they have, being honest with their own willingness to invest. Investors also have to ignore the *feeling* of risk in favor of the hard facts and data about where to spend their money. Even for the most risk-averse among us, there are methods and strategies to deal with risk that allow us to build our risk tolerance to a point where we're comfortable making sound investments.

Mitigating Risk

If you want to protect the money you invest, you need to use the right strategy to lessen the risk you face. In chapter 3, we will cover the various investing strategies that you can use and how to tailor these strategies to your risk preferences and investment objectives.

Mitigating risk is the act of adopting strategies to prepare for adverse effects. Once you learn to preempt the possible negative outcomes and calamities that could befall your investment, you can take steps to reduce your exposure. Certain investing strategies inherently involve higher risk. Other strategies may center around the same asset, but are inherently less risky.

NOTE

Talk to your tax accountant about the possibility of establishing a limited liability entity and how it could protect you and limit your risk by reducing your tax burden and protecting your assets from lawsuits and forfeitures. The ins and outs of forming LLCs is beyond the scope of this book, but for more information see the *LLC QuickStart Guide* from ClydeBank Media.

Decreasing Risk

By taking the time and initiative to read this book, you are already taking action to decrease the risk of your future investing endeavors. Learning about risk and studying risk factors is one of the simplest ways to improve your overall risk outlook—you can't reduce what you can't recognize. Learning to avoid the many mistakes made by less educated newcomers will go a long way toward your success in investing.

I am a student of success, and to me, there is no greater example of success than Warren Buffett. When Buffett was young, he already knew he would become a millionaire; he just had to figure out how to bring his vision into reality. And because his goal was to invest in the stock market, he devoted himself to learning as much as possible about stocks, companies, market trends, and everything else related to his field. Day and night, Buffett read the business sections of the newspapers and studied the profit and loss statements of various companies. He read every book available on the subject of investing in the stock market. He would often forgo seeing his own children because he was so deep into the study of investing. Absorbed in the companies and markets, what Buffett was doing was teaching himself how to decrease the risk of investing, and it was this commitment to minimizing risk that ultimately made him one of the wealthiest men in history.

You can accomplish this same learning through two means: studying and doing. But how much of real estate investing must be learned through experience may surprise you. While your road to success will undoubtedly be cushioned by rigorous and enthusiastic study, much of your skill-honing and instinctual knowledge will come through direct experience. And the more you do it, the more you will learn about it. And the more you learn, the less risky it becomes for you, both economically and personally.

Delegating Risk

If you have a high aversion to risk or you don't understand an investment well enough to take action, you can always choose to delegate the risk to someone else. I used the example of Bill Gates investing in a software company and how different the risk tolerance would be for me in comparison. I might not be willing to part with one hundred thousand dollars to invest in a software company, but I would willingly invest that same amount of money in Bill Gates himself and trust that he knows what he's doing with it.

In chapter 15, we will cover the possibility of developing partners to expand your reach as an investor. Using investing partners is also a very handy way to delegate risk to someone else. You can use the power of delegation to remove plenty of risk from your plate. Experienced *property managers*, for example, can be especially useful for screening and selecting good tenants, seeing to the day-to-day business of your rental properties, and removing the risk of excessive vacancies. If you feel that even with a solid understanding of real estate investing you are not quite ready to take the next step, it would be worthwhile to partner with a more experienced investor, shadowing their moves and joining them on your next venture.

Chapter Recap

» Real estate investors learn to define their expectations in terms of short- and long-term goals.

» Compared to other investing methods, real estate comes with many benefits, like building equity, developing a reliable cash flow, hedging against calamity, and diversifying your investments.

» There are no investments without risk. It's the key component in making money.

» Risk tolerances are different for everyone, but you can take steps to lower your risk tolerance.

» Mitigating, delegating, or decreasing risk allows you to identify and manage your specific tolerances, therefore allowing you to act on your first investment.

» There is a substantial difference between reading about real estate investing and taking action. Experience is a critical teacher, but reading and study will hasten your path to success.

| 2 |
The Vehicles of Real Estate Investing

Chapter Overview
» Explaining Residential Assets
» Explaining Commercial Assets
» Raw Land Deals

Before you start trying to work out which direction the property market is headed, you should be aware that there are markets within markets.

— PAUL CLITHEROE

Real estate is a broad term. Within that phrase, you have many types and classes of properties. What does it mean to invest in real estate? For one person, it may mean investing in the massive high-rises that line Madison Avenue. Another real estate investor may focus on leasing out the moorings on a riverbank. Still another may want to build tract homes in a brand-new neighborhood in an attractive part of town. Because there are so many asset types and classes, the practice of real estate investing varies mightily depending on the situation and the person doing the investing. As an aspiring real estate investor, you must take into account the current state of your finances, your location, your risk preference, and your experience level.

Although I'm going to present several different options for you, the best investment vehicle for a beginner is the simplest. Easy investments with little to no variables give you the maximum chance to succeed and learn something along the way while minimizing the potential of an early catastrophic loss.

You will make mistakes. That's the nature of investing. You learn as you go. And you certainly learn more when you fail. If you start out investing too much into a deal that is too complex for you, your failures will overwhelm you. You will probably feel like the whole concept of real estate investing isn't for you. You could end up quitting prematurely instead of learning from your mistake and preparing for your next deal.

A failed ground-up construction of a new luxury residence would be much more consequential than having to find a new tenant for your ready-to-move-in rental property. It is important to choose a real estate investment play in the beginning that limits your exposure to risk, and your "lessons" will cost you much less in the end.

In the broad sense, we can split most real estate assets into two separate categories: residential and commercial. I will touch on a third category, raw land, which can be residential or commercial, but the investing principles for land will remain the same.

Residential Real Estate

Most private investors, whether individuals or partners, focus on *residential real estate*. It's where most investors cut their teeth and develop their skills. Residential investing typically involves deals transacted at figures lower than $1 million (with exceptions to every rule). Besides being less capital-intensive, residential deals also benefit from a very broad network of properties and buyers.

fig. 9

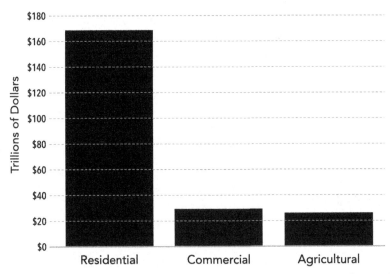

RESIDENTIAL VS. COMMERCIAL

Source: Savills

As of 2017, the worldwide residential market value was estimated to be more than five times greater than that of the commercial real estate market. That relates to *value*, but it doesn't account for the sheer numbers of opportunities; since most commercial properties are priced in the high millions, or even billions, there are many multiples more residential properties for you to invest in than commercial. With a large portfolio, residential investors can create true generational wealth and a healthy resiliency in this one asset type.

A real estate investor has two residential properties. If you add eight more properties, what does the investor have? They have freedom.

– ANONYMOUS

Single-Family Residences

Designed as one separate dwelling, the single-family residence is the most common and standard property type. There are no common areas on the property, there are no walls shared with neighbors, and the land upon which the building sits is usually included as part of the asset. The Case-Shiller Index used for all data research on housing values is based on this asset type being bought and sold between private owners.

MY TAKE

Single-family residences as rentals are one of the preferred asset types of beginner-level investors. They are simple to find. Growing rental demand supported by long-term demographic shifts makes finding a tenant painless in many markets. They present tax advantages and can help build long-term passive income, unlike short-term fix and flips.

A downside is that you won't make the same level of profit with a single-family residence as you would with larger properties. You can overcome this drawback, however, by building a large portfolio of single-family properties.

GRAPHIC

fig. 10

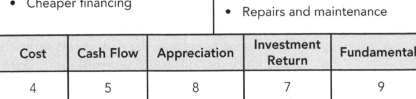

REAL ESTATE SCORECARD
Single Family Homes (SFH)

Advantages	Disadvantages
• Strong long-term fundamentals • Tax advantages • Easier to get started • Attracts quality tenants • Easiest to sell • Cheaper financing	• Limited profit potential per property • Concentrated tenant/property/market risk • 100% vacancy possible • Fewer financing options • Repairs and maintenance

Cost	Cash Flow	Appreciation	Investment Return	Fundamentals
4	5	8	7	9

All scores 1–10 (1 = worst, 10 = best)

fig. 11

Multiunit Properties

Like single-family residences, multiunit properties are single-family homes, but the properties share walls with each other. This category includes duplexes (two properties), triplexes (three properties), and fourplexes (four properties). You'll often find the owners of these buildings living in one property while renting out the other one, two, or three units. There are no common areas. Like the single-family residence, land is included in the asset. Developers like to build these types of properties on large lots in land-constrained markets to maximize *returns* from the same plot.

fig. 12

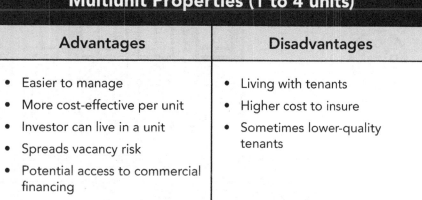

REAL ESTATE SCORECARD **Multiunit Properties (1 to 4 units)**				
Advantages		**Disadvantages**		
• Easier to manage • More cost-effective per unit • Investor can live in a unit • Spreads vacancy risk • Potential access to commercial financing		• Living with tenants • Higher cost to insure • Sometimes lower-quality tenants		
Cost	Cash Flow	Appreciation	Investment Return	Fundamentals
6	8	6	7	9
All scores 1–10 (1 = worst, 10 = best)				

GRAPHIC

fig. 13

Townhouses

When there are more than four homes in one building, it's called a townhouse. These are typically two-story buildings with shared walls between many homes in the same physical building. Small parcels of land in the front and back of the property are included with the asset. Units often have identical interior floor plans, or they may have small (or sometimes significant) variations as determined by the builder.

These townhouses are often part of a community, with common areas like pools, barbecues, spas, or tennis courts. Townhouse communities usually belong to a *homeowners association (HOA)* with rules and regulations pertaining to the cleanliness and visual appeal of the exterior, including upkeep of paint, trim, shrubbery, lawns, and fences. One must also adhere to HOA guidelines when renovating their property. As the owner of the property, they agree to meet all standards and pay the dues and fees imposed by the HOA.

fig. 14

fig. 15

REAL ESTATE SCORECARD	
Townhouses	
Advantages	**Disadvantages**
• Affordable • Good locations • Less repairs and maintenance • Easier to manage • Tend to be newer • Higher rental yields • More tenant amenities	• HOA fees • Costlier than condominiums • Tougher to finance • Lower appreciation potential • Subject to community restrictions

Cost	Cash Flow	Appreciation	Investment Return	Fundamentals
7	6	4	6	8
All scores 1–10 (1 = worst, 10 = best)				

Condominiums

Condominiums, or condos, are similar to townhouses, but are part of a larger multi-floor building. Condo units share walls and otherwise closely border neighboring units—above, below, and to the side. Condos also have common areas like parking structures, lobbies, elevators, halls, health facilities, and public rooms. Condo association fees imposed on the unit owners pay for these shared amenities. There is no land included with this asset.

Purchasing one or more condominium units is one of the most hands-off ways to own property. Even though everything inside of the condo is your responsibility, everything outside of the unit is the responsibility of the building manager. You are not responsible for trash collection, snow removal, landscaping, or similar exterior maintenance. On the downside, owners have limited ability to make improvements on the property and add value to the investment.

GRAPHIC

fig. 16

GRAPHIC

fig. 17

REAL ESTATE SCORECARD **Condominiums**	
Advantages	**Disadvantages**
• Affordable • Good locations • Least repairs and maintenance • Easier to manage • Tend to be newer • Extensive tenant amenities	• HOA fees • Harder to sell • Tougher to finance • Lower appreciation potential • Subject to community restrictions • Most sensitive to market cycles

Cost	Cash Flow	Appreciation	Investment Return	Fundamentals
8	7	3	6	6
All scores 1–10 (1 = worst, 10 = best)				

New and Developing Models

Some lesser-known and newer models for investing are popping up. One example is the *condotel*, a combination of condominiums and a hotel. These properties have been created to target the short-term rental market, which is still expanding every year. Condotels typically have a lobby where guests can check in and request services similar to those in hotels. Some condotels are managed by a live-in concierge under the employ of the property owner. In some countries, such as Australia, condotels are a common and popular option for holiday travelers.

Airbnb has partnered with developers to create condotels in various big cities around the United States to avoid the legal battlegrounds of short-term rentals in residential zones.

I've mentioned my experience with short-term rentals, and that may be an area where you'd like to focus. The idea of short-term rentals as investments is so relevant right now that I feel I need to address the topic.

On my blog I've covered some aspects of using Airbnb as an investment model, so if you have an interest in learning more than what we cover here, please do check out **www.symonhe.com/blog** for a more in-depth analysis.

The best way to think about using sites like Airbnb is to realize that it's not strictly an investment play; there's also an element of hospitality. You will learn the fundamentals of real estate investing throughout this book, but there's a whole other side to short-term rentals, such as dealing with guests, managing bookings, organizing cleanings, and abiding by hospitality regulations of your city and state. While many operators make a modest income, only a small fraction achieve lavish financial success. Much of it has to do with the region where the property operates. It's safe to assume that properties in bustling tourist destinations have a better chance of succeeding than those in rural areas. I would caution would-be investors in the short-term rental market to temper their expectations before jumping headlong into this relatively new investment field.

Another rapidly developing real estate asset model is the co-living properties now popping up in big cities. You may have heard of coworking spaces. Co-living is very similar. It involves a property where the common spaces are larger, with eating areas, gyms, and even shared bathrooms.

Think of a dormitory crossed with a hotel. These properties appeal to the younger generation who are more mobile, don't want to accumulate furniture, and/or can't afford the high rent of inner-city areas. Larger co-living spaces can house hundreds of people, and large companies are investing in entire buildings to offer these spaces. Rent for these co-living areas is cheaper than for traditional apartments or condos, and their popularity is rising. On the downside, the sheer size and expense of these assets make them inaccessible for most private first-time investors.

fig. 18

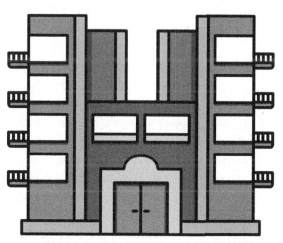

fig. 19

REAL ESTATE SCORECARD
Condotels (new and developing models)

Advantages	Disadvantages
• Good locations • Easy short-term rental conversion • On-site management • Extensive tenant amenities • Cater to new living demands	• New and unproven • Higher association fees • Subject to community restrictions • Potentially difficult to sell

Cost	Cash Flow	Appreciation	Investment Return	Fundamentals
7	8	5	5	9
All scores 1–10 (1 = worst, 10 = best)				

Commercial Real Estate

One of the best ways to understand *commercial real estate* is to study the key differences between commercial properties and residential properties. The first thing you will notice is the price differential. Unlike residential property, which is often accessible at price points lower than $1 million, commercial property deals tend to be worth $5 million at the low end, with higher-end deals going up into the billions.

NOTE

If a residential building has five or more units, it's technically considered a commercial property.

One of the best features of commercial property is that the owner has net or partially *net operating costs*. This means that the tenant is responsible for many of the ongoing day-to-day costs. Commercial tenants have a stake in the property to a much greater extent than do residential tenants. For the residential tenant, your property is a place to live. For the commercial tenant, your property is their means of doing business. As such, they have a vested interest in ensuring that the property is well-maintained, clean, and in good working order. Commercial real estate investors, much more so than residential investors, enter into long-term contracts with tenants, measured in years, not months. Unlike people, almost all businesses prefer to remain in one location and are willing to make longer-term commitments.

There is a broad array of asset types and asset classes under the umbrella of commercial real estate. We will cover commercial investing in much greater detail in chapter 14, but for now let's briefly explore a few of the more popular asset classes among commercial investors.

Multifamily

If you own one condominium, you are a residential investor. If you own the whole condo building, you are a commercial investor. Multifamily units are designed to house several families in one location. The multifamily property generally delivers the most stable returns among commercial property types because it is less sensitive to the broader economic cycle—businesses may forgo some office space, but people will always need a place to sleep. Multifamily properties include student housing (often privately run, even on university campuses) and senior housing complexes. Long-term demand for these multifamily units shows promise. The millennial generation is late to marry, have kids, and buy homes. Their delay in first-home purchases lowers the overall homeownership rate and drives up the demand for rentals. This is providing a strong "tailwind" for this type of investment in the future.

A new buzzword in community real estate is the "18-hour city." The big cities like New York, Chicago, and Los Angeles are known as 24-hour cities, but growing urban environments like Denver, Seattle, Orlando, and Nashville are being referred to as 18-hour cities. They are rapidly expanding with strong infrastructure, widespread urban growth, and lower costs of living. Look in these markets for expanding opportunities in multifamily investments.

Though multifamily properties have a reputation for stability and good return on investment, they also tend to be one of the pricier assets in which you can invest. In other commercial properties, many of the operating costs are passed along to the tenants, but that isn't the case here.

As buildings age, operating costs increase.

Banks and financial institutions love the multifamily property. It is reliable and produces a steady cash flow, great indicators of a good loan recipient. In fact, in many cases banks are more willing to issue loans for the purchase of multifamily properties than for single-family properties, assuming that the investor can exhibit sufficient property management experience. From the bank's perspective, the risk of foreclosure is very low with a multifamily, as it would be unlikely for all tenants to move out at the same time. The loss of a single tenant in a single-family property can be devastating, with weeks' and months' worth of unpaid rent adding up fast.

In some countries, governments offer insured financing for multifamily properties. By paying a small premium, you can lower the interest rate on a mortgage and enhance the returns.

Investing in a multifamily property is a quick way to expand your portfolio. While it might take years to create a portfolio of twenty-five residential properties, one multifamily property will instantly add twenty-five units or apartments to your portfolio, each of them generating monthly cash flow as a return on your investment.

If you are looking to be a hands-off investor, it's easier to pass the responsibilities on to a property manager for a multifamily property. By hiring a property manager or property management firm, you give up some of your income, but you also remove yourself from the headaches of managing tenants and maintaining the property. Consider what action you can take that will yield the most returns. Your energy is better spent looking for the next deal. Are you a property manager or an investor?

fig. 20

fig. 21

REAL ESTATE SCORECARD	
Multifamily (apartments)	
Advantages	Disadvantages
• More financing options • Additional income sources • Tax advantages • Strong long-term fundamentals • Lowest price per unit • Economies of scale	• Costs more • More sophisticated competition • More regulations than SFH rentals • More complex than SFH rentals • Concentrated risk in single property • More expenses overall

Cost	Cash Flow	Appreciation	Investment Return	Fundamentals
3	9	6	5	10
All scores 1–10 (1 = worst, 10 = best)				

Retail

Even within the overarching retail category, there is a wide variety of retail spaces. From large shopping centers to private one-store properties, retail real estate takes many forms.

Large enclosed shopping centers, also known as shopping malls, make their retail properties more attractive by, among other things, "anchoring" them with a well-known department store, such as Nordstrom or Target. These anchor stores, in theory, spin off foot traffic to the smaller mom-and-pop stores. The same model is used in strip mall properties, where the large anchor store is a stand-alone structure and a surrounding strip of real estate is used to house the smaller shops. The supposition is that the big store will draw traffic from neighboring roadways. Other retail developments anchor with grocery stores rather than department stores, and plenty of multi-space retail developments don't anchor at all. These anchorless developments run the gamut from tacky and hodge-podge to classy and high-end.

Besides *anchors*, retail properties have a lot of factors driving their success. Location, visibility, population density, local growth, and the income levels of likely patrons all play a role in the yields from the property. The economy is also a major factor. The retail space, in which so much commerce is conducted through discretionary spending, is often the first to feel the effects of a slowing economy. On the flip side, when the economy is growing, either nationally or regionally, retail investments will shine.

Historically, retail properties have performed very well. But shoppers' routines and habits have shifted over the years, and they increasingly favor online shopping. Every year, without fail, the news reports declare another drop in Black Friday sales at brick-and-mortar retail shops. As consumers change the way they shop, some retail properties close down, and commercial real estate investors face crippling *vacancy* levels of a magnitude they'd never have encountered fifteen to twenty years ago. Nonetheless, retail real estate is not a bad investment, not even in our present economy. The retail landscape continues to shift and much of the old retail space continues to be repurposed. Think of the Apple Store, where the primary purpose of the retail space is to allow customers to experience various products and access specialized services. The business model of the old big box stores with their sprawling inventories and now-digitized product catalogs may be gone forever, but the retail space itself—the real estate—still holds market value. Entertainment, lifestyle, and experiential businesses are upending old business models, repurposing the retail properties of old.

GRAPHIC
fig. 22

REAL ESTATE SCORECARD
Retail

Advantages	Disadvantages
• More consistent returns than office space • Generally long leases • More triple net leases • Many options in size and type • Opportunity for novel models • Higher rental yields	• Sensitive to current economy • More susceptible to obsolescence • Harder to find tenants • Susceptible to market disruptions • Growth of e-commerce • Experiencing "retail apocalyse" of store closures

Cost	Cash Flow	Appreciation	Investment Return	Fundamentals
3	9	6	5	10

All scores 1–10 (1 = worst, 10 = best)

GRAPHIC
fig. 23

EXAMPLE

CASE STUDY

In 1828, the Westminster Arcade opened in Providence, Rhode Island, as America's first mall. This was the original retail space that brought to America the concept of indoor shopping that was popular in the United Kingdom. The idea caught on quickly, and retailers and shoppers soon flooded the mall. Presidents and dignitaries would visit the Arcade to meet many people in one location. Retailers found success in an environment that thrived for decades.

The good times didn't last. In the 1980s, the Westminster Arcade reopened after several upgrades, but it closed again for good as a retail mall in 2008 when the Great Recession hit hard. But developers and investors continued to see potential in the retail space and brought the old building back to life. In October 2013, it was reopened as a mixed-use property. Retail and dining spaces are still found on the lower floor, and the upper two floors have been converted into micro 250-square-foot apartments. It has performed so well that there's a waiting list for retail and residential spaces within the repurposed property.

Industrial

Large industrial buildings are often used for shipping, logistics, manufacturing, storage, research and development, or as distribution centers. With an industrial property, the type of tenant you'll attract depends on a multitude of factors, such as ceiling height, the office spaces attached to the property, column spacing, availability and number of docks, and location. While other properties are measured simply in square footage, industrial warehouses must have overall volume factored in (including ceiling height) to determine their usefulness.

It may surprise many that industrial properties are less management-intensive, with operating costs that are often much lower than those of residential or office properties. Even though the capital investment can be large, it's an excellent investment to hold, with minimal energy needed to manage it on a day-to-day basis. Historically, investors find great industrial properties near major transportation arteries, like highways, railyards, and ports. In recent years, as the growth of e-commerce has been forcing businesses to locate warehouses closer to their customers, more investors are buying logistic warehouses in the *last-mile zone*, the final step in the delivery process.

NOTE

A recent PricewaterhouseCoopers study found that industrial properties had the best investment and development prospects. They performed better than any residential property as well, in terms of possible returns on investment. Something to keep in mind!

fig. 24

REAL ESTATE SCORECARD				
Industrial				
Advantages		**Disadvantages**		
<ul><li>Medium to long leases</li><li>More triple net leases</li><li>Many options in size and type</li><li>Lower operating expenses vs office and retail</li><li>More recession resistant</li></ul>		<ul><li>Difficult and costly to turn over tenants</li><li>Larger or single tenant risk</li><li>Low available supply</li></ul>		
Cost	Cash Flow	Appreciation	Investment Return	Fundamentals
6	9	3	7	7
All scores 1–10 (1 = worst, 10 = best)				

fig. 25

Office

The office space is the flagship of any commercial investor and can be very lucrative as an investment. Within this category is everything from the small neighborhood medical and dental offices to the high-rise buildings in the downtown core. Offices can be high-profile, as entire buildings can be leased out to corporations and businesses. But they also come with high operating costs.

Q: Who would need an office space?

Answer: The demand for office space is intricately linked with economic growth. When white-collar jobs are on the rise, there is a heightened demand for office space. Staying in tune with the economic temperature is an important aspect of investing in office space.

GRAPHIC

fig. 26

GRAPHIC

fig. 27

REAL ESTATE SCORECARD
Office

Advantages	Disadvantages
• Outperformance during strong economic cycles • Growth of shared office models • Medium- to long-term leases	• Underperforms in recessions • Poor space utilization • Concentrated sector risk • High capital expenditures per tenant • Growing work-from-home trends • Difficult and costly to turn over tenants

Cost	Cash Flow	Appreciation	Investment Return	Fundamentals
3	5	5	7	6

All scores 1–10 (1 = worst, 10 = best)

The economic performance of even a single industry can have a profound impact. For example, in cities such as Houston and Calgary, the oil and gas industry holds major economic sway. When oil prices crash, vacancies go up as companies lay off office employees and strive to stay afloat in hard times.

Losing a single major tenant due to an economic downturn can devastate an office investment. Conversely, when the economy is good, office investments do considerably well. You can charge much higher rents as businesses scramble to secure good office space. It would surprise you how the rent you can charge for office space will spike in the face of high demand. With office space investments, it's crucial to know where you are in the real estate cycle and where it's going in the future.

Mixed Use

With both residential and commercial properties in one building (like retail or office), there can be confusion about what defines a mixed-use property. The most common version is retail shops on the street level and residential apartments on the upper levels, but developers are testing out newer concepts.

Maybe it would help to understand the history of mixed-use properties and their place in our cities today. Before we lived in large urban sprawls, the concept of common commercial and residential spaces was typical; villages had homes and markets located right next to each other. But as industrialization spread, so did the commercial and residential properties. Cities then ordained different zones within their borders, creating residential and commercial districts, in order to reduce noise and pollution for residential housing.

But as demand for housing increased without an equivalent increase in supply, the mixed-use properties gained more popularity in large urban centers. Today, the future of mixed-use properties is bright, with many mixed-use developments becoming common in growing markets.

For investors, I see two sides to mixed-use properties. They can be advantageous for your portfolio, but there are some pitfalls to be aware of.

Advantages:
» **Lower infrastructure costs.** Investors get a discounted rate per unit on the infrastructure, such as utilities, internet, and waste,

compared to rates for individual units of residential or commercial property.

> » **More profitable use of available land in high-density areas.** A key goal for investors is to maximize the profitability of the asset. In high-density urban areas, mixed-use properties employ efficient layouts and provide two solutions to the demand from consumers.

> » **Better diversification of tenants.** The nature of these properties, with tenants in both residential and commercial units, allows for more resilience in market downturns.

Disadvantages:
> » **Requires special zoning permits.** One hurdle to getting approval for mixed-use properties is getting exemptions from outdated zoning codes, and this takes time to work through. Those zoning codes designed to separate commercial and residential are often unrevised until a proposed project unveils the obstacle.

> » **Difficult to finance.** Compared to standard single-use projects, mixed-use projects require greater expertise by lenders to evaluate and approve the finances. Because of the dual purpose, lenders need to evaluate each use separately.

> » **Requires more time to complete.** Generally, mixed-use projects take longer to complete than single-use projects. Therefore, the whole project is put at risk if market conditions change during the project period.

GRAPHIC

fig. 28

REAL ESTATE SCORECARD **Mixed-use**				
Cost	Cash Flow	Appreciation	Investment Return	Fundamentals
3	8	6	8	9
All scores 1–10 (1 = worst, 10 = best)				

Based on what I've seen, I expect mixed-use properties to expand in the future. New concepts and combinations in mixed-use properties (retail/

apartments, retail/offices/condos, offices/apartments, etc.) will meet the demand in the limited spaces of growing urban areas.

Specialty and Operating Assets

I'm presenting the following assets purely for informational purposes, as they are well outside the scope of a traditional private investor. These assets are highly specialized and often require operating experience, additional licensing or permitting, and potentially millions in investment capital.

- » Toll roads
- » Parking structures
- » Hotels
- » Airport hangars
- » Event spaces
- » Self-storage facilities
- » Surgery centers and medical offices
- » Agricultural land and facilities
- » Marinas
- » Mobile home parks

These are just a few of the types of real estate investments available. Each comes with its own opportunities and risks. These assets are not likely to become part of a typical private investor's portfolio through direct investment. Investors can gain exposure to these asset classes by investing in REITs or crowdfunded investment funds.

Raw Land

Buy land. They ain't making any more of the stuff.

– WILL ROGERS

Although most real estate investments operate with existing properties, either commercial or residential, there is a third category that I will touch on here. It is accessible to the private investor if they have the experience to work with it. Raw land is just as valuable a *commodity* for investment as any other property. The principle is the same. If you can add value to it, if you can let it appreciate, or if you charge rent for it, then you can make a return on your investment.

Adding Value

The main principle here is simple. When you add value to land, then that land will command a resale price higher than what you paid to own it.

Q: What am I willing to do to the land that someone else will pay for?

Answer: You can find raw, undeveloped land and move it through various predevelopment stages in order to enhance its value. For example, you can secure building permits for unpermitted land. You can resolve legal issues associated with the land, such as those related to *entitlements*, that are preventing development. You can add asphalt, gutters, or sewer and water lines. You can have blocks subdivided and complete all associated paperwork. Developers will pay more for land when they have fewer hurdles to clear prior to breaking ground.

Think of rehabbing land as an endeavor similar to rehabbing a home or other structure. You look for the potential investments that will add value to the property. Once the value is added, you can resell the property. The new, higher selling price is the market's way of confirming your value-added work—well done! Land or building, it's the same process.

But there are risks involved with land development deals. Some investors like to look at raw land as their first investment, thinking that if they control every variable from the beginning, then they can influence the returns to be much higher than with a standard real estate property play. The challenge with that way of thinking is that there is so much more room for things to go wrong than for everything to go right.

One of the issues is that land is purely speculative, meaning that you assume the land's value will increase over time, essentially gambling that nothing will go wrong and the investment will be profitable. I once read of a man who bought land, not as an investment, but for his personal residence. He thought he'd found a prime piece of real estate. The land was situated high on a hill, overlooking a golf course. He, of course, assumed that the hill was a permanent part of the environment, but after making his purchase he discovered that it was a man-made, bulldozed hill. It cost him an extra $40,000 in excavation just to find suitable solid ground to lay the foundation for his home. Imagine if he had lost that $40,000 on an investment strategy. There are legal, geographical, and geological elements at play with raw land, all exposing you to much more risk than you might be prepared to accept.

In the coming chapter, I'll introduce you to the investment spectrum of core, opportunistic, and value-added strategies, and I'll demonstrate which is the best solution for you at this moment.

Land Appreciation

If permitting and resolving complex legal disputes are not your cup of tea, another option for land investing is to sit on the land and let it appreciate. The parcel of land you own may eventually increase in value, and there are even ways to accelerate the process. In chapter 4, we will show you how to develop a dream team network of go-to consultants, business associates, and partners who will help you maximize the value of your investments. Among these key associates you will find a superstar broker and a superstar developer. These individuals will often have advanced knowledge of growth areas in a city. If you can purchase land due to be rezoned for a neighborhood expansion or a larger industrial area, that parcel could multiply in value very quickly.

In chapters 6 and 7, we will show you how to analyze a deal and assess the value of an investment. The problem is that many of the typical ways to assess value are inapplicable for raw land. So, a helpful technique to calculate the value of land is to look at the most profitable purpose for that land. In the investing world, this is known as the principle of "highest and best use." Is it an agricultural plot best suited for growing tomatoes? Is it located next to a large thoroughfare, ideally suited for an industrial shipping hub? Can the land be subdivided and sold off in lots? These are some questions to consider when determining the best raw land to purchase for appreciating returns.

fig. 29

Charging Rent

We are not technically in the food business. We are in the real estate business.
— HARRY J. SONNEBORN | Former McDonald's CEO

McDonald's Corporation does not follow the same franchising model as many other fast food restaurants do. While other corporations sell their ingredients (think the 11 secret herbs and spices or the components of the Frosty) and charge licensing fees to earn profits from franchising, McDonald's earns a large percentage of their profits by acting as landlords for the franchisees. This one small factor has made all the difference in their global expansion and dominance of the fast food model.

Across all their thirty-six thousand restaurants worldwide, they own 45 percent of the raw land upon which the restaurants sit. Think about the locations where you would find a McDonald's: in the middle of Sydney, in Times Square, next to Big Ben, within a couple of minutes of Red Square and the Kremlin. We are talking about incredibly valuable land, currently valued in total at over $40 billion, and it earns them a very tidy profit. In 2014, eighty-two cents of every dollar of profit earned by McDonald's came from rent paid by the franchisees (figure 30).

fig. 30

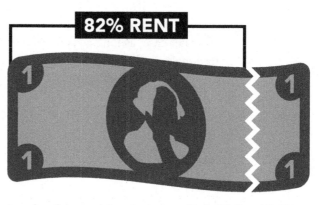

82% RENT

The proportion of profits earned from land ownership by McDonald's Corporation, 2014.

The McDonald's approach is one great way to invest in land—owning the land and renting it out for a source of income in perpetuity. But the challenge you will face is finding land that is available to buy that someone else will want to use, whether for industrial, agricultural, or residential purposes. Finding the right parcel of land takes experience, a lot of research, and a bit of luck as well.

Chapter Recap

» Even the term "real estate" is broad. Several asset types exist across different markets.

» Residential real estate is often the first choice for the beginning investor. It's cheaper, simpler, and more common than any other asset type.

» Commercial real estate is varied and complex, with deals often requiring at least $5 million and up to $1 billion in capital.

» Commercial real estate has the benefit of passing on operating costs to tenants, making maintenance easier.

» Industrial properties require considerations like volume, height, docks, bays, and access to main transportation hubs.

» Commercial real estate includes highly specialized properties, such as parking structures and self-storage facilities, that are often unavailable to the private single investor.

» Raw land can be invested in for residential or commercial purposes. In either case, as long as you can add value to the land, it can become a profitable investment.

| 3 |
Investing Methods

Don't wait to buy real estate. Buy real estate and wait.

— WILL ROGERS

Just as there are many types of properties in which to invest, there are many ways to structure an investment. If I said to you, "I'm investing in a single-family home," I could be referring to several different investment methods and strategies associated with that particular real estate asset.

There is no intrinsically superior real estate investment strategy. The best strategy for a given investor in a given situation will always depend on a multitude of variables. How do you determine which strategy is best for you in a given scenario? It depends on your goals, your capital, your risk tolerance, and the opportunities available to you. Broadly, investment strategies can fall somewhere along this continuum: core, value-added, and opportunistic.

Any real estate investment you make can be placed somewhere on this scale. On the opportunistic end, you have higher-risk investments with higher return potential. On the core end are lower-risk investments with lower return potential (figure 31).

A good example of a core investment is buying a brand-new home in an established, mature neighborhood with a thriving rental market. The tenant is already in the home and has a stable income and a good history as a renter. You also have a thorough understanding of the expected appreciation over time in that area. As you can tell, the risk for this particular investment is low. It's a new property. You have no additional structures to build or renovations to undertake on the site, and thus you have no need to apply for permitting. The market is tested, proven, and reliable. This is an ideal strategy for someone just starting out in real estate investing. Core investments like these are suited to investors who want stable rental income while minimizing risk as much as possible.

fig. 31

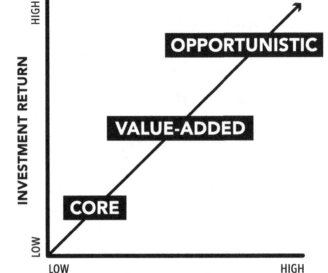

The Investment Strategy Scale.

On the other end of the risk spectrum, consider the following opportunistic investment. You buy an undeveloped lot with plans to build a property on the land and sell it. The land does not have any foreseeable development plans, but you're betting on future growth to increase the value of that property. You must have experience and know what you are doing to undertake an investment like this. There are risks in the permitting phase, risks in the construction phase, risks in the market, and risks in the execution; everything may not run smoothly from start to finish, so be prepared to put out some fires. But along with the high risk comes much higher return potential. If you get everything right, the returns may well be worth all the time and energy you put into the deal, and then some.

And in the middle of the spectrum, you have the value-added investment. Maybe you buy an older rental home in need of some repairs. Because of the dilapidation, the property cannot attract the level of rental income the market supports, but with some upgrades it will be desirable again. The risks inherent in this type of investment occur during the rehabilitation, or "value-add" phase. Even if you select a property in a good rental market, there is the risk that construction will delay your ability to earn rental income from it for weeks or months. You also risk underestimating total rehabilitation costs. If costs are higher than anticipated, they can eat into your bottom line, and if jobs take longer than anticipated, more time passes without tenants. But if you do it well, the value-added approach can lead to significant returns in the form of higher rental income as a percentage of your overall investment. You may also choose to sell the rehabilitated property right away for a profit.

Regarding this core/value-added/opportunistic scale, what's most important is knowing where you want to start. Your first investment will probably not be your last, and in order to be ready to move on to your second, third, and fourth investments, you want to minimize the complexity of your first one. Investments closer to the core end will allow you to experience firsthand what investing looks like without imperiling your chances to move on to more opportunistic models. I'm certainly not saying that every investor starts with core investments, but many do.

I want to touch on the different ways we can categorize the approaches to investments. Whether residential or commercial, there are a few options available to you.

Direct Investing

Direct investing is the most traditional, most common way to invest your money in any type of asset or property. It's what most people envision when they think about real estate investing. Whether you saved or borrowed the capital to invest, it's all your money. You hold the ownership to the property, whether it's the entirety of the property or just a part. Here are a few of the potential options in a direct investment strategy.

Buy and Hold

A "buy and hold" isn't much more complicated than it sounds. You buy a property and hold it in order to capitalize on its appreciation. Typically, this type of strategy favors the long-term investor whose goal is to create stable rental income over a long period of time.

In the residential space, tenant contracts tend to be shorter, with more upkeep and maintenance required on the property. The older the property, the more you should allocate for depreciation and repairs. Commercial property is a solid choice for the buy and hold strategy, as commercial tenants are long term. Traditionally, the newer the property, the more core that investment will be.

With commercial property, many of the operating costs are passed along to the tenant.

One of the benefits of the buy and hold strategy is that real estate markets tend to move through cycles. You will discover more about how this works in chapter 6. If you know the current cycle, you can plan accordingly for the type of property in which you're investing. You should also be able to accurately predict the expected returns from appreciation in a market, assuming the market is mature and established with good history and comparable properties around it.

Fix and Flip

The "fix and flip" strategy can be a fun and creative approach to real estate investing, which is why it's gained enormous popularity on television and other media. The impressive before-and-after shots of a property make it seem glamorous and achievable for the average investor. This type of deal starts to become more opportunistic as more renovations are required. I get questions all the time about my thoughts on fixing and flipping homes. I have two minds about it, and I'll explain both sides.

First, I'm all for it. I think the popularity of what we see in the media has elevated the perception of real estate investing as a means of creating wealth. I'm seeing more and more people looking into real estate investing as a viable way to reach their financial goals.

On the other hand, I do wonder if people realize that *reality* TV often fails to reflect reality. The producers on these shows play up the aspects that work for TV, and they downplay the aspects that are not so exciting to watch. The drama is exaggerated, and so are the results. Simple conversations are edited to look like major arguments. Slight delays are made out to be potential disasters. For a real aspiring investor, learning the art of the fix and flip from a TV show is the equivalent of styling your hair in a funhouse mirror.

The average investor looking at flipping a home will see an average of seventy-five to one hundred houses before making a decision to purchase. Television portrays these investors looking at just three options before choosing their favorite. Also not shown are the losses that flippers inevitably encounter. On average, three out of ten flips result in a loss due to bloated renovation costs and extended time on the market. Those types of deals always end up on the cutting room floor of TV shows that want to promote the excitement of a fix and flip.

Popular television shows portray buyers lining up to make offers on the completed property. In reality, investors will spend anywhere between five thousand and fifty thousand dollars to advertise the home before it sells.

But please do not mistake this reality check for discouragement. With knowledge and experience behind you, the fix and flip can be a lucrative investment. It does take increased knowledge and expertise to work with contractors, spot the potential returns on dilapidated houses, and properly assess a home's value in that market. If your risk tolerance allows you to work quickly (fix and flips are very time-sensitive) and manage an entire project, it's a great way to make profits in a short amount of time. The best way to dissect the returns is to look at homes that have sold twice in the previous twelve months. In 2017, the average gross profit was $68,000 per home. Some markets are extremely fruitful for fix-and-flippers; Baltimore, Jacksonville, and Knoxville have all recently posted returns on investment of more than 75 percent of the initial home purchase price.

BRRR(R)

One of the more popular approaches to direct investment is the BRRR(R) method. The acronym stands for Buy, Renovate, Rent, Refinance (and Repeat). It's almost like a buy and hold and a fix and flip combined, although you are using the improved value of the home as increased equity, improving your leverage to borrow from banks. This also tends to be more opportunistic as an investment.

The goal is to purchase a home that—usually due to disrepair—is underpriced relative to other homes in a given area. When *financing* a project like this, you need to account for the purchase price of the home as well as all costs involved with the renovation project. The home is then renovated, and the property may be rehabilitated as well—overdue permits may need to be acquired, sewer lines may need to be repaired, etc. With elements like execution, permitting, and construction risks, it's very similar to a fix and flip approach. With the renovated property, you can attract higher-end tenants willing to pay more in rent, which will hopefully allow you to recoup the debts incurred through both the property purchase and the renovations.

Here is where this method of investing differs from the others. Once you have acquired the right tenants, and once your improved property has been appraised at a higher value, your property can now command a bigger bank loan.

Banks can *refinance* at a loan-to-value ratio of, at most, 80 percent, so you need to significantly improve the property value if you want to execute the BRRR(R) strategy properly. The new loan will pay off your original purchase price plus the costs for rehab, and then—assuming you were sufficiently shrewd and skillful in your execution—there will be cash left over, hopefully a lot of it.

It's important to find a bank that has a short *seasoning period* (the length of time you need to hold a loan before you can refinance it), because you need to refinance from the new appraised value of the property, not at the purchase price when you acquired the property.

Imagine that an investor in Kansas City is looking to use the BRRR(R) strategy on a single-family home he found in a reputable neighborhood. Soon after purchasing the property, the investor remodeled the outdated kitchen, replaced some windows, and made minor repairs throughout the entire home. The process took two months, and now he wants to reevaluate the value of the property with his new renovations. Figure 32 breaks down the key numbers in play for the BRRR(R) strategy.

The profits from a fix and flip are typically not considered capital gains, given their short project cycles, and are therefore taxed as ordinary income. The cash profits secured through the BRRR(R) strategy typically take more than a year and are therefore taxed as capital gains on the property. Capital gains taxes are assessed when you sell the property.

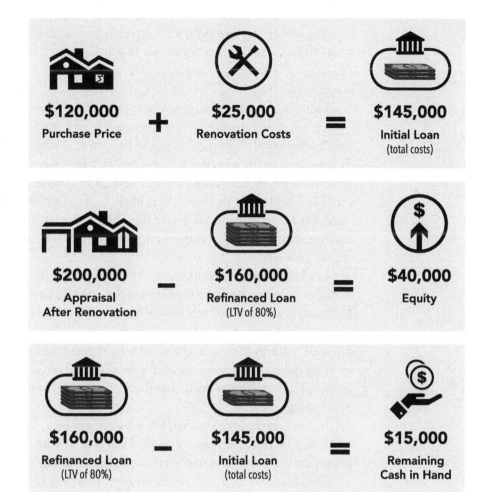

GRAPHIC

fig. 32

$120,000 Purchase Price	**+**	**$25,000** Renovation Costs	**=**	**$145,000** Initial Loan (total costs)

$200,000 Appraisal After Renovation	**−**	**$160,000** Refinanced Loan (LTV of 80%)	**=**	**$40,000** Equity

$160,000 Refinanced Loan (LTV of 80%)	**−**	**$145,000** Initial Loan (total costs)	**=**	**$15,000** Remaining Cash in Hand

 **Original Home**
Rents for $1200 →  **Renovated Home**
Rents for $1600

After paying off the purchase price and renovation costs with the refinance, the rest of the
cash is yours to keep.

Indirect Investing

It is possible to invest money in real estate without owning the asset.
This method is called indirect investing, because you aren't putting your
investment capital directly into a property.

REMEMBER

If you are not comfortable with risk, you can delegate it to an investor
you trust. This is considered an indirect investment.

The money you spend on an indirect investment is invested with funds, with trusts, or with other investors. If you pool your money with partners to secure a greater investment property, you would be using an indirect investment.

Indirect investing gives you greater liquidity with your investments. Let's say you own a rental property and you need access to some cash. If you wanted to sell your rental property, you would have to deal with the tenants, prepare the property, list it, advertise it, negotiate with buyers, wait until closing, and then you'd finally have access to your cash. It would take months before you could be liquid, and that's not always ideal. Indirect investments, on the other hand, can be bought and sold much like shares of stock in the public markets, making it easier to cash out the equity you have in your investment at a time of your choosing.

In addition to better liquidity, another thing I love about indirect investing is that it gives you more range with your capital. Let's say that you have $100,000 in capital to invest. It would be hard to invest that $100,000 across several rental properties. Ordinary investors can't gain exposure to several different markets at once in the same way high-net-worth investors can. But by using indirect investing, the average investor has access to more properties in more markets, dramatically increasing their experience in different fields of investing.

Indirect investing is incredibly easy to get into, even if you have no strategic investment experience at all. However, as with any investment, it is important to do your research, so that you know exactly what you are buying.

The downside to indirect investing is that it comes with a decreased amount of control. Direct investments put you in the driver's seat, giving you control over your asset and how you use it. You can control the renovations, the time taken on a project, how you advertise, who your renters are, the timing of the market, and so on. Indirect investing gives you less control, so you need to invest where you can trust that your investments are being managed according to your standards, principles, and objectives.

Public REITs

Real estate investment trusts, or REITS, are very much like shares in a company. But instead of a company, you are investing in a portfolio of different properties. As such, REITs come with the standard advantages of diversification; if you have one underperforming property in the portfolio, your bottom line isn't affected as much. The risks are lower, as are the rewards.

You are placing your trust in the manager of the fund as well as the properties in the portfolio. The rental incomes and capital gains (profits made from selling the properties) are distributed as dividends to shareholders in the REIT. But unlike stock shares, which confer an equity share in the underlying business, your REIT shares do not confer ownership in the REIT's properties. You are investing in the profitability of the portfolio and betting that the properties will remain profitable and gain value over time. A benefit is that REITs don't tend to correlate with the stock market, so investing in REITs is a way to diversify your stock portfolio with lower-correlation securities.

REITs are very steady long-term performers. According to the National Association of Real Estate Investment Trusts (NAREIT), from 1979 to 2018, the average return of REITs was 11.8 percent. That draws investors who are looking for that built-in diversified asset for their portfolio. Investors also love that REITs are required by law to pay out at least 90 percent of their net income as dividends to the investors. The only problem is that a REIT's dividend attracts a higher tax rate because it's assessed as ordinary income rather than capital gains.

Some other forms of REITs that you may have heard of are private REITs and mortgage REITs. At this end of the spectrum, investors must meet net-worth and income requirements in order to participate. These REITs are still public but often out of range for typical private investors.

For more in-depth discussion of REITs, both public and private, refer to ClydeBank Media's *Investing QuickStart Guide*.

Other Forms of Indirect Investing

Alternative forms of indirect investing include the following:

» **Notes:** These are private loans that investors can make to others involved in real estate deals. They may or may not be secured against the property to which the loan applies. With indirect investing the investor is inherently lacking in control, but this method allows investors to have more control and see better returns than other indirect options. But be careful—private loans are unsecured, with no protections to back you up should the borrower default on the loan. This option is costly and time-consuming for the lender.

» **Crowdfunding**: Though similar to REITs in nature, crowdfunded investments are open to the public on a specific property for a limited number of investors. Several platforms have made opportunities available to investors for as low as ten dollars or as high as ten thousand dollars. You also have more choice over the type of property you wish to invest in with a crowdfunded project. These types of investments are generally less liquid because of the long-term commitment required. Many of these platforms also restrict investors to those with some form of accreditation, putting it out of reach for the typical private investor.

» **Private Investment Funds and Syndications**: Participation in this indirect option also requires accreditation. Partners in these private equity funds pool their resources to invest in a property, usually commercial property, with high capital at the outset. This limits the participation to wealthy investors with the ability to commit at least five years to the investment. Investors are considered limited partners in the pooled fund, with general partners managing the investment and paying returns. These can be very lucrative, as many private equity firms achieve higher-than-average market returns on their investments.

» **Real-Estate-Related ETFs and Mutual Funds**: If you want to keep your investments in the field of real estate, there are exchange-traded funds and mutual funds that hold stock in companies related to the industry—for example, construction firms, development companies, hotels, commercial real estate, or any of the publicly traded companies closely related to real estate. Just as with REITs, it's very easy to get started in these funds; only a small amount of capital is required to invest. The brokerage fees associated with trading the funds, as well as management fees, can sometimes eat into the profits you make—therefore, it's important to first determine that the expenses for the funds are not prohibitively high just for the right to invest in them.

Non-Investing

How do you invest in a property without investing in the property? This is what I call non-investing: your money is not used to purchase a property but instead you negotiate deals that are associated with property, keeping you at a distance. You still gain exposure and experience with real estate investments, but as a non-investor you are acting as a middleman in the investment. Compared to direct and indirect investing, the non-investing approach requires a lot more work and a lot more luck to succeed.

Investors with little to no capital may find themselves drawn to non-investing deals. A word of caution here. A non-investing deal is often sold by "gurus" as easy, fast, and profitable, but the reality is that the results are atypical. What these gurus fail to mention is both the timing of the deals and the market where the deals were done. Maybe the homes were worth less than $100,000, or maybe the deal was finalized eight years ago. Often, the results are unrepeatable in today's *economic cycle* or in the markets where you live.

Wholesaling

One example of non-investing is the ever-popular wholesaling option. Your job starts by finding a motivated seller who needs to sell a house. There is either something wrong with the house or something wrong with the seller. Maybe the seller is in a bad financial situation and can't pay the mortgage. Maybe the property needs massive upgrades and the seller cannot afford to undertake the project. For whatever reason, you are negotiating the purchase of the property from a seller who needs to get out.

At the same time, you are also negotiating with a buyer who wants to take on the project. Maybe they want to undertake the renovations needed. Maybe they want to capitalize on the lower purchase price. Your role is to connect the two parties. You can either "double close" (buy it and sell it without taking possession) or you can temporarily take possession and then assign the property to the buyer at a negotiated price.

You're not the investor in a wholesaling deal. You are the facilitator for the investor. But you can still make profits from your involvement.

When pursuing wholesaling deals, young investors often work with mentors. The young investor, the mentee, will locate prospective deals on behalf of their mentor, who will iron out the finer points and oversee the execution. This practice of chasing down prospective wholesaling opportunities is known as "bird dogging."

Why would a newcomer to real estate investing pursue wholesaling? For one thing, it's a great way to get your feet wet in the game and to make acquaintances in the community. You do not need a real estate license to get started. You don't need much (if any) capital to make a deal happen.

The broad strokes of wholesaling are simple to understand with a little study. But, fair warning, just because something is simple does not mean that it's easy. It takes hard work and a strong commitment to search through potential listings for the right deal. There is a real risk that deals will fall through and your hard work will be for nothing. But, on the flip side, the rewards can be well worth the effort and then some.

As a motivated investor, Joe wants to learn more about real estate investing, but he does not have sufficient starting capital. In order to learn more about the whole process and make some cash on the side, he decides to place an advertisement seeking a motivated seller who wants the cash right now. After some time, he finds Paula.

Paula is behind on her mortgage by a few payments and does not want her house foreclosed on. After seeing Joe's ad, she calls him over for an assessment of the property. Joe thoroughly examines the home. It's fallen on rough times, and there is a lot of work that needs to be done. Paula can't afford to fix it, so she needs to sell—*fast*.

Joe makes her an all-cash offer of $75,000 for the home in its current state. The offer is lower than the home's market value, but it is a quick and easy sale. Joe knows that the expected market value for a home in that neighborhood is $125,000. And, given that it will need about $25,000 worth of repairs, the $75,000 price point will likely appeal to an investor who wants to rehab the property and make a profit. Paula accepts the deal and agrees on a contract.

Once the property is contracted to Joe, he negotiates with an investor who has been looking for a new project. The investor has a good understanding of the area, and he believes that Joe's projected returns on the property are accurate. Joe offers to sell the property to the investor for $80,000 in its current condition.

In the preceding scenario, everyone got what they wanted. The homeowner, Paula, got out from under the home that was weighing her down. The buyer/investor was able to renovate and sell the home, presumably for $125,000, making $20,000 in profits ($125,000 - $25,000 - $80,000). And Joe walks away from a few weeks' worth of work with $5,000 in his pocket for negotiating the whole deal without having ever taken ownership of the property. Just imagine what might be possible for Joe if he could juggle two, three, or more deals like this over the course of a few weeks.

Chapter Recap

» Investments can be broadly categorized into a sliding scale of core, value-added, and opportunistic.

» The more opportunistic the investment, the greater the risk, but also the greater the potential for profits.

» Most investors begin with a core investment to learn the ropes, moving up the scale to find more value-added or opportunistic properties for their portfolio.

» Direct investing is the most common investment method. Investors spend their own money and own the property directly. Within that framework are the buy and hold, fix and flip, and BRRR(R) methods.

» Direct investments give you more control over your investment.

» Indirect investing allows you to invest in real estate without owning the asset.

» Indirect investing limits your control, but you can diversify your investment across several opportunities.

» Non-investing strategies allow you to get involved in real estate without actually investing.

» Strategies like wholesaling can be difficult to find and negotiate but may be one of the few options for investors with little to no starting capital.

| 4 |
Recruiting the Dream Team

Chapter Overview
» Team Players and Their Roles
» Recognizing Different Perspectives
» Building Trust with Your Team

No man is an island.

–JOHN DONNE

You will never do this alone. Many would-be real estate investors think that success in real estate investing means that they no longer have to work with other people. They are their own boss. They have the control over their lives. They can steer their own course. Yes, that is true in a sense, but it doesn't mean that you're going to be alone. Great investments happen when you have a great team working with you.

What does your team do? You'll find out that assistance is required at each step of the investment journey. If you are working on a fix and flip, you need reputable contractors that you can trust. If you want to get to know your market, there is no better source than a local broker or agent who knows the area. As you read through the coming chapters, you will find that you can greatly benefit from the experience and wisdom that comes from having the right team around you.

It takes two flints to make a fire.

– LOUISA MAY ALCOTT

They say that you make your profits when you buy. That simple phrase means that the best investors know that the most important phase of the whole process is at the beginning. If you can set yourself up for success with a wise purchase, you will make greater profits. In order to make that happen, you need to have the ability to find great deals. You would be amazed to know where investors get their leads to find the best deals on the market. We'll touch on that later in this chapter (hint: it's not where you'd expect). When you have a variety of people working on your team, you expose yourself to deals and investment opportunities that will never be advertised on a multiple listing service (MLS) site or in the newspaper.

Surround yourself with the right people, those who have the experience and specialized knowledge to catch problems and spot opportunities that you would otherwise miss. In many cases, the perspective of someone on your team can make or break a deal that you had your eye on.

Josh Altman, star of the TV show *Million Dollar Listing Los Angeles*, tells stories of having his team around him when he makes his deals. One story concerned the home of a very famous TV personality in the '90s.

This person was certain of the long-term value he had accumulated, thanks to a custom-built home he owned in the Hollywood Hills. It was unique, more like a castle than a house. The celebrity's fame had faded quite a bit since his prime. He was asking $9 million for his palatial house, but there was no interest in the place. The crux of the matter was that the home was too offbeat and unconventional; it had been built for him and not anyone else. It was very hard to capture anyone's interest, so the price started to drop. Eight million. Seven million. All the while, Josh was watching the home stagnate on the market and was thinking to himself, "Wow, with that incredible view and ample square footage, this property has huge potential."

So, Josh turned to a developer he trusted for advice. Josh wanted to see what this developer noticed about the property. After looking through the house, the developer had a radical plan. This was not a seven-million-dollar house. This was a plot of land that was the best deal on the market. Even though the cost to buy the home and tear it down was exorbitantly high, the potential profits were enormous. Josh went all in. He negotiated the price of the house down to $6 million and worked with the developer to tear it down. The developer then designed and built a home that perfectly maximized the square footage and the view, and Josh was able to list the home again at $25 million. That's the power of having the right team around you.

It's one thing to have knowledge and experience, but you must know your limitations as well. I only know what I know. I can't know everything about an investment deal, so I rely on the advice and experience of the people around me. Not only do they fill in the gaps of what I need to know, they can often spot elements of a deal, or maybe an entire strategy, that I could never have understood on my own.

I also find that the right team makes the investment process quicker. Although deals can pop up in unexpected places, you might be in direct competition with other buyers looking at a particular property. Timeliness could make the difference between landing a great deal and missing out on it. Building the right team improves your flow and speed, which markedly improves your chances of securing the property you want. Let's cover some examples of the members to include on your investment team.

Agents and Brokers

Say what you will about the real estate agent, they can quickly become a real estate investor's best friend. Real estate agents love investors because they can represent a constant source of income and business if the relationship is built on trust and mutual help. Investors represent volume. They offer repeat business. Investors can elevate the comparable asking prices of homes in a neighborhood. They look at the properties that homeowners would pass over. Homeowners buy a house every five years; investors can do multiple deals in a year. Which do you think would appeal more to an agent? How do you cultivate a good relationship with an agent or broker in your area? Simple. You just ask:

> "Hi, my name is [your name] and I'm looking to invest in some properties in the area. Would you be available to have a chat about the properties you currently represent?"

In chapter 5, we will discuss how to research and analyze an area to locate deals. Adding good agents to your network is a key component of that research and analysis. Agents bring localized knowledge that you can't find on a spreadsheet or a census report.

I suggest you find an agent who has personal experience with investing. They will be more aligned with your own interests and will possess demonstrable proof of the successful investments in the area.

Agents are good sources of two unadvertised elements of a good investment: the pocket listing and the motivated seller. A *pocket listing*, or an unlisted property advertised only through word of mouth, is usually purchased by serious investors with the cash and motivation to buy quickly. These properties can turn out to be lucrative investments due to the comparative lack of public awareness about them. A smaller pool of potential buyers (coupled with motivated sellers) makes it easier to negotiate an excellent purchase price. Thank your real estate agent—she's the one who makes deals like this possible.

Architects

Whether in residential or commercial, you are going to need the services of a professional architect to draw up plans for your property. Once you begin to invest in more value-added deals, you will need more plans and *permits*. Having an architect on your team speeds up that process. Permitting, especially in markets like Los Angeles, can be a major time delay for your project. Use the power of a reputable architect to keep this process moving.

I'm also in favor of having the phone number of my architect on speed dial for when I need advice on the potential profit I can make on a major rehab project. As I said earlier, I only know what I know, and I'm not a professional designer or builder. I don't have the capacity to see the potential add-ons and improvements in a property. I can analyze the price and value, but to create a new design requires someone outside of my skill level. I use the experience and skilled eye of an architect to offer suggestions and ideas for improving a property. They can also quickly answer questions of legality, such as whether the council will approve of additions or renovations.

Some markets have properties that are classified as Heritage or Historic. They come with stipulations on what is and is not permissible to improve in the home. Work with a knowledgeable professional to be aware of any restrictions that could apply to you.

Legal

As you work through an investment, you will find that you are in contact with the legal profession again and again. With every paper you sign, every agreement you make, every time you buy, sell, adjust, negotiate, or alter a deal, the legal team for that deal will contact you again. You'll quickly discover that the right legal team will be indispensable for timely and profitable deals.

I'm in no way an expert on zoning laws, on financing laws, on construction laws, on contract law, or on any other legal matter. And because you'll be working with several different areas in one deal, you could require more than one legal professional. Just like with agents and brokers, it is in your best interest to find a legal team that you can trust to be timely and principled. They want the repeat business of an investor just as much as you would appreciate the quick return on contracts or zoning concerns.

Contractors and Developers

I cannot emphasize this enough: if you are interested in any investment that requires a value-added approach, you will need to vet the contractors that you use on the project. The more opportunistic your investment, the more you will come to rely on choosing the contractors and developers that will work best with you.

One of the problems I come across regarding contractors and developers is that investors are too focused on the bottom line of the investment. They work with three, four, or even five contractors a year because each time they're focused on getting the cheapest price for the work they need done. That mentality does nothing for the long-term relationships that you should hope to be building with your contractors. Rather than thinking of how to best use a contractor, think instead about how you can contribute to the relationship.

The benefit of working with one contractor that you trust is that you can develop a good understanding of the quality that works best in a property. If you don't have to consistently train a contractor on your preferences to fit out a kitchen, to properly landscape, to efficiently rehab a property, then you reduce the time you spend on each project; you are freed up to find new leads, analyze other properties, and make more lucrative investments.

Don't work with contractors that want to bury problems and take shortcuts on the workmanship, because although you'll save money up front, that lack of quality will take a toll on the life of the asset and the type of tenant you can attract. Find a contractor with the same goals you have—goals of quality, trust, reliability, and continued work. They want more work from you, so it's in their best interest to give you the best possible quality on the job.

Q: Would you trust the contractor you're dealing with to work on your own home? Or on your mother's home?

As I showed in the Josh Altman story I provided earlier, a contractor and a developer aren't there just to do work for you. They have an invaluable perspective on the investment property and the potential for returns you can make from it. I seek the advice of my contractor for any investment I consider, discussing the assessed price of the property, the potential value it can achieve, and the time it will take to do the work. I can estimate pretty well after working with many different investments, but I always want the advice of a professional.

Property Managers

Seek to eliminate tasks that take up your time and energy, such as the active management of your property. Let a property manager handle the daily operations, dealing with things like tenants, repairs, and rent collection.

For the residential core investment with a solid tenant, it might be easier to manage the property on your own. After just one investment, you will have learned valuable lessons about what makes a good tenant, how to vet the potential applicants, how to collect rent, how to negotiate contracts, and so on. But there will inevitably come a point when you no longer find it profitable to use your own time to manage your property (or properties).

Sometimes, it's just not practical to manage your investments, such as when you have a multifamily property with many tenants in one building. When that time comes, you need to hire a property manager with experience and a good reputation for handling large-scale investments like your multifamily property. If your goal is to create passive income, hiring a property manager buys back your time, so you can pursue activities more exciting and more lucrative than being a landlord.

A qualified and trusted property manager will also find the tenants for you that maximize the returns on your investment. Buying an asset is not just about the equity you build but also the rental income you intend to make. That rental income depends on securing the right tenant, one that has long-term goals, one that is reliable and pays on time, one that is interested in maintaining the integrity of the property they are letting from you. That tenant is not common, and intensive filtering and research are required to find them. This is where a property manager can come in handy. With a network of tenants and a good grasp on how to spot and approve good tenants, competent property managers are well worth their expense.

We'll go into greater detail on property managers in chapter 9 when we talk about the practical day-to-day business of handling investment property.

Partners and Private Investors

Getting involved in real estate investing still might sound like an overwhelmingly scary idea to you as a beginner. Let me reassure you that it is completely natural to be apprehensive about taking the leap into this new world. But there is a way to get started in spite of all the concerns you may have about investing. As a beginner, consider working with financial partners to learn the craft.

For one thing, working with partners allows you to pool your resources. If you have little to no starting capital, your choices are to pursue the non-investing options or to wait until you have saved enough to get started. Another way is to pool your resources with a partner and get started quicker on your first investment. And even if you do have the starting capital, pooling your resources will open up more investment opportunities to you both.

As a single investor, your limitations are defined by what you possess, and not just in terms of money. Your time and expertise are also assets that you bring to the investment table. If you can work with a partner, your combined expertise and time can expand the range of investment choices available.

Having another person to examine your deals is of incalculable value. You can identify the risks and find ways to mitigate, delegate, and decrease those risks. The division of tasks allows you to focus on your strengths while leaving your partner to cover your weaknesses.

Your skill set can be the perfect complement to that of your partner. For example, I tend to be more talented at the analysis and number-crunching aspects of investing, so I look for partners with complementary skills, such as negotiation, networks, and experience that I lack. You could even potentially form partnerships with some of the professionals I've already mentioned, like contractors, property managers, or agents. There is no rule that says an agent can't be an investor, or vice versa.

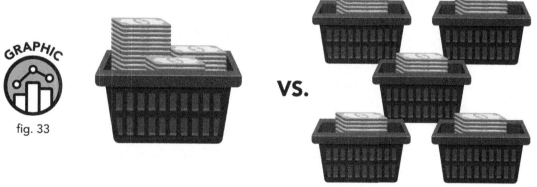

GRAPHIC

fig. 33

VS.

Protecting your capital by spreading your risk.

One of the greatest benefits of working with a partner is risk mitigation. As you can see in figure 33, if you have all your capital in one investment and it goes sour, you stand to lose it all. But if you had, let's say, five partners and that same amount of money was pooled into five different investments, your capital would be better protected. If one of the investments went sour, you would only lose one-fifth of your capital.

One of the risks is that disagreements can cause major rifts in the partnerships. If one partner feels unheard, or their effort goes unrecognized, it can lead to the dissolution of the entire partnership. It is crucial that all members of the team are on the same page from the very beginning, so that expectations and goals are agreed upon before a single dollar is spent.

MY TAKE

As a beginning investor, it's tough to know who should be on your team. In chapter 7, I include a due diligence checklist (a resource you can also download as a bonus) to assist you in figuring out which experts can help with your investment properties. Get your copy of the checklist now by going to **www.clydebankmedia.com/rei-assets**.

Others

Who else could you recruit into the cast of your investment journey? Who else might benefit you and help you along the way? The answer is everybody!

Consider every group, every organization, every association that you belong to as a potential source for investment help. You can find leads where you least expect it:

- » Family
- » Friends
- » Alumni associations
- » PTA
- » Gym
- » Colleagues
- » Friends of friends
- » Neighbors
- » Tenants

One of the keys of being an investor is to let everyone know that you are an investor. I think there is a mental element to this that really helps as well. Jeff Goins, in his book *You Are a Writer*, talks about the phenomenon of going from being an aspiring writer to landing paying gigs. The one shift he made was that he started handing out business cards, telling people that he was a writer. Once he began doing that, he found that people were willing to pay him to write, and his dream of becoming a working writer was finally fulfilled.

Q: **Who in your circle knows that you have plans to be a real estate investor?**

You simply never know where leads and deals will pop up, and when you make it known that you are a real estate investor, you're opening yourself up to deals that you never knew existed.

For example, did you know that divorce lawyers are a great source of investment deals? They represent clients who want to sell off the assets from a dissolved marriage, and they are aware of potential leads before they ever go up for sale. They are a great source for unlisted properties that need to sell quickly. Accountants can also help identify clients with the means to buy assets or with the desire to sell off an asset they hold. There is no way to list all the potential avenues for finding leads, because they can truly come from anywhere. And the way to make yourself open to these deals is to start introducing yourself as a real estate investor, letting it be known that you are the interested party for any real estate investment opportunities in their networks.

Chapter Recap

» Real estate investors rarely operate alone. The best strategy is to have a trusted team around you.

» A team can give you perspective on the deals you find, helping you to see things with new eyes.

» Having a team allows you to complete projects quicker and save more time and money on each investment.

» Agents and brokers are excellent resources for leads and unlisted properties. Their networks are invaluable for finding both buyers and sellers.

» Architects can advise on the potential profit from rehabbing an investment and can draw up plans to estimate costs on any work done on a property.

» Every step along the way requires a legal team, which can advise on what's permissible and hasten the deals you want to land.

» Contractors make great partners, working on mutual goals with a long-term relationship in mind. Investors must choose wisely to find the right contractor.

» Property managers make it possible to have a passive income. They also remove the hassle of securing good tenants for your property.

» As you make it known that you are a real estate investor, leads and deals can come from everyone and anyone.

PART II

ANALYZING YOUR INVESTMENT

| 5 |
Finding Your First Deal

Chapter Overview
- » Where to Find Potential Deals
- » Explore Advantages of Investing Locally
- » Develop Opportunities in Long-Range Investing

The trick is that you can't find the hidden treasure until you start digging.
— DEBBI FIELDS

Your first investment will likely have very different goals and outcomes than your next ten investments. It is important that you have a good framework in place and understand that you want to find an investment that limits risk and does not jeopardize your chances to continue investing well into the future. You want to take precautions to find the investment that will maximize your learning potential but also minimize the risks you take. It's a balancing act. The more complex your first investment, the more you will learn. But as complexity increases, so also does risk.

The primary goal of your first deal is to be able to do a second deal.

But before we talk about deals that use the investment strategy you want to employ and the capital you have to spend, we have to first talk about the location. Where will you find your first deal? Chances are that while you may have one or two ideas about how to find available investments, you aren't yet aware of the multitude of ways investors source their best deals. You also might not be aware that your next best investment opportunity isn't even in the same location as where you live right now.

I want you to be open to the possibility that your best investment deals aren't necessarily in the same town or city as you are. As you widen your search field to broader markets, you will discover the ways in which investors narrow the options for potential investments. You will be exposed to the tools and formulas that investors use to compare different markets according to their needs and experience. You will also learn how to look at real estate markets in the broadest sense, from region to city and all the way down to the neighborhood level.

In order to help you grasp this concept, I want to introduce a fictional character, a hero if you will: Neil Hector the Real Estate Investor, who will be using the same process as you to find his first investment. Neil lives in Las Vegas, and he is ready to begin creating his real estate portfolio. Our hero has been diligently saving in order to invest, cutting his spending and even making some wins in the cryptocurrency market. He now has $75,000 in hand for his first investment, and he is ready to find property in a market that suits his needs.

NOTE

I've chosen $75,000 for purposes of this analogy, but depending on your circumstances, you might find that you need much less or more for the investments you want to make. The number might be different, but the principles are the same regardless of the amount you have.

Although Neil is fictional, the data he uses to find his first deal is not. As a beginner investor, he's looking for that deal that will give him the experience he sorely lacks. He is also intent on finding a deal that does not expose him to too much risk, as he does not want to get in over his head. And finally, our protagonist is very much like you; he'd like to make some money.

Where Should I Look?

Maybe you've lived where you live for your whole life. Or maybe you've only been there for a year. The question most investors ask is "Should I invest where I live?" The answer is "It depends." Familiarity is very important in real estate investing. You have an advantage over other investors by virtue of the intimate knowledge you have about where you live. But the familiarity factor doesn't always play a major role in your final decision.

The decision of where to invest is also influenced by how active you will be in managing the property. If you are using the services of a property manager, then distance does not play that much of a role in your investment. The use of property managers has allowed me to maintain several successful investments in different parts of the country. But some investors prefer to be hands-on with their deals. These active investors tend to find properties that are close to them, giving them more managerial opportunities to control the investment and its outcome.

MY TAKE

If you are a first-time investor, then you should find an investment that requires your active management. Simply from an educational standpoint, you gain much more experience through active rather than passive engagement with your investment.

Even the experience of evaluating different markets will open up opportunities without exposing you to too much risk. Comparing the investment opportunities in your own backyard is easier if you have some context by which to compare. When you look at how your own community's properties are behaving compared to those in the rest of the country, then you have a better appreciation of how to understand your own market. You are not simply looking at the investment from the close-up property level; you are developing a deeper grasp of the larger market forces in play, affecting your selected property and all the others.

Real Estate around You

One of the obvious advantages of having an investment nearby is that you can be there. It's not costly to travel to your investment, and it's easy to do your research. And with properties in your local area, that research can be a lot more in-depth and comprehensive.

One of the first pieces of advice that I give to my students when a couple of properties have caught their eye is to spend some time in the neighborhood. I advise them to visit the community, possibly a coffee shop, and speak to the people living in that community. They can talk to people who've lived in the area for years as well as maybe finding someone who's moved there only recently. I also advise people to drive through the neighborhood at different times of the day: mornings before rush-hour commute, afternoons when everyone is returning home from work or school is letting out, weeknights and weekends. These are all great times to experience the ebb and flow of the community and uncover facets of the neighborhood that facts and statistics on paper cannot convey. Are there major traffic snarls that could impact your schedule? What's the noise level like at different times during the week? How do people feel about their community? What are some of the hidden benefits and pitfalls that only a local resident could show you? This kind of information is invaluable to an investor.

Another upside to looking for local properties is that you will have the benefit of a great network through which you can uncover better leads.

You can cast your figurative net wider with the help of people around you who also know the neighborhoods and the potential deals coming up on the market.

Use your team of experts (you recruited them in chapter 4) to help you find those deals, because their local knowledge is invaluable.

In our case study, our fictitious investor, Neil Hector the Real Estate Investor, is using non-fictitious data to look for properties within his own town. Las Vegas is a unique city with a large tourism industry impacting the local economy, and it's big enough to find good deals. Having lived there for his whole life, Neil has an intuitive and comprehensive knowledge of the neighborhoods around the city. He knows the best roads. He knows where the good schools are. He knows where the affluent and the blue-collar residents like to live. So, as he finds potential deals, he can quickly sift through the good and bad opportunities using his local experience as a guide. Neil also has several friends who are residents of the city. Their firsthand experience, combined with his own, makes our hero think he'd be wise to remain within the city limits for his investment deal. But even with all of the seemingly obvious advantages, is staying local Neil's best bet when considering the capital he has available and his limited investing experience?

The only concern I have about local investments is that the attractiveness of their convenience might prevent the consideration of alternative investments that could generate higher returns. An investor who only considers local properties obviously limits his prospects. Again, the experience of actively managing your first investment is valuable in its own right, yet the best formula for selecting optimal property deals relies on having as many leads as possible. Even if you must add the expense and hassle of dealing with a property management company into the equation, it's still quite possible that your net return will be significantly bigger when you venture beyond your backyard.

Long-Distance Real Estate Investing

I like to imagine that the difference between local and long-distance investments is like a pilot landing a small airplane in different conditions. If acquiring a successful, profitable investment is the goal of the investor, the pilot's goal is to safely land the aircraft on the tarmac. However, the way in which they achieve that goal can differ, even though the end result is the same. On a clear and sunny day, pilots are able to land a plane with the aid of their eyesight. They will also consult their instruments, but the ability to use their own vision helps tremendously if the conditions allow it. This is what analyzing a local investment is like. You have the figures and facts before you, but there's nothing quite like using your own senses to evaluate whether an investment is viable.

When the conditions are cloudy or dark, pilots must transition from using their own senses to relying primarily on their instruments. They use gauges, altimeters, and the voice of the flight controller as substitutes for their obscured vision. Think of long-distance investing like this. Although you can't rely on your own senses to gauge your investments, you can rely on data and other people to replace the lack of sensory input. Can you fly a plane at night or through fog? Of course you can. You simply rely on a different strategy to succeed. The same goes for investing long-distance. Can you successfully invest in different cities? Yes. It just requires a different strategy to analyze your investments. But in both cases, the goal and the outcome are the same.

As you expand your search to include non-local properties, you gain the benefit of having more leads to consider. The downside is that everything you could do with a "boots on the ground" approach for local investments is now something that you have to trust to a third party; you must now acknowledge that your investment will be based on analysis of remote data. Long-distance investments require an element of faith, trusting in the data and analysis without the input of your own senses. That puts these investments outside of the scope of some first-time investors without the risk tolerance to outsource some of their data mining to third parties.

One ironic advantage of remote investing is that your reliance on cold, hard data may help you make more rational decisions. You lose your local knowledge advantage, but you can gain an ability to analyze investments in a detached manner without personal opinions getting in the way. For instance, say you grew up with the belief that a certain neighborhood had a poor reputation. It's possible that even if it underwent *gentrification*, your own beliefs would still cause you to undervalue the neighborhood. Or maybe you have a family member who's tried investing in your town and tells you that all the tenants are bad, leaving a bad taste in your mouth about rental properties. It's entirely possible to be too close to an investment to make a good decision about it. I don't believe that you should dismiss the idea of looking elsewhere when you can use the distance to help clarify your own analysis process.

With long-distance properties, you have no choice but to use a property manager for the management and control of your investment. Consider this another advantage rather than a loss of control. You have the ability to employ an experienced manager who replaces your lack of local knowledge. If this is your first investment, then working with a good property manager can also help mitigate your lack of experience. There is freedom in the ability to outsource your investment inexperience to a property manager who's done it all before.

It helps that Neil's new job has exposed him to a new group of people, because they've encouraged him to look at real estate investing in a new light. One of his colleagues has invested in cities all over the West Coast with great success, and it's encouraged our hero to look beyond the borders of his city. It will give him validation about his own market and ease his mind about possibly overlooking investment opportunities that he didn't know existed. He wants to expand his opportunities without stretching too far. He would also like to travel to his investment when necessary without too much hassle. He decides to limit his search (for now) to the southwest United States, focusing on three major cities that are close to him: Los Angeles, Reno, and Phoenix. Although they differ greatly in size and economy from his own local Las Vegas market, he still wants to determine if they hold potential investment opportunities that suit the capital and investment strategy he wants to use.

Sources for Finding Potential Deals

Whether you are looking locally or all over the globe for prospective investments, it is important that you generate your leads with the aid of multiple sources. Let's cover a few of those now.

» **Multiple Listing Services:** *Multiple listing services (MLS)* are *the* source for active listings in North America. It's where investors go to find the newest listed properties in a market. The problem until now has been that there were hundreds of MLS networks, most restricted to local options. If you wanted to see properties, you'd have to subscribe to several services for local and regional listings. You'd also need a real estate license to directly access the networks, but most agents pay for the right to list properties on their own sites. MLS sites are slowly consolidating, with the goal of offering investors, buyers, and agents a national database, but that's still some time away. For now, you need to know that MLS sites are reputable and trusted as a source to be used by governments, economists, financial institutions, and appraisers to determine property value. It's a quick way to narrow down your own search based on factors like square footage, price, or location.

fig. 34

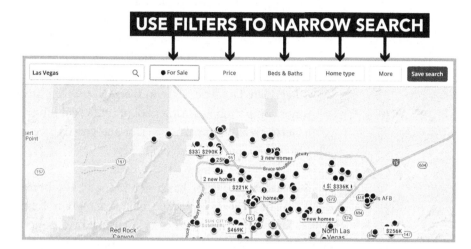

Zillow.com is one of many websites that utilize MLS data to allow users to search for properties based on a number of different attributes.

» **Newspapers:** While it's not as popular as it once was, the newspaper is still a great source for finding properties for sale. Agents and brokerages advertise in papers, often highlighting recent price reductions or brand-new listings. Most agents understand that newspaper listings are more for the seller, showing that their agent is diligently working to sell the home. The primary reason for agents to use newspaper listings is to generate calls and inquiries into their brokerage. I would advise using the newspaper more as a way to get to know the agents in an area than to discover the properties available.

» **Craigslist:** It may seem a bit old-school, but Craigslist still has a real estate property search that can unearth some gems. One of the reasons people list on Craigslist is that their property is ineligible for a standard mortgage and therefore only appealing to select buyers. If the property is currently unfit for residents (uninhabitable), then it presents a potentially great deal to the investor who is looking for a quick flip or renovation project.

» **Pocket Listings:** Not every deal on the market is publicly viewable. The private listings that won't show up on the internet or in newspapers are known as "pocket listings." These occur when the agent agrees to use their own private network (or the network of the seller) to find a suitable buyer. They can also be known as For Sale by Owner deals (FSBOs) when there is no agent to represent the seller. I knew of one real estate investor who would regularly drive around town looking for the "for sale by owner" signs on lawns or in windows. He called it "driving for dollars" because he was able to negotiate fantastic deals on these properties, simply because he was not competing against a pool of interested buyers. Develop a solid network as a reputable investor and you'll discover pocket listings that were once hidden from view.

Now that Neil Hector has a good idea of the best investment markets around him, he creates a spreadsheet for each market: Las Vegas, Los Angeles, Phoenix, and Reno. He begins by focusing in on one market, Las Vegas, home turf. He starts with Zillow.com and Trulia.com, both trusted MLS networks that consolidate listing information. Because our hero knows the city, he is easily able to narrow down his search to a few neighborhoods. In these neighborhoods alone there are hundreds of options. He filters them by inputting his target price range as well as his desired age range for the home. Since it's Neil's first investment, he doesn't want to risk older homes with much higher upkeep costs. In his results, Neil notices a few properties that pique his interest, including some pre-foreclosure homes with prices in his range.

NOTE

For the purpose of this book, I've used property and sites specific to the United States where data is generally available and accessible online. For online resources in other countries, please refer to Appendix I.

Moving on from the MLS sites, our fearless investor protagonist browses the newspaper for listings. It's not as easy to filter out the properties, but a couple of homes catch his eye with recent asking price reductions. He finds a real estate agent that sells in the neighborhoods he's looking in, so he writes down the number to contact the agent later on.

Craigslist is next, with Neil browsing through the private listings of homes there. But he clicks out after a few minutes of browsing ads, as it seems a bit riskier to consider these investments right now. Many of the homes listed require intense work and don't match his price criteria.

Having worked some on his own, Neil's next step is to call the agent he found in the paper and let him know that he'd like to invest in a certain type of home. Immediately, the agent highlights two homes that Neil had overlooked in his search. The agent also promises to email him with any new opportunities as they come up. After all that, Neil's Las Vegas spreadsheet includes six potential homes that could be worth his investment, and that's just in one city. Looks like it's time to do some driving.

Over the next couple of days, Neil diligently adds potential deals onto his spreadsheets from a variety of sources. He's getting better at pulling out the properties that match the type of investment he's planning to make. The Los Angeles market is considerably more expensive, and the Reno market doesn't have as many listings. Phoenix has a few listings with potential, and the price seems right. But how does Neil compare each of his properties? How can one market be compared to another market? What's important to know and what can be ignored? What data does he need to make a decision about where to invest?

Comparative Analysis of Markets

This may be a new concept for you, but I want to recommend that as an investor, you start your first comparison at the market level. What I mean by that is that rather than shopping through the available properties and comparing one house to another, let's take a step back and compare one entire market with another market.

ANALYSIS FUNNEL

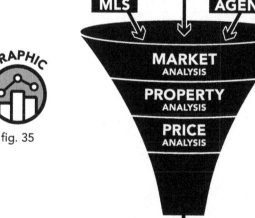

GRAPHIC

fig. 35

The analysis funnel—the more leads you put in the top, the greater your chances for better results out the other end.

When I talk about analyzing at the market level, it's not enough even to say city by city. We have to look at the market a bit closer, neighborhood by neighborhood. The neighborhoods in Los Angeles vary enormously, from the run-down South Central and Watts to the upper-class Beverly Hills and Malibu. You can't put a blanket generalization over an entire city when there is so much variance between its regions.

It's not just the economic class of a neighborhood that we care about, it's also the barriers between different regions that make such a difference. Maybe a highway or rails divide up a city into sections. Maybe different school districts divide communities into different categories. Maybe it's proximity to the industrial areas, the shore, or the closest amenities. All of these "barriers" can delineate different markets within the same city.

Our hero, Neil, now has a mountain of data in front of him. His four spreadsheets (one for each city) contain dozens of homes for his consideration. The task of narrowing down all these options seems monumental. Our investing pioneer needs to stop looking at the trees and first take a look at the entire forest. If his goal is to find a birch tree, he can't find it if he's looking in a pine forest. What is required is a broad look at the four markets (forests) themselves to compare them to each other. Neil's goal is to eliminate markets quickly, only selecting those that can support the properties he's interested in pursuing.

Case-Shiller Index

The Case-Shiller Index provides us with a suitable starting point for market-by-market comparative analysis. It's a simple tool that allows an apples-to-apples comparison of different markets (figure 36).

fig. 36

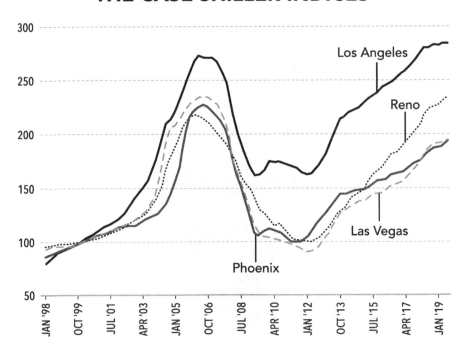

The Case-Shiller indices for Los Angeles, Las Vegas, Phoenix, and Reno.

Normalized to the year 2000, each index shows us the average trending house prices over the last thirty years. In Los Angeles, if a home was worth $100,000 in the year 2000, then by the year 2006 it would be worth nearly $280,000. You can clearly see the housing bubble in the mid-2000s as well as the subsequent housing price crash of 2008 and its steady recovery. Looking at markets like this, we can see how each city has recovered after the 2008 *global financial crisis*.

The Case-Shiller Index gives the investor a snapshot of where the market is right now but also how it has performed historically. Investors use this data to determine whether entering the market is likely to offer good results, or if it's not the best time to invest. For instance, if the market is at an all-time high compared to historical records, and it seems to flatten out after a rise, this could be a sign that it is slowing down or peaking. But if the market is at a low compared to historical performance, and it's flattening out after a fall, that's a good sign that it's stabilizing from the downturn and could present an attractive entry point for investing.

Q: If you were investing in Phoenix real estate, when would be the best year to invest? How do you know?

Hindsight is always twenty-twenty, but were we to look at the Case-Shiller data on Phoenix from 2011 and 2012, we would notice that the market had been flat for some time and was beginning to perk back up. Investors who bought during this period would likely have enjoyed sizeable profits from their assets appreciating, not counting rental income.

Turning back to our fearless investor: to aid in his comparative analysis, he pulls up the graph for each market and starts to take note of the trends of the cities. Looking at Los Angeles, he notices that the housing prices in 2019 show complete recovery from the crash of 2008. In fact, current housing prices have *exceeded* the bubble's peak prices of 2006. The crash also had noticeably less effect in the stronger LA markets compared to those of Reno and Las Vegas. In Las Vegas, homes bottomed out with less value in 2012 than they had in 2000. Phoenix's index shows that a home worth $100,000 in 2000 was worth $100,000 in 2012, but the steady recovery has been consistent since then.

The volatility of the Los Angeles market is concerning for Neil, a first-time investor. Also, the scale of each recovery is interesting. In Reno, Phoenix, and Las Vegas, housing prices have doubled since 2012 when the market began to recover. Los Angeles has not doubled, even though that market has the highest prices of the ones he is evaluating.

Rental Price Index

As an investor, you will need to know how the rental market is doing in each market you're analyzing. There are very in-depth analyses that we can perform to determine the expected returns from rental properties, but for a broader market analysis, we just want a general indication of the entire market's ability to sustain renters.

A simple rental index, a guide of average monthly rental prices over time, should provide us with enough of a bird's-eye view to capture and examine the market (figure 37). In big cities, there are usually municipal reports or real estate reports from brokerages or research groups from which to glean rental data. I'd start there if you're in a big city market. Alternatively, you can usually get this kind of data from your local real estate agents as long as you present yourself as a serious investor with intention to invest in multiple properties.

fig. 37

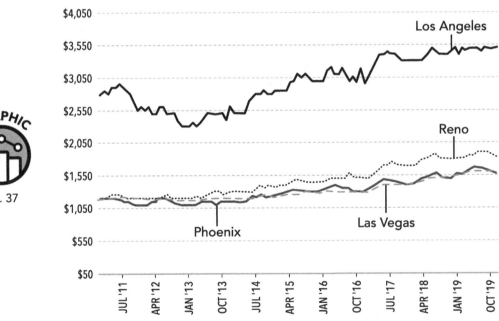

MEDIAN RENTAL PRICES

The rental price indices for Los Angeles, Las Vegas, Phoenix, and Reno.

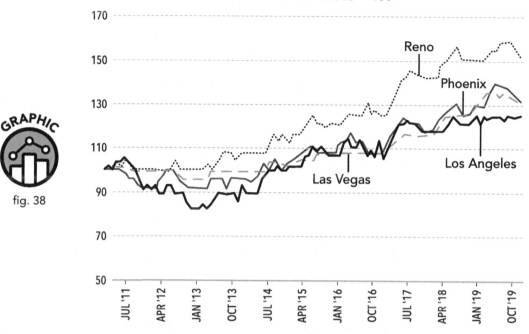

MEDIAN RENTAL PRICE GROWTH INDEX
OCT '10 HOME PRICES = 100

GRAPHIC

fig. 38

It's not just the rent figures we need to analyze, because, although the rent prices in LA look appealing, you can see that it had the lowest dip and the slowest growth compared to the other markets.

Neil's investing strategy, at least for his first investment, is to find a nice property with minimal work needed and to find a suitable tenant for steady income over the next three to five years. Neil's investor colleague has been bragging about getting $2,850 each month from just one average-sized property in the Simi Valley, on the outskirts of Los Angeles. That seems too good to be true, so Neil checks out the numbers to see what's possible (figure 37). This might be a rental market that Neil should tackle later in his investing career. Or, if he is dead set on this market, he can look for older homes, knowing that with the proper renovation strategy he can get high rental returns for his investment. The problem is that high rents are entirely possible, but the purchase prices of those homes are very close to the edge of his comfort level. He *could* afford an older property, but it seems that he could use the same capital to buy two or three properties in his hometown. Conclusion: Los Angeles is a "maybe," but it seems like a thin chance.

Phoenix shows a growth pattern quite similar to that of Los Angeles, with housing prices much closer to Neil's expected price range. The rent values are increasing at a faster rate than housing prices, a very good sign that it's a healthy market with plenty of room in the future for growth. Reno's growth rate is very similar, showing a healthy increase over the last six years with good average rental prices, better than Phoenix at any rate. Vegas, Neil's hometown, has seen a slower increase in rental rates relative to the other markets. But does that mean that Las Vegas still has room for more growth? With the rental price index, our investor hero, Neil, can see that while the growth rate for Vegas is less dramatic, it's still on a healthy trajectory.

After careful consideration, you should be able to eliminate some markets and focus in on the ones you want to target. Prices should *not* be considered in a vacuum but compared to those of the other markets around you. Neil has been actively looking in different markets, but in his discovery phase he's concluded that with his available capital he's priced out of the Los Angeles market at this time. That's not to say that he can't pursue it later, and he'd like to because the growth rate is very healthy, but he will keep his eye on the ratio of rent to housing price for future deals. Remember that the primary goal of his first investment is to not jeopardize his ability to make a second investment. Even if everything went perfectly with an LA-based property, he could afford two or three investments in less expensive markets like Phoenix or Vegas for the price of acquiring just one property in a solid-growth neighborhood in Los Angeles.

Our protagonist has also been quite surprised by what he's found out about Reno pricing. Though it's a smaller town than Las Vegas, housing prices are substantially higher. The tech boom has hit Reno, with rental prices and Case-Shiller indices both showing tremendous growth rates. Neil *could* afford a property there, but he could find cheaper properties in Las Vegas or Phoenix making similar returns. Simply because this is a first investment, Neil is aware that his risk tolerance is lower, and he wants to maximize his experience without paying too much for his first attempt. It was good practice to look at Reno property, but at the end of the day, the risk exposure boots Reno from Neil's list of possible investment options.

Chapter Recap

» Real estate opportunities exist beyond the area where you live.

» Deciding where to look depends on your approach to the deal, whether you want to be active or passive in the management of your property.

» Local real estate investments give you the advantage of doing the research on your own in the actual neighborhoods you are considering.

» Looking for real estate in other markets requires the use of a property manager, but it opens up many more possibilities.

» Using broad indices like Case-Shiller and rental price reports, investors can visualize the entire forest instead of the individual trees.

| 6 |
Deal or No Deal?

Chapter Overview
» How to Analyze the Investment Market
» Calculate the Return on an Investment
» Study the Market Cycles to Know When to Invest

It is not the answer that enlightens, but the question.
— EUGÈNE IONESCO

Invariably, as I talk about real estate investing with my students, I am asked this question: "How do you find the deals you do?"

Over the course of nearly fifteen years, I've directly worked on real estate deals that exceed $500 million in completion value, but the process I currently use to discover potential investment opportunities has not evolved much from what I'm explaining now. I still follow, in essence, the very same model that I advise all beginning investors to follow with their own investments. The only real difference is that I have teams of agents looking for deals for me. Using the same principles I talked about in the last chapter, I search markets throughout the country and ask agents in those markets to use the criteria I lay out in order to send me potential investment opportunities. Some of the variables I ask for include the year a house was built, its relative location in the city (close to X school district, east of Y highway, etc.), the number of bedrooms, and so on. From that, I get multiple properties sent directly to my inbox, which I sort and organize for further analysis.

After I get the property details, I use the broad indices to look at potential markets, just like what you did in the last chapter. In the end, I always find that the properties I like are clustered in the same neighborhoods, or at least the same vicinity (figure 39).

The first logical question I ask as an investor is "Why are people choosing to live there?" and then "Why would I want to live there as well?" You are no longer looking at the broad macro view of multiple markets. You have now come closer, narrowing your search to investigate and analyze a specific individual market. Your job is to understand what makes that area so appealing, why people live there, and whether it makes sense for you to invest in a property there. That's what we aim to do in our next analysis.

fig. 39

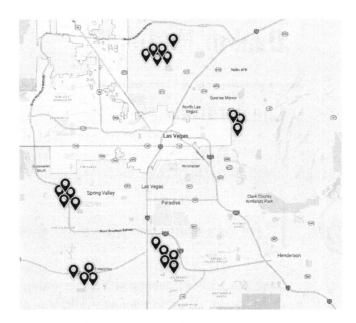

In this step you are going to take a cold objective look at the money. It's the fun part, to begin to really figure out how much you could make from an investment. My approach does not involve one simple formula, but a collection of different ways to gauge the potential returns from a property. Essentially, I'm comparing properties to other properties, looking at comparable sales, lot sizes, and more. Combined with the time frame you established with your goals, you can plot out the actual returns per month, per year, and overall that you can expect from your investment.

We also want to look at the forces of timing. I want to be clear here that I'm not advising that you attempt to "time the market." That's not practical. But one of the outside forces that affects the returns on your investment will be the economic cycles that we see in real estate. We can observe them, and we can also (to an extent) predict what's coming up in the next few years. Having a knowledge of those cycles allows you to set your expectations about your investment. Part of the concept of timing concerns when you receive money and when you have to pay. Delayed income and early expenditures will hurt your investment returns. Money in your hand right now is worth more than money coming in ten years down the road.

But before you do further analysis, you need to gather as many leads as you can find that fit your criteria. It's a numbers game. By driving lots of leads in through your analysis funnel, you increase the chances that you'll uncover the best investment for you. Your goal at this stage is not to find deals but to discard them. If you can get rid of all those risky, opaque, or bad deals, then you can focus your energy on analyzing better deals and actually making those investments.

I've created an entire online course on this very topic. It covers everything you need to know for a pre-investment analysis of your prospective investment properties. We venture into topics that extend beyond the scope of this book. Find my course along with your Digital Assets at **www.clydebankmedia.com/rei-assets**.

This is no time for a gut decision. This is time for a systematic, data-driven analysis to determine if the property is worth the investment. The best returns come from a strong fundamental of investment "number crunching" to weed out the nonviable investments.

Many of my students assume that their number one goal is to spend their capital on an investment. I want you to reframe that by making it your primary goal to eliminate leads. You will find many more opportunities for investment than you have time or money. Your job is to whittle down everything you gather and say no to as many leads as you can. Spending your money on the first lead that comes your way usually turns out to be a bad (or less profitable) investment.

External Market Analysis

fig. 40

Analyzing the forces that affect your return is easier when you separate them into categories.

There are so many variables that affect the properties you analyze. It can easily get overwhelming to try to compare different properties unless you have a way to categorize them. Let's create three different buckets to help keep track of the variables that affect your decision. In the first bucket, we have everything at the regional level. In the second bucket we move closer, looking at the neighborhood. And finally, we examine the investment from the property level, seeing how individual homes compare to other homes.

Regional Analysis

fig. 41

REGIONAL   NEIGHBORHOOD   PROPERTY

The whole point of this analysis is to quickly throw out bad candidates. We're still focusing on working through many different properties and finding efficient ways to eliminate most of them while pulling out the gems. To do that, we ask very general questions at the beginning, and as we eliminate more and more properties, the questions become much more detailed.

Some of the questions might be these:

» What is the general economic condition of the area?
» Are businesses opening or closing?
» Are there good shopping centers around the region?
» What's the density of the area?
» What are the typical household units?
» Where are the job sources for the people living here?

The big questions all revolve around three major elements: jobs, people, and money. To start with, let's look at jobs. What are the job sources? Are these jobs coming from healthy, dynamic industries or industries in decline?

To give an example, Neil was curious about the housing prices in Reno, which seemed higher than expected for the size of the city. It is less than half the size of Las Vegas and yet housing prices and rental prices are much higher. Neil discovered that Reno has experienced quite a tech boom, with a number of big companies establishing factories and corporate headquarters in the area. Apple and Tesla are two of Reno's biggest employers. Many other tech giants have footprints in the area as well. With high-income positions aplenty, the housing prices reflect that strong economy.

Consider two different markets, Detroit and San Francisco, and how they looked at the exact same time in the early 2000s. In size, these two cities are comparable, and yet housing prices were dramatically affected by the industries that provided jobs. In Detroit, a crashing automotive manufacturing industry put a blight on the real estate economy, with home prices plummeting in a very short time. Vacancy rates exploded. Homeowners and unlucky investors were left with dead assets. At the same time, San Francisco's tech boom caused the opposite effect. San Francisco's housing prices were exponentially climbing as the very healthy technology industry boosted the real estate economy.

Q: Are there booming (or dying) industries in the region you're considering that could affect property prices?

And a closely related question: what about unemployment rates? Not just as a static number, but what's the movement of that rate? If unemployment is climbing in the area, it's safe to say that real estate will have a glutted market with prices stagnant or dropping. This is a very easy metric to track and study, much easier than analyzing an area's individual employers one by one. If it's hard to get a read on the underlying job market, you can at least take some cues from the employment numbers. A higher-than-average unemployment rate tells you that something is keeping people from finding jobs. What is it?

Household income is an easy metric to study as well, and you'd be surprised to learn how many early investors fail to consider that tenants must be found who can afford to pay their rent.

Buying an investment in a costly neighborhood might be outside your price range, but consider as an alternative the surrounding neighborhoods. Proximity to high-income areas can increase interest in your property.

Ask the question about who lives in the area right now. Is it heavily populated with families? That's a good sign of safety and long-term trust in a neighborhood. Are there high numbers of single occupants? This could be healthy for a strong rental market, especially if it's close to schools or a major metropolitan area. Also, consider the *net migration* into a neighborhood; "negative migration" means more people are leaving than arriving, and "positive migration" is the opposite.

Municipal authorities often issue *zoning maps* that can help you visualize which areas in your region are approved for which kinds of development. One useful tip is to look for recent changes to these zoning maps to discover updated zoning codes. For instance, if your local council decided to rezone a plot of land for housing, but it's currently undeveloped, that presents a good opportunity for investment. Also, zoning maps help explain some of the future plans for retail, business, and industrial areas. Exploring this data will help you zero in on areas that are primed for growth.

Neighborhood Analysis

fig. 42

How can you be confident that you are investing in a good neighborhood? What are the crucial factors at play that matter to your investment? And more importantly, what are the key distinctive traits of that neighborhood that set it apart from other neighborhoods?

As you look at properties within a neighborhood, here are some of the factors you should investigate.

» **Schools:** School districts affect property value, especially those with high-performing schools. An area with perceived high value in the schools will help to attract good tenants with higher incomes.

» **Major Developments:** One of the best ways to know that a neighborhood is worthy of investing in is if other investors have established developments there. It's a big vote of confidence when major developments like offices, infrastructure, and retail are located in the neighborhood.

» **Transportation:** Use websites like Walk Score (walkscore.com) to get useful insight into the transportation available to the community. Does the neighborhood have roads in good repair that are well-maintained?

» **Desirability:** Do people want to live there? Are there natural elements like rivers or parks that increase the desire to live in that area? Age of the community and of the housing are also factors that help determine desirability.

» **Amenities:** Do you have to travel far to get what you need? Or is everything right at hand within the community? Easily accessible supermarkets, professional services, and dining options all make for a better neighborhood atmosphere.

Comparable Analysis

fig. 43

Up until this point, you've been asking very general questions, eliminating the areas within the targeted cities that don't quite add up to a great investment. By this stage, you should have narrowed it right down to a handful of properties, because comparable analysis examines the individual properties on a case-by-case basis. From here, the analysis gets much more involved with actual figures and statistics. Can you see why it's important that you're not analyzing dozens of properties at this stage? Your time is best spent focused on the most likely investment properties. You don't want to waste time by focusing on those that don't meet your initial standards.

Before we look at the property units around you, we need to consider supply and demand and how it affects your ability to make a profit.

SUPPLY VS. DEMAND

GRAPHIC

fig. 44

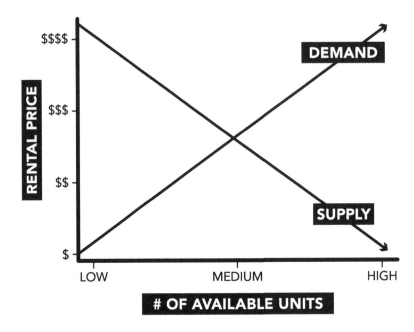

As you can see, as supply (the number of vacant units for sale at any given time) increases, the demand for those units is decreasing. This pushes the price downward. But if the supply is low and demand is high, the price is pushed up. The pricing of each property is going to be calculated considering the available supply in the community.

Let's return to our fictional investor, Neil Hector the Real Estate Investor. He's been steadily evaluating the two markets he's decided would be suitable for investment: Phoenix and his hometown of Las Vegas. As he's looked at the regions of Vegas and Phoenix and then compared the neighborhoods of each city, he's whittled his list down, eliminating many properties in neighborhoods that have bad job prospects, poorly performing schools, and no major developments or growth potential. After all that, he's left with only two properties, both in Las Vegas. Right now, Phoenix doesn't appeal to him. He can't identify any advantages Phoenix can offer that are sufficient to overcome the proximity advantages offered by Las Vegas, his base camp. Our intrepid investor wants to remain as hands-on and active as possible, at least for his first venture, to maximize opportunities for learning.

It's difficult to look at two different investment opportunities and compare them to come up with the amount of rent you can expect to charge. With so many variables, not only between markets but even in the same neighborhood, taking the rental price into account can cause confusion about which investment is better. How can you compare a property that costs more but will command higher rent to a property that costs less and will bring in lower rent? The goal of the next exercise is to help you gain confidence about what rent you can charge. You can use comparable properties within your market to get an accurate idea of expected rental prices. But our main goal in looking at comparable properties is not for the rent, at least not right now. We want to evaluate how much we should pay for the property. Rent prices are good for income projections, but they are also informative regarding the market price of a property.

If you can be confident about the rent you can charge, then you can be confident about the price you should pay for the property.

How does Neil go about comparing his potential investment properties to other properties in the area? What information does he need to track to create a side-by-side comparison that will help him make the final decision? Let's assume that if he's looking to buy a one-bedroom apartment, then he's only going to look at one-bedroom apartments. But even within that category there are a number of variables, like amenities, incentives, features of the home, and so on.

I'll give you a demonstration of what it looks like to make the comparison between seemingly different properties to come up with an expected rent as well as a good indicator for the price of the property.

» **Market Rental Prices**: What are the actual market rents right now?

» **Amenities**: What does your unit offer? A common room? A pool? An enclosed garage? List the amenities on offer in the area and in your unit.

» **Incentives**: To remain competitive, you will need to see what others are offering, such as one free month, waiving of the security deposit, or similar bonus incentives.

UNIT TYPE	BATHS	S.F.	ASKING RENT	ADJUSTED BASE RENT	DEDICATED PARKING SPACE	WATER	ELECTRIC
1B	1	900	$1,000	**$990**	0	1	0
2B	1.5	1100	$1,150	**$1,090**	1	1	0
1B	1	975	$1,050	**$990**	1	1	0
2B	1	1050	$1,250	**$1,190**	2	1	0
1B	1	1000	$1,075	**$975**	2	1	0
2B	2	1200	$1,050	**$1,015**	0	1	0
Studio	1	650	$700	**$640**	1	1	0
1B	1	850	$950	**$890**	1	1	0
Studio	1	700	$750	**$670**	1	1	1
1B	1	875	$975	**$905**	1	1	0
2B	1.5	1150	$1,100	**$1,040**	1	1	0
3B	2.5	1151	$1,101	**$901**	2	2	1

GRAPHIC

fig. 45

DIGITAL ASSETS

You'll find a copy of this Rental Comparison Worksheet in your Digital Assets available online. Access this worksheet and more by going to **www.clydebankmedia.com/rei-assets**.

On this spreadsheet, your target property will go up at the top and you'll enter the comparison units in the area below. In the example, Neil is looking at a one-bedroom apartment with one bathroom; it's nine hundred square feet, and the asking rental price is $1,000 a month. He starts plugging in the data from units in the area similar to what he's analyzing. Notice that he's also making note of the included amenities on the side, such as dedicated parking, water, electricity, balcony, view, oven, fridge, and so on. Everything listed here will affect the desirability of that unit, so he wants to be as thorough as possible.

Part of the worksheet is a section called Adjusted Base Rent. Arriving at this figure is somewhat subjective, but it is easy to calculate. Let me show you how it works.

For simplicity, let's say that our investor hero has selected three units in the area to compare with his own target property. They are all one-bedroom apartments, and Neil has listed all their square footages and asking prices and has made note of as many amenities as he can find. His job now is to assign a value to each amenity. In other words, what would that amenity be worth, each month, to the prospective tenant (figure 46)?

GRAPHIC

fig. 46

	S.F.	ASKING RENT	PARKING	WATER	OVEN
Neil's Unit	900	$1,000	No	Yes	No
Unit A	975	$1,050	Yes	Yes	No
Unit B	850	$950	Yes	Yes	No
Unit C	875	$975	Yes	Yes	Yes

REMEMBER

The market price is not an objective figure. The market price is the price people are willing to pay.

GRAPHIC

fig. 47

	S.F.	ASKING RENT	ADJUSTED BASE RENT	PARKING ($25)	WATER	OVEN ($10)
Unit A	900	$1,000	$970	No (-$25)	Yes	No (-$10)
Unit B	975	$1,050	$1,040	Yes	Yes	No
Unit C	850	$950	$930	Yes	Yes	No
Unit D	875	$975	$980	Yes	Yes	Yes

To assign a value to an amenity, we must look at how the market is pricing units with different amenities. Let's look at Units A and B in figure 47. Unit B has more square footage, as well as dedicated parking. The price difference here is $50 a month. Neil calculates that to mean that dedicated parking is worth $25, and the extra square footage is valued at another $25 each month.

Now let's look at Units C and D. There is only $25 per month difference in rent, and Unit D is slightly larger and has an oven. The extra $25 a month makes sense, so Neil calculates that any unit with an oven is worth maybe $10 extra per month. It is a subjective estimate, so there is some freedom here to decide the ultimate figures.

After doing this, you then adjust the rent based on what amenities the unit has or doesn't have. Once you've done that, you take the average of all the base rents for that same unit type.

$$(970 + 1040 + 940 + 975)/4 = \$980$$

You get an adjusted base rental rate of $980 for units of that size in that area. When Neil Hector the Real Estate Investor looks at his own property, he adds in all the amenities that come with his unit to help him understand the rate that people will pay in that market. Does it have a view? That's worth an extra five dollars. Does it have a balcony? That adds another ten. Does his unit have parking? That adds twenty-five dollars. His unit also comes with a washer/dryer, an oven, and a fridge. That's an extra twenty. After accounting for all amenities, he calculates that he could ask $1,040 a month in rent for his property. It's more than the base rental rate, but his unit offers a lot more amenities that make the price acceptable within that market.

Measures of Return

At this point, let me break the fourth wall for a minute. If you're just glancing through this book, maybe eating lunch and checking messages on your phone while reading, I would encourage you to stop here and finish what you're doing before continuing on. This section is very interesting, and it needs your undivided attention. This section, in my opinion, will separate the serious investors from those who are just dabbling without intention.

Let me give you two simplified investments, two options, and you can choose to invest in only one.

> » **Option A:** You make a $100,000 investment, and after two years you sell that investment for $150,000.

> » **Option B:** You make a $300,000 investment, and after four years you sell that investment for $375,000.

Which is the better investment? It's hard to intuitively say, isn't it? On one hand, Option A gives you just $50,000 in profit, whereas Option B offers you $75,000. Option A pays out sooner, while Option B makes you wait a further two years to receive your payout. Option A is an initial investment of $100,000 and Option B requires that you spend three times as much.

In the real world, investments are complicated with different payment schedules, different capital requirements, and a whole host of variables to break down and analyze. The question the investor is always asking is "How can I compare apples to oranges?"

Simple. You don't. By using metrics called measures of investment return, you can equalize several different options to make the comparison an apples-to-apples analysis. You use these metrics to inform and give you a tool (or tools) to analyze investments much more complicated than the simplified example I gave previously. Although we are talking about real estate investments, the measures of return metrics that we are talking about here apply to any investment you could make, such as in stocks, a business, or a three-bedroom home. Some of the measurements we were looking at earlier apply only to properties with a rental income, but what if you're investing in a fix and flip? Or what if you can't collect rent for six months? No problem, because we can analyze all the investments and compare them, no matter the differences.

We must divide an investment into three separate categories: efficiency, magnitude, and risk. How efficient is your investment? How large is your investment's return likely to be? And how risky will it be to undertake this investment? But before we get into the metrics that we'll use to look at these three categories, you need to understand a simple concept: a dollar today is worth more than a dollar tomorrow. If I asked if you wanted one hundred dollars today or tomorrow, you'd likely say today. Easy, right? And this simple concept frames our entire discussion of how to compare each of our investments, knowing that money today is worth more than money in the future.

I'm going to show you a few ways to calculate costs, but I've included much more detail in my companion course, a free bonus available to my readers. Learn more by going to **www.clydebankmedia.com/rei-assets.**

Internal Rate of Return (IRR)

How do we best understand *internal rate of return*? It's a measurement of how efficient your investment will be. Although the official definition describes IRR as "a discount rate that makes the net present value (NPV) of all cash flows from a particular project equal to zero" (which doesn't sound like anything intuitive), I want to simplify it for you. Because no matter how you receive money on an investment (rent earned over time, money earned after the sale of the investment, etc.), the IRR will allow you to equalize the analysis so that you can determine the best course of action.

I've included a spreadsheet for calculating the IRR for your investment as well as the other key metrics mentioned in this section. Download it at **www.clydebankmedia.com/rei-assets.**

The actual formula to calculate IRR is complicated. Rather than attempt to work through this formula with pen and paper, it's much more efficient to use a program or software designed to calculate IRR for you. I want to stress that the "how" of the calculation isn't as important as the "why." Let me show you what I mean. In figure 48, we have eight hypothetical investments of $200 (shown as "-200" since it's cash flow out from you, the investor, into the investment). All these investments return a total of $1,000 within a ten-year period, but, as you can see in the table, the amounts and timing vary for each investment by year. It is this variance that influences the IRR.

fig. 48

Investment	IRR	DAY 1 1/1/20	YEAR 1 1/1/21	YEAR 2 1/1/22	YEAR 3 1/1/23	YEAR 4 1/1/24	YEAR 5 1/1/25	YEAR 6 1/1/26	YEAR 7 1/1/27	YEAR 8 1/1/28	YEAR 9 1/1/29	YEAR 10 1/1/30	Total Cash Flow
#1	49%	-200	100	100	100	100	100	100	100	100	100	100	1,000
#2	51%	-200	100	100	100	200	0	100	100	100	200	0	1,000
#3	54%	-200	100	100	200	100	0	100	100	200	100	0	1,000
#4	59%	-200	100	200	100	100	0	100	200	100	100	0	1,000
#5	69%	-200	200	100	100	100	0	200	100	100	100	0	1,000
#6	27%	-200	0	0	0	0	500	0	0	0	0	500	1,000
#7	28%	-200	0	0	0	0	500	0	0	0	500	0	1,000
#8	31%	-200	0	0	0	500	0	0	0	0	0	500	1,000

Money earned today is more valuable than money that will be earned in the future, and money earned next year will be more valuable than money earned five years from now, etc.

As you can see in figure 48, the original amount of the investment is the same ($200) and the total cash at the end of the investment period of ten years is the same ($1,000), but each investment offers payouts at different times. How can you select the best investment? Simple. You can use the IRR to equalize the investments to create a fair comparison. When you do that, you can see that Investment 5 is the superior choice, because getting more money back earlier is better than getting money back later.

IRR is not always the best ROI measurement, at least not on its own. If you look at investments A and B in figure 49, they both have the same IRR of 86.2 percent. But obviously, Investment B is better because for a $200 investment in the beginning, you get $100,000 after ten years. In Investment B, the year-ten cash flows, so far out into the future, are deeply discounted by the IRR formula, enough to generate an IRR value that is identical to that of Investment A despite the staggering differential of total cash flow over the life of the investments.

GRAPHIC

fig. 49

Investment	IRR	DAY 1 1/1/20	YEAR 1 1/1/21	YEAR 2 1/1/22	YEAR 3 1/1/23	YEAR 4 1/1/24	YEAR 5 1/1/25
A	86.2%	-200	172.7	172.7	172.7	172.7	172.7
B	86.2%	-200	0	0	0	0	0

Investment	IRR	YEAR 6 1/1/26	YEAR 7 1/1/27	YEAR 8 1/1/28	YEAR 9 1/1/29	YEAR 10 1/1/30	Total Cash Flow
A	86.2%	172.7	172.7	172.7	172.7	172.7	$1,727
B	86.2%	0	0	0	0	100,000	$100,000

If we want to factor in timing as well as the final payout (as is clearly warranted in the figure 49 scenario), then we need to look at an additional measure, either the cash multiple or the net present value, in addition to the IRR. Where the IRR measures how efficiently an investment returns cash to the investor (the timing), the cash multiple and the net present value determine different magnitudes of the investment returns.

Cash Multiple

If you put one dollar into an investment, how much money will you get back? This is what the *cash multiple* metric evaluates—the magnitude of the investment. Some beginner investors are drawn to this very simple metric. If you invest one hundred dollars and you get two hundred dollars back, it's a very easy 2x cash multiple. But over what time period?

CAUTION

Be wary of investments that offer only the cash multiple equation. It doesn't factor in the timing of the return.

As we've learned with the previous metric, timing of the returns matters to investors. A 2x multiple return in a year is far better than a 2x multiple return in ten years. But they both have the same cash multiple to show return on investment.

To solidify this concept and to help explain the need to use all three metrics, I like to ask investors a question. Answer this honestly for yourself. Would you rather know how much you're going to get from an investment but not know when you're going to get it? Or would you rather know exactly when the investment payouts are coming but not know how much you'll receive (or have to pay if the investment is a loss)?

Neither sounds like a very good deal. You wouldn't want to risk your capital on either investment, which is why you need to know both factors going into your investment: the when (efficiency) and the amount (magnitude).

Net Present Value

We've covered the timing of your investment and the amount of money you can expect to make as a cash multiple. But we haven't yet evaluated the very important matter of risk. Two investments with identical IRR and cash multiples aren't identical if one is inherently riskier than the other. This is why we introduce the concept of the risk profile, factoring in a measurement that can equalize the risk for a better grasp of the investment. If Investment A has a higher IRR than Investment B but is significantly riskier, it still may be in your best interest to choose Investment B. Here's how we do that.

Before we can look at the net present value, we must understand the *discount rate*. The discount rate is a way that investors can assess and gauge risk. The higher the risk, the higher the discount rate we should use. But each investor has their own risk profile. What do we do about that?

Think of your baseline discount rate as the nearly risk-free alternative return that you would get if you did not invest the funds into this particular property. The reason this number is different for each investor is because we all have a different opinion about what is risk-free and what is achievable. For someone whose only option is to put the funds in low-interest CDs or treasury bonds, their discount rate may be only 2 to 4 percent. But if an investor has lots of investment options and has historically achieved a blended return of, say, 8 to 10 percent overall, they may use that as their discount rate.

Basically, ask yourself, "If I don't put this money into this investment, what return can I confidently expect elsewhere?" You want to know that your investment will do better than if you had taken the safe alternative. Otherwise, it's not worth your time to undergo the process.

If you have no investment experience, the only alternative you have for your money is a savings account, maybe a 2 percent rate. For most people investing in a blend of equities, bonds, and other alternatives, I would guess their discount rate should be between 4 and 10 percent. Let's say you settle on 5 percent. Then add up the additional risk your project presents. Perhaps it has construction risk. Maybe it's in a poor rental market but presents some possible upsides after your rehab is completed. Adjust for construction risk by adding 3 percent, and add a further 3 percent for the rental risk. With this metric, you know that your personal discount rate for this particular project is 11 percent (5 percent base + 3% + 3%).

Now that you understand the principle of the discount rate, let's discuss how to use it for your risk profile metric. The basic premise of *net present value (NPV)* (figure 50) is that one hundred dollars today is worth more to you than one hundred dollars tomorrow (or in ten years).

NET PRESENT VALUE

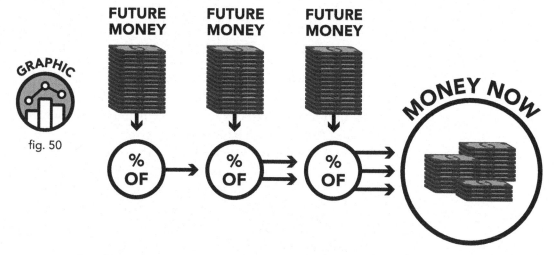

Investments pay out at different rates at different times. The calculation of the discount rate allows investors to visualize all of those payments in one number: the net present value.

That's very intuitive, isn't it? But real-life investments are rarely that intuitive. This is why professional investors choose to use the NPV to help clarify their decisions. Money has different value at different times, that much is clear. Now is better than later, almost always. But you'd also prefer investments that fall within your personal risk profile. By using the discount rate, you can compare the cash flow coming in at different times and convert that future cash into its respective value today. This is called the net present value.

Although the amount you receive each year might be the same (for example, $5,000 returns every year), the discount rate takes the timing of those payouts and discounts it back to the present day. The further out the payments, the more discounted the final amount will be. For example, $5,000 a year from now will only be discounted once, but the Year 5 payment will be discounted five times before arriving at the net present value.

Again, the how of the calculation is not as important as the why. To illustrate, let's look at those investments from the earlier section.

GRAPHIC

fig. 51

Investment	D.R.	NPV	IRR	DAY 1 1/1/20	YEAR 1 1/1/21	YEAR 2 1/1/22	YEAR 3 1/1/23	YEAR 4 1/1/24	YEAR 5 1/1/25
A	8%	$959	86%	-200	173	173	173	173	173
B	8%	$46,119	86%	-200	0	0	0	0	0

Investment	YEAR 6 1/1/26	YEAR 7 1/1/27	YEAR 8 1/1/28	YEAR 9 1/1/29	YEAR 10 1/1/30	Total Cash Flow
A	173	173	173	173	173	$1,727
B	0	0	0	0	100,000	$100,000

Let's go back to the analysis of two investments with identical IRRs. Now, take into account the NPV as shown in figure 51, with an identical discount rate of 8 percent applied for each investment. For Investment A, the NPV is calculated to be worth $959. In other words, if you could get all those payouts in one lump sum of $959 today, it would be equivalent in value to waiting ten years to get $1,727. Fascinating, isn't it? But as for Investment B, it is very clear that it's a far better deal than Investment A, with an NPV of $46,119 for your $200 investment. Which would you prefer right now, $959 or $46,119? That's an easy one.

ROI for Rental Properties

In the last chapter, we talked about how to compare properties against other properties and how to compare neighborhoods and regions alongside one another. Now, we are going to compare properties by their potential returns. Even in identical markets, neighborhoods, and assets, the variables between investments are large. When we're looking at properties with rental returns, we can use metrics to create that apples-to-apples comparison that we're always looking for.

We need consistent measures to equalize all the variables that come with each investment, variables like renovation costs, rental returns, time on the market, and so on. This is so you can do a side-by-side comparison and say without a doubt, "Yes, this is the investment for me."

The previous metrics applied to any investment opportunity, even outside of the real estate world. These next measures apply specifically to any investment with a rental potential.

Net Rental Yield

The first and most common way to evaluate a rental property is by the rental income you expect to make compared to your total investment. The *net rental yield* compares your annual rental income to the total value of your property. The best part about this metric is that taxes and any other expenses have already been considered. Basically, this is the money that goes into your pocket. The calculation is simple:

(Monthly Net Rent x 12) / Property Value = Net Rental Yield

Your net rental yield is expressed as a percentage. The higher the percentage, the better the deal.

Let's say that you have a property from which you're collecting $1,000 rent each month. It's a studio apartment in the middle of downtown Las Vegas. You also have a property in Phoenix, another one-bedroom apartment, this one collecting $1,100 in rent. Is one performing better than the other? Are you charging the right amount for rent? How can you tell? It all depends on the value of the property.

Don't confuse the value of the property with the purchase price of the property. If you have invested in a solid property, newly built, no problems, well-maintained, then, yes, your purchase price is fairly close to the value of the property. But if you paid to make major repairs and some key upgrades, then such costs should be factored into the value.

Let's say that for your Phoenix property you bought a well-kept apartment, and you didn't change anything before you began renting to your first tenant. In Vegas, the apartment had to go through a few renovations to bring it up to code and to modernize some of the tired décor and amenities.

» Phoenix Property Value = $135,000 purchase price
» Las Vegas Property Value = $72,000 purchase price + $32,000 renovations

The value of the Phoenix unit is $135,000, as you didn't change anything. The value of the Vegas unit is $104,000 after all the work you put in. Here is what the net rental yield looks like for each of your units:

» Phoenix Net Rental Yield: ($1,100 x 12) / $135,000 = 9.78%
» Las Vegas Net Rental Yield: ($1,000 x 12) / $104,000 = 11.5%

At first, it looked like your Phoenix investment was doing better, earning you an extra hundred dollars a month. But after calculating the net rental yield, we can see that the Las Vegas investment is outperforming the Phoenix investment by almost 2 percent. Essentially, what this ROI measurement is telling us is that for every dollar invested in the Las Vegas property, you can expect to get 11.5 cents back each year in rent, as opposed to 9.78 cents back from the Phoenix property.

Added Value Potential

Think about all the ways a property investment earns income. Rent earned is just one way of bringing in cash. The appreciation value of the property is another. And one of the things I really love about real estate investing is that you as the investor have the control to add value to your own investment. You can directly control the amount your asset is worth as you increase the perceived value of it.

When analyzing a property, savvy investors take note of its untapped potential. Let me show you what this looks like. Let's say you are interested in investing in a multifamily complex with six units with an asking price of $700,000. The average rent per unit is $800. It could do with some major repairs, and you are not sure if the price is worth it. But in your research, you see that other multifamily units in the area are 100 percent occupied, with rents as high as $1,200 for a unit of similar size.

In other words, you have the potential of realizing an extra $2,400 per month if you can do the repairs. But how much could you spend without decreasing the return on your investment?

Using the same net rental yield calculation we just talked about, you can determine the repair budget you would need to bring your multifamily unit to a better valuation.

» Current Net Rental Yield: ($800 x 6 units x 12 months) / $700,000 = 8.22%

To figure out the budget and maintain that net rental yield, you reverse the calculation with the new expected rental rates.

Repair Budget = (Rental Income/Net Rental Yield) – Purchase Price
($1,200 x 6 x 12) / 0.0822 = $1,051,000
$1,051,000 - $700,000 = Repair Budget of $351,000

Now you know how much you can spend on repairs and still get the same investment yield on your money. By making all the necessary repairs within this budget, you'll end up getting a higher overall return on your investment.

Choosing Your Best Investment

fig. 52

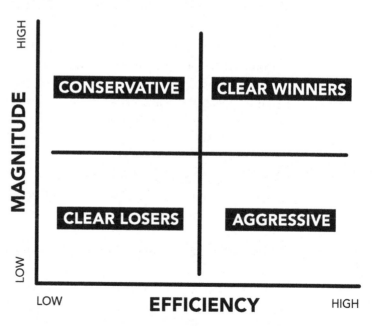

The efficiency (or timing) as well as the magnitude of your returns matters. Your investments will likely fall into the bottom right or the top left quadrant, dependent on your risk tolerance. The "clear winners" are really hard to find unless you have the metrics to measure them (figure 52).

To summarize this chapter: you need to consider the full force of the magnitude of your investment and the efficiency of the returns, balanced against the amount of risk you're willing to accept. I always advise beginner investors to select a property that allows for minimal risk of failure so they can move on to their next investment. You may be tempted to select properties with higher risk factors because of the higher magnitude and efficiency of returns, but will that potentially harm your future as an investor if you lose your initial investment capital?

To close off this section, let's return to our now-familiar investor hero pursuing his glorious fortune; I know you're anxiously waiting to see what Neil does with his investments. After all his analysis, Neil is left with two properties, each with its own advantages and disadvantages. One property is very appealing, on the east side of Vegas in a good neighborhood with a great school district. It is considered new, built in the last four years, with a long-term tenant already living there. He would not have to spend anything on rehabbing the property and could simply take over the existing lease without any disruption to the current tenant. The lease would net him $1,000 per month after all expenses.

The other property under consideration is closer to town and presents some challenges. The interior is old and worn out and needs some work. The property could do with some exterior work as well to spruce up the curb appeal. But rental prices in that area show Neil that with some core improvements, he could add equity to the home as well as increase the expected rental rate to make $1,400 per month, after all expenses.

Both properties have a $350,000 price tag, which is within Neil's budget, but for option B, Neil estimates that a further $40,000 would be needed to complete the repairs.

He starts with the net rental yield to help quantify both investments:

» **Option A:** ($1,000 x 12) / $350,000 = 3.42%
» **Option B:** ($1,400 x 12) / ($350,000 + $40,000) = 4.30%

Option B has a greater net rental yield, which demonstrates that the work necessary to put into that option would be worth it for the return he would expect to get. He begins working through the key metrics to help equalize the two returns on investment. Making some assumptions, Neil figures that he will be able to sell Option A for $500,000 in ten years. But Option B will likely sell for the same amount in just five years with his improved property value assessment (see the Year 5 and Year 10 columns in figure 53).

fig. 53

Investment	IRR	DAY 1 1/1/20	YEAR 1 1/1/21	YEAR 2 1/1/22	YEAR 3 1/1/23	YEAR 4 1/1/24	YEAR 5 1/1/25
A	6.6%	-350,000	12,000	12,000	12,000	12,000	12,000
B	8.3%	-390,000	16,800	16,800	16,800	16,800	500,000

Investment	IRR	YEAR 6 1/1/26	YEAR 7 1/1/27	YEAR 8 1/1/28	YEAR 9 1/1/29	YEAR 10 1/1/30	Total Cash Flow
A	6.6%	12,000	12,000	12,000	12,000	512,000	$620,000
B	8.3%	0	0	0	0	0	$567,200

Neil also assumes that since Option B is older, he'll wait to do major upgrades in Year 5 just before he sells; thus, no rental income will be collected in Year 5. The total cash flow is higher for Option A, giving Neil a greater cash multiple on that option. But Option B is much more efficient—it returns less money but in a quicker time frame. Therefore, the internal rate of return for Option B is significantly better.

fig. 54

Investment	D.R.	NPV	Cash Multiple	Annual Yield	IRR	DAY 1 1/1/20	YEAR 1 1/1/21	YEAR 2 1/1/22	YEAR 3 1/1/23
A	5%	$49,617	1.8	3.4%	6.6%	-350,000	12,000	12,000	12,000
B	7%	$23,398	1.5	4.3%	8.3%	-390,000	16,800	16,800	16,800

YEAR 4 1/1/24	YEAR 5 1/1/25	YEAR 6 1/1/26	YEAR 7 1/1/27	YEAR 8 1/1/28	YEAR 9 1/1/29	YEAR 10 1/1/30	Total Cash Flow
12,000	12,000	12,000	12,000	12,000	12,000	512,000	$620,000
16,800	500,000	0	0	0	0	0	$567,200

Neil decides to calculate the net present value to help him understand that IRR number. Option B has to include more risk because of the construction, so his discount rate is higher on Option B than on the safer Option A. With his calculations, Neil determines that the NPV is $49,617 for Option A and $23,398 for Option B (figure 54).

Overall, his two options look like this (figure 55):

	OPTION A	OPTION B
Net Rental Yield	3.4%	4.3%
Total Profit	$270,000	$177,200
Internal Rate of Return	6.6%	8.3%
Net Present Value	$49,617	$23,398
Cash Multiple	1.8	1.5

Seeing it like this, Neil can determine the best course of action. Ultimately, although Option B has the benefit of being more efficient, Option A presents less risk. He's willing to forgo the higher returns in favor of starting with a solid investment that shows great promise over the long term. And with that, Neil decides to put in an offer on Option A to begin his investment journey.

NOTE

In his eagerness to get started, Neil did not even consider financing. But, fortunately, he will end up securing financing that ultimately helps him to achieve higher-than-expected returns. In chapter 8, we'll explore how debt financing can help or hurt investment returns. In chapter 12, we'll look at Neil's actual performance.

Market Cycles

QUOTE

> *Be fearful when others are greedy and be greedy when others are fearful.*
> – WARREN BUFFETT

If I told you about a man who accurately predicted the 2008 financial crisis back in 1997, would you think he was worth your attention? I certainly do, which is why I included this section, based heavily on the writings of Fred Foldvary, a brilliant economist who evaluated and wrote about real estate *market cycles*. The housing crisis of 2008 is all anybody can think of when the subject of real estate investing comes up. Unless you were among the few who saw it coming, it seemed to come out of nowhere. Suddenly housing prices were crashing and hundreds of thousands of homeowners and investors were left upside down on their investments. What might surprise you is that the rare Wall Street savants and hedge fund managers were not the only ones capable of anticipating this period of recession. Though no one can predict the magnitude of a crash, seasoned market investors do learn how to analyze trends and assess the risk of recession. In fact, with a little bit of background and awareness, you can do this as well.

In the late 1800s, a man named Henry George noticed a pattern with housing prices that was extremely consistent. It was a cycle that real estate would move through in a repeatable and (more important to our discussion) predictable fashion. While not exact, the market cycle of real estate has closely followed this same pattern since Henry George discovered it. Major global events can disrupt the pattern (like World War II and the hyperinflation of the 1970s), but, barring such events, we can predict the peaks and booms to be expected in real estate.

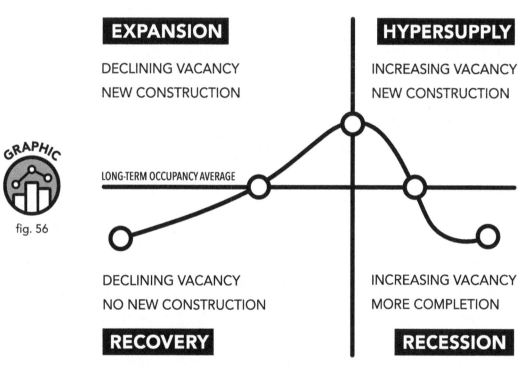

fig. 56

The 18-year typical market cycle.

The market cycle can be explained in four phases, each with its own attributes and warning signs (figure 56). To work its way through the cycle, real estate seems to take around eighteen years, but that time frame is by no means rigid. I'd rather we don't focus on the actual length of the phases and instead focus on interpreting the data to know how to find out where we are currently and what's likely to happen in the next few years.

When we're on the upward trend of a market cycle, it's a great time to get into the investment market with full confidence of seeing excellent returns. But if we're in the downward trend of a market, it's time to be wary. Being aware of the current phase makes a decision to buy or sell assets clear and straightforward. In other words, just as the stock market will tell you to buy low and sell high, understanding the real estate market cycle can show you when the value of your investment is high or low.

Be mindful of the fact that market cycles don't just affect housing prices. They also affect rental prices as well as vacancies. Be sure to include contingencies to counteract the effects of the expected vacancy rates of the various phases of the cycle.

Phase I: Recession

When occupancy rates fall below the national average, it's a sure sign of a recession phase. And when it comes, it comes on fast. The market is inundated with vacant units that were built in the previous cycle when construction peaked. This abundance in supply will drive housing prices down and vacancy rates up. Supply exceeds demand and investors suffer because of it.

CHANGES IN HOUSING COSTS

fig. 57

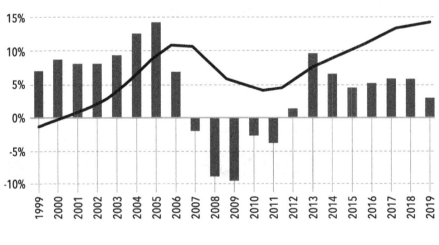

At this stage, most construction halts, with new projects starting very rarely and sporadically. But the projects that have begun are continued through to completion, even though the need for them has diminished. This leads to a very interesting trend being displayed in recessions.

In the graph in figure 57, the line represents the change in housing costs from year to year. The bars represent the actual figures showing the change in prices from year to year. You can see that from 1999 to 2005 housing prices dramatically increased in value, as much as 15 percent from one year to the next. But by 2007, housing prices had started to lose value. In 2008 and 2009, they were plummeting. It wasn't until 2012 that prices truly began to recover. That's almost six years of recession. Why did it last so long? Part of the reason is that the previous cycle had such an enormous boom, with many projects oversupplying the market with new units. There was simply too much extra inventory. It took almost six years for the demand to catch up with the supply on the market, finally stabilizing and improving housing prices.

Besides a glut of inventory, other economic factors also play a role. In an effort to curb a hyper-expansion phase, the Federal Reserve will raise interest rates, an almost certain sign that they believe there is going to be a recession. Higher interest rates will halt new projects because financing is just too prohibitive to start anything.

During a downturn, the investor must be patient. When we look at recessions of the past, we can see that they often take three to five years before hitting bottom. During that time, investors should hold on to their assets, maybe building up cash reserves before the recession hits to cover any vacancies and loss of income. The best course of action would be to exit from all your investments prior to the recession's arrival; however, the ability to perfectly time a recession is nearly impossible.

One way to endure and even lay the groundwork for future prosperity during a recession is to set aside some cash. Investors who manage to be flush with cash during a recession can pick up new properties for just pennies on the dollar. It's very possible to do deals during a recession, but because it's a buyer's market, you must negotiate very aggressively. You should negotiate a deal that will allow you to secure good returns in the market as it is. You should not accept a deal that forces you to assume any significant improvements in the near future. Such negotiations may not be easy, but they are very possible, assuming you can find motivated sellers.

Phase II: Recovery

Everyone is aware of what a recession looks like, having just lived through one of the worst since the Great Depression. But what does it look like after the worst is over? How can you begin to recognize the signs that you're through a recession phase and into a recovery phase?

In the United States, the market bottomed out nationwide in 2011, and in 2012 in some places. But since then, it has been in a steady recovery phase, with many markets bouncing back to pre-recession prices. Not only does the demand meet the supply for available units in the market, it's also fueled by lower interest rates, making investors more likely to find new projects.

When interest rates start to go lower, businesses start to grow. They hire more people, they expand into new markets, they build more office space, they create more jobs. Overall confidence grows, causing increased demand for new homes. Vacancies drop as businesses and newly hired employees start to move into those empty properties.

Although vacancies will drop, new construction is very slow to begin again. But as investors see improved returns, they are more willing to fund those new projects. Also, when vacancies drop and occupancy begins to jump over the national average, the construction industry will move to take advantage of the growing demand.

One way to interpret this data as an investor is to look at the increase in permits issued for new developments.

LA METRO AREA BUILDING PERMITS

fig. 58

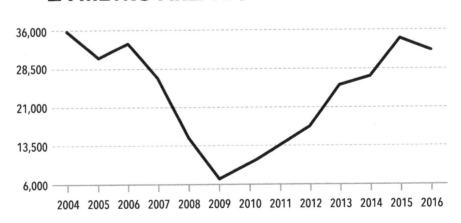

As an example, look at the housing permits issued in the metropolitan area of Los Angeles (figure 58). In 2009–2010, the permits were at an all-time low, but as the recession began to ease, more permits were issued. Los Angeles is a mature real estate market that recovered quickly after the recession, but you can see how the trend in building permits signaled the recovery phase quite accurately for investors who were paying attention.

Accumulate investments quickly during a recovery. This is the time to be aggressive about finding new properties. You have the advantage as a buyer, with many people looking to get out from under bad deals done during the wrong phase. Use your buying power to negotiate prices down very low, as competition for the available properties will be nonexistent at this phase.

Phase III: Expansion

As occupancy stays above the national long-term average, the recovery phase gives way to the expansion phase. New building and construction really ramps up during this phase as more investors see the profits to be made from these deals. A good way to determine whether you're in an expansion phase is to look at rental rates. When demand begins to outstrip supply, rental prices can really expand. In many markets, double-digit rental growth is quite common after the recovery phase. This is because building new properties to satisfy the demand takes time. Deals need to be negotiated. Projects need to get funded. Permits need to be acquired. Land needs to be developed. Time is needed to complete new construction. And during this rapid expansion of new projects, supply has not yet caught up with the rising demand. By the time the supply of available units starts to meet demand, the recovery phase has been well underway for four to six years.

Another indicator of this phase is the ease of financing. Straight out of a recession, banking institutions are hesitant to fund new projects. But as the market tension starts to ease and recovery is evident, financing becomes easier to secure. As the rules get relaxed, you know the expansion phase is in progress. As an investor, you should be able to secure better terms on your investments by taking advantage of the bank's willingness to lend.

This can also be a worrying time for investors. Many people make calculations based on the rapid growth they've seen in the past. But that can leave them expecting greater future results when the bulk of the growth has already happened. The expansion phase doesn't last long but leads very rapidly into the last phase.

Phase IV: Hypersupply

When builders and investors see that rent prices are rising exponentially every year, they are motivated to enter the market to get their own piece of the pie. This isn't present only in new construction; housing prices will begin to grow as well when people start to outbid each other on existing properties. Everyone wants to be in real estate, and everyone is fighting to get their own share.

As construction from the expansion phase begins to oversaturate the market with new units, the supply becomes far greater than the available demand can support. Vacancies level off from their decline in the previous two phases and sharply increase. When you see this, it's a sure sign that the market is in the hypersupply phase.

REMEMBER

Your job as an investor is not to react to the current market conditions, but to recognize them and preempt them by your actions.

The temptation to stay in your investment, or even to begin new ones, is very real in this phase. Rental rates and housing prices are still rising, though they are rising more slowly than in previous phases. It still looks good from one year to the next, but that difference begins to shrink. Your job is to see the next phase coming—the recession, when everything comes crashing down again. The hypersupply phase is a good time to exit from your investments and hold cash positions with plenty of liquidity in preparation for the upcoming downturn. If you can identify weaker-performing investments, those are the first ones you'll want to pare from your portfolio.

I want to echo Warren Buffett's sentiment that good investors don't act in accordance with the market. They anticipate the next phase and plan their actions based on that, not on the current conditions. By recognizing where you are, you can take the appropriate steps to be ready for the next phase, not doing what everyone else is doing. In this way, you're not timing the market, but instead you are identifying the market's current phase and anticipating future phases.

Chapter Recap

» The goal of market analysis is to eliminate candidates.

» Begin by thinking of the different forces that affect returns, narrowing in from a wide view to the actual property itself.

» Begin comparing neighborhoods with careful analysis from a variety of sources.

» By creating an apples-to-apples comparison, you equalize the measurements used to evaluate properties.

» Use key metrics to calculate the expected return on your investment despite all the variables you will encounter.

» Use calculations to determine the efficiency, magnitude, and risk profile of your investment, prioritizing those properties that make more money quicker.

» While it is not possible to perfectly time the market, you can analyze the different phases (recession, recovery, expansion, and hypersupply) and take appropriate action.

| 7 |
The Deep(er) Dive Analysis

Chapter Overview
» Turning Estimates into Actuals
» Verifying Your Analysis Assumptions
» Counting Up the Whole Cost of Your Investment

What gets measured gets managed.

— BUSINESS PROVERB

I heard a story about Leo Babauta, author of the Zen Habits blog (zenhabits. net). He was trying to figure out why he wasn't able to start running. As an overweight guy trying to get into shape, he would read constantly about techniques and methods. But no matter what he tried, he couldn't find a way to actually begin running. In the end, he tried a radically simple technique. Every morning, Leo would put on his running shoes and get out the door. That was his only goal for the day. He didn't have to run a mile, around the block, or even to the end of his driveway. He simply had to put the shoes on, lace them up, and walk out the door. On some days, he just turned around and went back inside, but on most days, he would do a run. When he became consistent about going for short runs, he upped the ante. He had to run to the end of the street every day, but that was it. He made it decidedly easy to take action, and because he did, he was able to overcome that analysis paralysis and start working on his goals.

Why am I telling you this? I want you to avoid the temptation to get stuck in this analysis phase. As you've discovered, there are a lot of analysis techniques and tools that investors can use to study their options. But it's very easy to get stuck working through spreadsheets, charts, and graphs. I don't want you to forget that the whole point of this analysis is to find the right course of action and then to *take* it. It's just too tempting to rationalize away action because of the possibility of getting something wrong.

There is no such thing as "perfect" for an investment, so I don't want to put forth the idea that we're working toward that goal. But anything that impacts your cash flow is worth the analysis to get as close to good as you can get. By this time, you have narrowed down your investments to just a couple of options, which is good, because we're going to be looking not in a general way but in highly specific areas for that individual property. That was impossible before, with the huge number of leads you were working with.

What does cash flow mean? For the investor, it speaks to both sides of the investment: the money going into the property as well as the money coming out of it. Think about some of the cash flow outputs that you have to consider, such as the actual purchase price, any rehab or renovations you have to undergo, repairs and maintenance that happen during the life of your investment, as well as the cost of having a vacant unit. For cash inflow, you are already familiar with the equity you build over time and through paying down the principal. There is also the rental income you get, and possibly other sources of income—maybe you own a multifamily property with a coin-op laundry, or you provide room rentals in common areas for parties and other events. Assessing and optimizing all the cash flows, both incoming and outgoing, is crucial to analyzing the health of your investment.

Development Costs

Unless you are taking over a new or recently renovated property, there's a good chance that part of your investment will involve working with contractors. You did your estimates in the last analysis, but now it's time to assign actual costs to the work you intend to have done.

In development, there are two types of cost that you'll have to include as part of your analysis: soft costs and hard costs. The hard costs are sometimes called the "brick-and-mortar" costs, anything that has to do with the physical construction or upkeep of the building (materials, labor, equipment, etc.). Typically, you'll find that a large percentage of your costs come from these brick-and-mortar elements—things like paving, landscaping, carpets, lumber, steel, drywall, and site excavations.

The soft costs of development are things related to the property that are less tangible than the hard costs. Consider elements like loan interest, project management, inspections, insurance, architectural fees, legal fees, permitting, and any studies that need to be done.

You may have to update your running cost estimates based on improvements you make. For example, if you are planning an addition, it will lead to higher utility costs as well as increased property taxes due to the higher assessed value of the property.

Depending on the amount of work you're likely to need, you could be engaging the help of several different professionals, so be sure to budget for architects, lawyers, planners, surveyors, civil engineers, and specialist services like environmental reports or traffic engineering.

Due Diligence

Trust, but verify.

                                        –RONALD REAGAN

You may not recognize the name, but Stanislav Petrov is the ultimate proof of the efficacy of doing your due diligence. He was a Russian soldier during the Cold War era. His role was to personally oversee the Russian countermeasures if he saw any sign of the Americans launching nuclear weapons. Tensions were very high as both countries came extremely close to an all-out nuclear attack on each other. In 1983, during the absolute height of this tension, Petrov was manning the station when he received word that the Americans had launched a missile toward them. Immediately following, he received word that four more missiles were launched and headed directly for Russian airspace. Protocol for Petrov was to alert his superiors of the imminent threat and to take decisive counteraction. But Petrov decided instead to use his judgment and undergo one of the world's best examples of due diligence.

He decided not to report the missiles and instead assumed that the reporting system was at fault. His reasoning was that, should the Americans launch an attack, it would not be a mere five missiles. It would be an all-out assault. He went to investigate his reporting system and found that there was indeed a fault with the computing mechanism. Had he followed protocol, there is no doubt his superiors would have launched what they thought to be a counterattack, but Petrov's diligence spared the world from a cataclysmic event.

After a thorough analysis of the investment opportunity you have before you, you want to engage in a process of due diligence to uncover what you've been assuming to be true throughout the process. The reason for undergoing due diligence is to avoid catastrophe and loss with your investment (albeit not as severe as the example I gave!). As you've seen, many of the analysis tools at your disposal are subjective, relying on you to gather neighborhood comparables and market data and to acquire information from sources that you hope are reputable. The due diligence process is to verify those key drivers that could greatly impact your ability to make a good return on your investment.

To aid with this whole process, I've created a Due Diligence Checklist as part of the digital assets available for readers of this book. Note that this includes many items that cover various commercial real estate scenarios, so many of the elements may not be applicable for a residential rental property. They are provided to give you a more complete list of potential due diligence items. Download by visiting **www.clydebankmedia.com/rei-assets**.

Let me cover some of the key components to consider as you work through the assumptions and questions related to your investment.

> » **Are you getting what you think you are getting?** You would be amazed to discover how many investors have planned out their investment on paper only to discover, often too late, that what they thought they were buying was not what it really was at all. Unless you can visit your investment, be extra cautious about verifying that you are buying what you think you're buying.

> » **Is the market what you think it is?** Verify elements like the demographics in the area, typical incomes of residents, and schools in the vicinity. Source data can sometimes be out of date, so double-check everything so as not to get left in the lurch.

> » **Are your rents and expenses realistic?** Trust but verify the elements you used to determine rent, like vacancy, other rental properties, and delinquencies. Also, are your tax calculations correct? Are your management fees and marketing costs accurate?

> » **Are your rehab cost estimates accurate?** Add *contingency* buffers to any estimate you get to keep from running out of cash before the end of your project.

> » **Is your property in the stated condition?** Agents can sometimes be "generous" with their descriptions. Before closing your purchase, I encourage you to get a full property inspection report to verify the condition of all major elements, like the roof, foundation, electrical and HVAC systems, whether there's termite or water damage, and many more factors. This can easily affect your rehab costs.

» **Are you buying from the seller?** Although it's not as common anymore, scam artists have been known to put on a whole show for a buyer, receive payment, and then disappear. Only after the scammer has fled does the buyer realize that they were never dealing with the seller. Always check the names on the title to ensure that the right person is the seller of your investment.

» **Are there lease contracts?** Verify that there are no underpinning leases that have been contracted with third parties. You don't want a nasty surprise that leaves you handcuffed to a very cheap rental agreement for the next few years.

» **Is there environment contamination?** If you have an industrial property, it's possible that the previous tenants have been less scrupulous than they should have been, leaving dangerous contamination for you to manage. You can mitigate your risk by taking out insurance that covers you or by including clauses in your contract that make the previous owner legally accountable for cleanup costs for any contamination.

Many of these checks can be done very quickly and easily, but I would caution that you don't want to do this for every property you are looking at. You want to be just one step away from making the investment before doing your due diligence.

Adding It All Up

At this point, you have done everything in your power to conduct a thorough analysis of your investment. You've also conducted an in-depth due diligence process where you've examined the major and minor assumptions you've made about the property. All of that leads you to this point where you are ready to say yes to the investment. But how much will that yes cost you?

» **Purchase Price.** This is the easiest cost to factor in. Negotiate hard to arrive at the best purchase price for this investment.

There is no such thing as the "right" price for a property. The market is subjective, and the value of the home is only what you are willing to pay for it and what the seller agrees to accept for it—meaning you can sometimes present a strong case to the seller to accept less than they asked for.

» **Closing Costs.** When the title transfers from seller to buyer, there are some final costs, not all of which you have to pay. Although it varies from deal to deal, estimates show that buyers pay an average of 2 to 5 percent of the total purchase price as closing costs. Some costs are negotiable. Some are owed by the seller. And some might not apply in your situation. You can include any closing costs in the loan. I would advise working with lenders who offer the lowest closing costs, or who at least are up-front about what costs you are expected to pay. These can include the following:

- Loan application fee
- Credit reports
- Home inspection
- Homeowners insurance
- Private mortgage insurance (if paying less than 20% deposit)
- Property tax (varies from state to state)
- Transfer taxes
- Recording fees

» **Professional Fees.** These costs go toward architects you employ, the legal team and their efforts, property management of any long-distance investments, and any inspections (if you've arranged it privately). Other specialty professional fees, such as for traffic studies, environmental impact reports, or civil engineering costs, could also be relevant for commercial properties.

» **Construction.** Factor in the quotes provided by the contractors and builders as part of the total price you're paying for the property. If you've used the net rental yield to help budget for it, you can plan this cost well in advance.

» **Contingencies.** Using some of the neighborhood data from previous analyses, you can make some assumptions about the expected vacancies in your unit. Maybe you need to set aside four weeks out of every year to account for vacancies. But it could easily be eight weeks. Plan for the worst-case scenarios and what that would look like on your bottom line. Include any repairs and maintenance during the life of the property. Consider the age of the property to determine major upgrades likely to be needed during your ownership, such as plumbing overhaul, roof replacement, HVAC unit repair, new window installation, exterior repainting, or mold testing.

» **Commissions.** If you have a larger property or an investment in another city, factor in some of the commissions you're likely to pay to brokers and property managers to find tenants and manage the property. Ideally, you'd like those fees to come out of the lease itself, but just make sure that it's part of your deal analysis.

» **Other Costs.** Any number of costs could crop up during your ownership, costs that aren't common or that you aren't thinking about at this stage of the investment. Consider the holding costs that you'll have year after year, like property taxes, insurance, bills, interest owed on your loan, and so on. This is also the time to consider the exit costs you will be liable for later on. These will include staging the property, agent fees, marketing, and commissions for selling the home. Your sale of the property may be more than five years down the road, but it's important to include this information in your final account now to estimate investment performance.

Chapter Recap

» "Analysis paralysis" is the enemy of real estate investing. The point of analysis is to work toward a decision, to uncover the easiest path of action.

» Work on gathering exact figures for development costs, both hard and soft.

» Due diligence allows you to verify all the assumptions you made during the analysis process.

» Once you are satisfied with the analysis and due diligence, and you are ready to pull the trigger on your investment, calculate the entire cost of that action.

| 8 |

Right on the Money: Financing

An investment in knowledge pays the best interest.

— BENJAMIN FRANKLIN

The year was 2006. Banks were enthusiastically handing out *subprime mortgages*—loans that were given to people with poor credit scores—and they felt comfortable enough doing it. AIG, along with many other insurance companies, was backing these banks and their investments, so that in the event borrowers defaulted on their loans, the banks were insured against the losses. Thousands and thousands of mortgages were handed out to people who, if not for the subprime criteria, would never have had the chance to invest in real estate or own a home.

To help you understand just how relaxed the banks were, let me tell you the true story of Clarence Nathan, as reported by Planet Money and This American Life. Clarence was an average homeowner who had three part-time jobs from which he earned a combined total of approximately $45,000 a year. He was able to secure a loan against his house when he needed some money. The loan was called a no-income-verification loan, which meant that the banks were not concerned about Clarence's income or his existing assets (other than the house), yet they were still willing to loan him a whopping five hundred forty-thousand dollars. Clarence himself said, "It's almost like you pass a guy in the street, and you say, will you lend me $540,000? He says, OK."

It gets worse. Banks were also offering "no income, no asset" (NINA) loans, meaning that you were not required to have a job at all, and the banks would still give you a mortgage. It seems that the rules for getting loans were written in pencil, and if you didn't qualify for a traditional loan, then the banks created new products that they could offer you to bypass their own regulations. It might seem foolish on the banks' part, but remember that everything was driven by national greed. These poor mortgages were then bundled together, rated highly by rating agencies with good credentials, and sold to investors as reputable investments.

And then the Fed started raising interest rates. If you recall our discussion from chapter 6, then alarm bells may be going off in your head. When interest rates start to go up, it's one of the signs that the market is about to enter the recession phase. Higher interest rates made it impossible for these low-credit loan holders to repay their exorbitant loans. And in one swoop, many of those subprime mortgages were defaulted on all at once. And the insurance companies that were receiving insurance premiums to safeguard banks against this very event? They did not have enough liquid capital to pay out the insurance claims, and they also defaulted on their promise to pay. The combination of all these factors led to the crash we saw starting in 2007 and very rapidly becoming a long recession, the worst since the Great Depression of the 1930s.

Why am I telling you this? Because you should know what money lenders were doing just a few short years ago to understand how the rules have changed. Lenders are much stricter with their requirements. They have controls and measures to prevent people from getting easy access to money. And you can see why they would be so cautious, given their past experiences with lending.

Although the financing world has tightened up as of late, you can still find great financing options for your investments. This is, in part, what we were doing in the last section by adding up the costs. If you can demonstrate to lenders that you know what you're getting into, show the finances you need for a project, and prove that you have a good grasp of your total costs, you will have access to better financing for your deals.

There is nothing worse than coming up short on your projections and not having enough money. Not only do you lose valuable credibility with banks if you have to secure a second loan, but you might find that the rates are exorbitantly high, costing you much more than your pride. In this chapter, I want to cover the basics of financing, both the benefits and the options you have at your disposal.

Before going any further, I do want to make a disclaimer. I make no claims to be a financial expert or advisor. Even from the time of this writing, banking rules could have changed. And as we continue to wrestle with the economic fallout of COVID-19, we find ourselves facing recession in an environment where interest rates are lower than ever. You should seek the advice of a professional before securing any financing of your own. Use the following pages as information and general advice that may or may not suit your own financial needs.

The Double-Edged Impact of Debt Leverage

"Give me a lever long enough... and I shall move the world." That's what Archimedes said about the power of using leverage. Although he was referring to the physics and mathematics of real-world levers, the concept is not that different from the financial way in which we talk about leverage.

In basic terms, the more money you have access to, the more you can do with it. And by using your capital, you can secure greater financing, and then you can realize greater returns with your investments. Let's look at a simple analogy to help illustrate the power of using financing to secure your investments.

An investor has a total of $100,000 in capital that he would like to use for real estate investing. He is considering three options.

> » **Option A**: He can buy a property worth $100,000 without using any financing at all.

> » **Option B**: He can buy a property worth $200,000 and finance $100,000 to cover the rest. This creates 50 percent leverage.

> » **Option C**: He can buy two properties, each worth $200,000, using financing to cover the shortfall. This creates 75 percent leverage ($150,000 financed compared to $50,000 capital for *each* $200,000 property).

In our very simple example, let's imagine that after one year, each property has increased in value by 10 percent. How well does our investor do on each investment, just looking at asset appreciation alone?

> » **Option A**: The property is now valued at $110,000, giving the investor a profit of $10,000.

> » **Option B**: The property is now valued at $220,000, giving the investor a profit of $20,000.

> » **Option C**: The two properties have a combined value of $440,000, giving the investor a profit of $40,000.

Although we haven't factored in the cost of the debt or the extra rental income from the two higher-value investments, it is still clear to see that the amount earned per dollar invested can be greater using the power of leverage. As I covered in chapter 1, if the leverage is positive (the return on investment is greater than the cost of the debt), then the use of debt to finance your deals will be advantageous (figure 59).

POSITIVE LEVERAGE

fig. 59

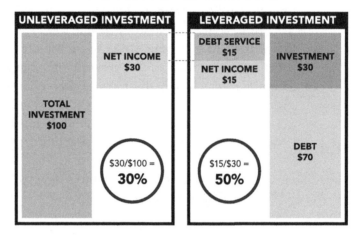

But when debt is too costly, it can actually hurt your investment returns. This is called negative leverage. The debt service amount is the cost that the investor incurs for using financing, usually in the form of debt repayments on the interest or principal. The net rental income is the money that goes into the investor's pocket after all the expenses are counted (figure 60).

NEGATIVE LEVERAGE

fig. 60

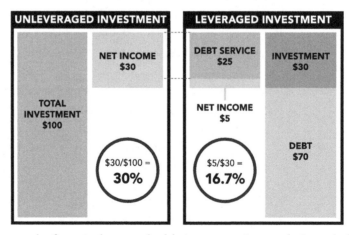

An example of negative leverage: the debt is too expensive to make it worthwhile.

It's invaluable to consider the leverage of a deal as a tool for investing. When you increase the leverage, you increase the risk, and you also increase the potential returns from the investment. There are many different financial products that can increase the complexity of your deal, so consult with a broker or professional lender about the best option for your situation.

Benefits and Risks of Leverage

You will notice that there are other significant advantages to using debt to leverage your investments. The first is that you can put your capital into several investments rather than one, multiplying rental income and diversifying your portfolio. In our simple example, the investor held two properties using the same amount of invested capital. If one property had an extended vacancy, some major repairs, or didn't perform as expected, his capital would be protected against excessive loss by the other investment.

Another benefit is that the investor has the option to invest in properties that would be prohibitively expensive to purchase outright. In the example, the investor had only $100,000 capital and could not afford the $400,000 price tag for two properties. But with the leverage that debt financing offered, he was able to multiply the impact of his money, extending his investment to higher-value properties.

Tax-wise, having a mortgage on a property can save you thousands per year. Check your local laws, but here in the United States, the interest portion of mortgage payments is tax-deductible, providing an effective tax shield, especially in the first few years.

There is also the risk of over-leverage, such as was the case for hundreds of thousands of people during the 2008 recession. Many people were leveraging and refinancing their properties at a ridiculous 90–95 percent loan-to-value ratio. The problem with this is that if you have a house at 90 percent leverage, a 10 percent drop in prices would wipe out 100 percent of your equity in the home. This over-leveraging puts your investment at a massive risk of going underwater. As a comparison, if you had only 50 percent leverage, the housing prices would have to drop five times more to wipe out your equity—a rare occurrence, but still possible.

In 2008, Lehman Brothers collapsed for this very reason. They were over-leveraged to the point where a 3 percent drop in the market would bankrupt them, which is exactly what happened. When the housing prices did drop in 2007–2008, homeowners and investors were left with excessive debt service costs, defaulting on their mortgages and declaring bankruptcy in an attempt to get back on their feet.

Securing Financing

As we covered, the many types of lending and loans outnumber the types of real estate deals you can make. Given this breadth of available and ever-changing options, it's best to consult with one or more trusted financing experts in your area.

You would never go into McDonald's to ask for a steak dinner. They will only sell you their own products. It's no different in the lending world. If you visit a bank, the only products they will offer are their own, but these products might not be best for you. My advice would be to consult with a broker who has access to a variety of lenders with hundreds of financial products. Then you can look at all the options, not just the services of one lender. It makes sense to shop around to find the best deal in the market.

Before we get into the sources of financing, let's see if you can answer these questions that a lender will ask about your investment plans.

Q: What is your debt service coverage ratio (DSCR)?

This is one of the key metrics that lenders will refer to when they ask about your plans for investment. The debt service coverage ratio is a guide for the lender to determine if the income you make from the property will be able to cover the debt you will incur to finance it. It's very simple to calculate.

$$DSCR = \frac{NET\ OPERATING\ INCOME}{TOTAL\ DEBT\ SERVICE}$$

fig. 61

If the DSCR is anything above 1, it means that your expected income will cover the costs of servicing the debt, both principal and interest payments. As a rule of thumb, lenders want to see a DSCR of at least 1.25–1.35 to classify it as "good" and worthy of the loan. If the DSCR is too low, that means the property is costing you money, which puts a lot of risk on both parties. Lenders would like to see DSCRs as high as 1.6 or 2.0, especially with inexperienced investors or with riskier properties in less established rental markets.

Kathy is preparing her documents to get a loan. She projects making $30,000 a year from rental income on her investment property. In order to reach at least a 1.3 DSCR, she needs to get a loan with a yearly total debt service of just under $23,000, or less. But, in a stroke of good fortune, the loan she is seeking will only cost her $15,000 in total debt service, giving her a DSCR of 2.0 ($30,000 income / $15,000 loan repayments). The bank will appreciate that high ratio and will likely give her the loan she needs.

The DSCR doesn't account for the appreciating value of the property, only the actual money coming in and going out from annual rental income and operating expenses.

Q: What is the loan-to-cost ratio you need?

Typically, you'll see lenders advertising the loan-to-cost ratio (LTC) for their loans. This is the amount that lenders are willing to lend in proportion to the total costs of the project.

$$\text{LOAN TO COST} = \frac{\text{LOAN AMOUNT}}{\text{TOTAL PROJECT COST}}$$

fig. 62

Let's say that a loan is offered at an LTC of 80 percent. If the total cost of the project is $100,000, the bank is willing to lend out $80,000. The total cost of the project includes many line items, such as purchase price; soft costs (legal, architectural, surveying, etc.); furnishings, fixtures, and equipment (FF&E); closing costs; and liability insurance costs. This is a different calculation from the loan-to-value ratio, which banks offer against the value of the property. As you can imagine, the value of a property often exceeds the cost of purchase and rehab; therefore, you might have access to more funding with the LTV.

Kathy is calculating the LTC for her investment to see if it will comply with the bank's 80 percent LTC loan requirement. She has a total of $50,000 in capital available for this investment. That leaves her with enough room to borrow up to $200,000 if she can demonstrate that her total project costs are $250,000 or less. The property has a purchase price of $190,000, and she estimates that she'll need $30,000 for rehab and a further $5,000 for soft development costs.

» Total cost of the project: $225,000
» 80% LTC loan amount: $180,000

Kathy will invest $45,000 of her $50,000 in investable capital, and she meets the LTC requirement set out by the lender. Life is good.

Interest-Only and Amortized Loans

Before we look at the different loan options available, let's talk about the elements of every loan. No matter if they're interest-only or amortized, every loan has principal, the amount you are actually borrowing from the bank. There is always going to be an interest rate associated with a loan. That's just the cost of borrowing, the price the lender charges you for the privilege of borrowing money. Another element is the term of the loan. This is the time frame for which you will be servicing the loan, whether six months or thirty years.

GRAPHIC

fig. 63

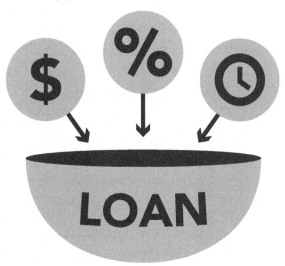

For interest-only loans, you borrow the principal amount and you make repayments consisting only of the interest calculated on the loan. At the end of the term, you repay in full all the principal borrowed, in one balloon payment. An investor would likely use an interest-only loan when doing fix and flips. One of the benefits of interest-only loans is that monthly repayments are smaller, so even if there is no rental income coming in, it won't be so hard for the investor to service the loan. Also, the repayment structure assumes that the borrower can make the big balloon repayment at the end of the term. For rehab projects, you would likely use the profits from the resale of the home to make that final payment. Interest-only loans only make sense with short-term projects, when the principal is paid back within months of taking out the loan. The risk is that if the project is delayed (if the property doesn't sell by the end of the term) or if it sells but at too low a price, then the borrower will be unable to pay the large balloon payment at the end (see figure 64).

fig. 64

An interest-only loan visualized.

The amortized loan is slightly different. You borrow a principal amount, but the repayments are structured in a way that incorporates two elements (see figure 65).

fig. 65

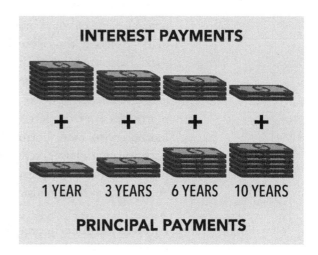

A fully amortized loan schedule visualized.

One important point to note is that the repayments for fully amortized loans are larger than those for interest-only loans with the same principal and the same term, because they include both interest and an increasing amount of the principal. There is no balloon payment at the end of the term; the final payment pays off 100 percent of the interest and principal at the same time. If a project has rental income to offset loan costs and the investment is held for a long period of time, the amortized loan is the best option. The benefit is that the interest is paid on the basis of the remaining principal. So, you have an advantage if you can make significant payments early on toward the principal of the loan, because it will effectively reduce the total interest you will need to pay. Be cautious, though, as many lenders like to base their own financial projections on receiving the interest they calculated at the outset of the loan, and they may charge you penalty rates for early repayments.

Knowing what's out there is all good and well, but where do you go to find these loans?

Conventional Mortgages

When you approach a banking or lending institution for a loan, you're typically going to be offered the conventional mortgage, which is backed by a private lender rather than by a government entity such as the Federal Housing Administration (FHA) or the Department of Veterans Affairs (VA). Unlike government-backed mortgages from the FHA or the VA that sometimes allow for 3.5 percent or even 0 percent down payments, conventional mortgages typically require a down payment of at least 20 percent. Conventional mortgages are common; from 2016 to 2019 they made up nearly three-fourths of all mortgages, according to US census data. There are "conforming" and "non-conforming" types. Conforming conventional mortgages meet the guidelines established by Fannie Mae and Freddie Mac, two government-sponsored enterprises that buy mortgages from lenders to give lenders the liquidity to provide more mortgages to more borrowers. Non-conforming loans typically go to borrowers with lower credit and have lower loan-to-value ratios, resulting in less favorable loan terms for borrowers, such as higher interest rates and private mortgage insurance premiums.

Although it differs in every case, the investor's down payment or deposit is typically between 20 and 30 percent. First-time home buyers have access to lower down payment schemes but only if it's for their primary residence. Properties that aren't single-family homes will have higher down payment requirements. The down payment the borrower is expected to supply also depends on whether the interest rate is adjustable or fixed.

Be aware that if you're planning on supplying less than 20 percent of the purchase price, you will be required to take out ***private mortgage insurance (PMI)***, the insurance that protects your lender should you default on the loan. Your PMI expense can be included, or "rolled into" the loan amount. Once you have more than 20 percent equity in your property, PMI is no longer required.

Conventional mortgages have stricter credit requirements than government-backed loans, such as those insured by the Federal Housing Administration (FHA) here in the United States. Lenders will want to see your debt-to-income ratio (the monthly debt repayments divided by your monthly income) at less than 50 percent. Loan sizes vary as well, state by state. Anything larger than the conventional mortgage limit is classified as a "jumbo mortgage" and is subject to different laws and restrictions. Lenders accept more risk when offering larger loans and that risk is passed on to you, the investor, through higher interest rates.

Federal Housing Administration Loans

While it's not exactly common, I do want to introduce the FHA option of getting a loan that meets strict guidelines laid out by the government. The *Federal Housing Administration* does not issue these loans; they are issued by federally qualified lenders. The FHA simply insures them.

These loans are usually offered to low-income home buyers or those with credit difficulties. While typical home buyers must supply about 20 percent as a down payment, buyers with FHA loans pay just 3.5 percent. That can make a huge difference up front. On a $400,000 property, an FHA loan would require only a $14,000 down payment, and with a typical 20 percent loan the investor would be expected to put up $80,000.

One of the stipulations of the FHA loan is that the property must be used as your primary residence for the first twelve months. Remember that this loan is intended for home buyers without the option to raise the capital for a traditional down payment. If you want to use it as a rental property, you'll need to live in it for a year, but after that you have the freedom to rent it out as you would any investment property. Alternatively, investors can use the FHA loan to finance a property with up to four units. They can purchase a duplex, a triplex, or a fourplex and then live in one unit and rent out the others to make rental income.

There is a big difference between laying out just a few thousand dollars for an FHA loan and tens of thousands for a traditional mortgage. But there are risks with the FHA. First, with a very small down payment on the property, any drop in value can instantly wipe out the equity you have. Second, if you supply anything less than 20 percent of the purchase price, you will be paying higher insurance premiums for the life of the loan—however, those insurance premiums will drop off eventually as you continue to pay down your principal. You could also choose to refinance the property after some time to eliminate that high mortgage premium. Finally, the FHA loan has a limit, restricting you from purchasing properties at higher values. This figure changes from year to year.

Although an FHA loan is usually not the best option, it might be the only chance for low-credit buyers or investors with little capital to directly purchase a property.

Hard Money Loans

Besides the big-bank lenders offering conventional loans, you can find private lenders willing to make loans to fund your investments. These are called *hard money loans*. Stepping outside of the protection offered by insurance companies and big banks does present its own set of challenges. In hard money loans, the lender accepts most of the risk, and so the loans these private investors offer will be much more expensive. But they may be good options, especially if you have an insufficient credit score or little experience with investing. Hard money loans are also known as asset-based loans, because they are often based on the use of the property itself as collateral for the loan. Therefore, the lender wants to see that your property has enough value to protect them by offering good collateral against the possibility of defaulting on the loan.

Finding a hard money lender can be difficult, especially if you have not established good contacts in the business. But it's not impossible. Hard money lenders are often very experienced with real estate development deals. They know property. They understand market value. And if you come to them with a good plan, a detailed set of financials for the project, and even a respected contractor as a partner for the deal, it's very possible to secure a private loan through these lenders.

John's freelance career puts him at odds with the traditional lenders who want to see pay stubs for proven and trusted income. The conventional model won't work for him, because he doesn't meet the lenders' standards. But John has access to a property that he wants to remodel and flip. His exclusive rights give him the credibility and weight to seek out a hard money loan. Because the loan is based on the potential of this property, and not on John's credit score or income, he's able to finance the deal with a reputable private money lender for an interest-only loan.

Hard money loans are also an option for the investor who has miscalculated the amount needed for a project. If you come up short on the amount you need to complete your deal, going to the banks will cost you credibility and trust in their eyes. Investors who find themselves in this secondary position can use the services of a hard money lender to cover the extra costs needed to close out the project. These hard money deals are often interest-only, with short terms in which to make full repayment of the principal borrowed.

Chapter Recap

» With a good analysis and accounting of your finances, you can start to seek out sources for the financing you need.

» Using debt as leverage opens you up to higher-value investments, greater returns, and better results.

» Banks want to know the key metrics of your debt service cost and loan-to-cost ratios.

» All loans, both interest-only and amortized, have the same elements of principal, interest, and term.

» How you structure your financing depends on the deal you plan on making.

» Conventional loans must often meet strict standards to secure financing.

» Hard money loans from private lenders can be more expensive but may provide a viable option for some investors, such as those who require a secondary loan to cover their costs.

PART III

DAY-TO-DAY OPERATIONS

| 9 |
Landlording Essentials

Chapter Overview
  » Controlling Your Investment to Maximize Your Potential Returns
  » Managing Your Property (Self-Managed and Outsourced)
  » Securing Great Tenants
  » Outlining Your Success with Strong Contracts

I'm not really a control freak, but can I show you the right way to do that?
— ANONYMOUS

I think the whole concept of this chapter revolves around the question that all investors ask when they buy their first property: *Now what?*

In part II, we talked about analyzing your prospective properties. You've done a lot of work to determine the right property, the right price, the right financing plan, etc. When you pay for that purchase, when you finally pull the trigger on the investment, you set your profit or your return potential. You paid X amount and you'd reasonably expect to make Y profits from that investment. At this stage, however, all that profit that you've been calculating and analyzing is just potential. None of it is in your pocket yet—you must do the work to turn that potential into reality. When you start to manage your own property, when you become the landlord, you can determine how much of that potential you can achieve.

This is where real estate, the formerly alternative asset, comes into its own. Investors are realizing the potential of controlling their own investments. If you buy stocks in a company, that investment is not under your control. The only thing you can do is watch as the company makes the right moves or the wrong moves, and the option you have is to buy or sell portions of that company. Unless you own a controlling proportion of the shares, you have no say about the direction of your investment. But with real estate, it's different. Investors can operate their real estate investments with a greater degree of control, maximizing the potential returns they can make.

Being a landlord isn't a passive role. You don't make your money by finding it in the couch cushions. But with smart, informed decisions, your rental yield can be healthy and consistent. I want to elaborate on the areas where you can exercise the most control and realize the profit that you planned to earn. While there is no room to go deep into the weeds of owning and operating a *secondary property*, there are some fundamentals that you should know. How do you track the income and expenses? What should you do at the beginning to set yourself up with a great tenant? How do you manage the property in such a way that it doesn't take up all your time, especially if you're still employed in your day job? And how do you secure your property against those potential profit-killers like vacancies, costly repairs, damages, and sub-market rental returns?

In part I, we touched on an adage that investors like to use: you make your profits when you buy. That's an aphorism that applies to every part of your investment, from the analysis to the day-to-day operations of your property. Do the hard work up front to maximize the potential success, and you will reap the rewards along the way. If the question on your mind at this point is "Now what?" then the answer is to set yourself up for success by mastering the fundamentals of owning and operating a property.

I want you to succeed in operating your real estate investment, so I've left you with as many resources as I can to prepare you for success. You'll find a number of downloadable checklists, templates, and samples to use so that you are as prepared as possible. Keep an eye out for them throughout this chapter.

Property Management

You will walk a fine line as you start to manage a secondary property. And it all depends on how active you want to be with it. You can choose to be a handyman, making all the little repairs that come up. You can be a collections agent, constantly worrying about the rent and dealing with late payments and lack of communication. You can be an on-call guide, answering the (sometimes mundane) questions that pop up about your property. Of course, you can wear all those hats as a property manager, but that will take time. If you're still working full time at your day job, or even part time, that can present a challenge, especially if serious concerns come up. The main question to ask yourself is what is the highest and best use of your time. In other words, can you maximize your returns by remaining active in the daily operations of your property, or would you be better off looking for the next property, analyzing the leads that come your way, and planning on making your second, third, or tenth investment?

Do you try to maximize the return on your time as an investor or on the return from your investment? Investors need to figure this out as they go. If it's your first investment, it could be more beneficial to gain experience, remaining an active investor that self-manages the property. There is no teacher like experience, and there is no better experience than working with tenants and properties and everything that comes with them. On the other hand, if you believe that you could earn greater returns by spending your time looking for the next investment, maybe you need to outsource your property management to a third party. You might sacrifice some of your profits in fees, but if your time will be more valuable when spent chasing the next deal, the sacrifice is worth it.

Seneca, the great Stoic philosopher, wrote an entire book about the concept of time. He remarked that the one resource that is most precious to us is the one resource that we frivolously squander away. Not only do we let others waste our precious time, but we don't spend it well ourselves, often wasting it on things that don't matter and don't offer the best returns. Seneca points out that if someone stole a piece of your personal property, you would be upset about it. But stolen time doesn't affect us nearly as much as it should. The whole philosophy he teaches is that since time is the most valuable resource we have, we should use it to the best of our ability. Money can come and go, but if our time is wasted, there is no way to recover what we've lost.

There is no right or wrong answer to the question of managing your property. Every choice is just a set of trade-offs—you give up one aspect in return for something else. Let's look at both options to determine the course of action that will return the most money for the time spent.

Self-Managed Properties

When it comes down to it, nobody cares about your property as much as you do. No one else will have your best interests at heart, so it makes sense to self-manage your property simply because nobody is as invested as you are in realizing greater profits. Having control over the property is what some investors need, especially in the beginning. But even long-term investors often like to retain control over their investments because they understand that nobody will ever care as much as they do.

You know the property better than anyone. You've spent time analyzing the area and the comparable properties around it. You know that squeaky stair. You know the rental returns you can make. You know the curb appeal that the property offers. When you self-manage your property, you get to be involved in every aspect of its operation, including finding tenants, signing contracts, collecting rent, making repairs, and improving the value of the property. That sense of control is powerful when it's your money at stake. Self-managing investors are asking "How can I make this better?" because they have the power to do just that. Let me tell you a story.

CASE STUDY

In the 1970s and '80s, Toyota started to dominate the car market. Up until then, it was the American industry making all the vehicles that people drove. But out of relative obscurity came this Japanese car company, partly because they were doing something different in the way they built cars. In fact, it was so revolutionary that American car company executives would tour the Toyota plant, trying to determine just what Toyota was doing that was making them so successful.

It seemed that every aspect of Toyota manufacturing was counter to the way Americans were building cars. Toyota had mantras like "Reform business when business is good" and "No change is bad." Above all else, Toyota would never say "This is how we do things here." They were always looking for the next best improvement. One of the major incentives for any Toyota employee was to find new ways to make the process faster. Although other car companies kept the conveyor belts constantly moving at any cost, Toyota installed large STOP buttons so that each employee had the responsibility and the directive to halt production if they could come up with a way to shave two seconds off a certain procedure.

One American executive touring the plant watched how a door was fitted to the frame of a chassis and was then moved down the belt to the next station. The American asked, "Why don't you hit that door into place? We put our doors in and have workers hit them with rubber mallets, so they sit just right."

The Toyota executive just smiled. "We don't need to hit them with hammers. We've already designed the door to fit perfectly the first time."

When you manage your own investment property, you can have the same mentality as Toyota, looking for the small improvements to be made in every facet of your investment, looking for ways to make the whole process smoother, easier, and more valuable for you.

It makes sense to self-manage your property because property management comes at a cost, often between 8 and 12 percent. If you're not paying anyone to do the work, you get to keep more of the profits from your property. It's also incredibly handy to have a direct line of communication with your tenants, your agents, or your contractors. An intermediary can slow everything down as well as cause miscommunication, which could result in loss of funds on your part.

There is no doubt that self-managing a property also comes with a heavy time cost. Although some owners thrive on this level of active involvement, it's not for everyone. The cash flow that you projected in your analysis may require more work than you anticipated, making the trade-off to self-manage not worth the returns you're getting. In other words, if this is your first investment, your lack of experience could cost you some of the profits as you make mistakes, but this could serve as the best way to gain valuable experience that will benefit your next investment.

Although self-managing properties looks different for every type of investment asset, a single-family home could require significant work up front. The better you are at securing an excellent tenant and preparing a great property, the less ongoing work you'll have during the life of your investment.

Professional Property Management

Naturally, if you want to create a passive income source, the option of finding a professional property management service makes sense. If you aren't physically able to be present, as with out-of-state investments, it could be the only option you have. Hiring the right professional manager is paying for peace of mind.

An experienced manager fills in the gap of your lack of experience. They know the local laws and taxes (especially handy for out-of-state investments), they know the right way to market your property to find tenants, and they often come with their own Rolodex of contacts to find reputable tenants or even buyers when the time comes to exit your property.

Your decision to hire a property manager will factor into your analysis before you decide to buy. The cost of a professional service will usually skim one to one-and-a-half months of rent from your bottom line. You need to account for that in order to remain profitable. If the margins are too tight, professional management might be a luxury that you can't afford. Also, the concept of completely passive income isn't quite accurate, since your presence and response are still required for major issues. Disputes and problems arise, and critical decisions still need to be made. Don't imagine that hiring a professional property manager is a "set it and forget it" deal where you no longer need to do anything.

One of the easiest ways to make a professional property management service a nightmare is with poor communication. Although you may have the number one manager in your area, they still aren't *you*. Establish early your requirements, objectives and end goal for easier communication all along the way.

MY TAKE

Ensure that the contract is based on actual rental income rather than pro forma rent, or the rent that it *could* be achieving. There is little incentive for your property manager to find the best tenants for you if they are paid regardless of whether there is a paying tenant. Also, keep all communication with your property manager in written form. Emails may be impersonal, but they are great for keeping everyone on the same page and for serving as a reference should anything go wrong.

Tenants

There is no such thing as being lucky about finding a good tenant for your property. You have to trust that there are solid people with great credit ratings looking for reputable properties. The more work you do up front in finding that perfect tenant, the less you will have to do over time.

It's a common saying among investors that a bad tenant costs more than a vacancy. You are better off having an empty unit for an extra month or two while you find the right tenant than selecting someone that will end up costing you time and money. Evictions alone can cost thousands of dollars and wasted months while your property remains unused. Excessive repairs can also cost money and time while you undo the damage caused by having the wrong tenant. No matter what type of property you have, another cost that all investors have to contend with is turnover. Bad turnover—property that sits vacant for months between tenants—can set you back on your long-term goals.

I'm not trying to scare you; I'm merely pointing out that the effort of finding and keeping the right tenant pays dividends in the long run. Long-term tenants are the lifeblood of your investment, so use care to secure the right ones. One horrible tenant could cost you years of investment returns.

Marketing

Even if you've purchased a property that's in perfect condition, you will need to market it to attract great tenants. Don't look at marketing as merely making the property look as appealing as possible. Think about *how* you market it, finding the right agents and the right listing sites and using the best strategies to secure the best tenants. All the work put into finding a great tenant happens at the outset, starting with how you market your property.

Preparing the Property

It all starts with how you prepare the property itself. Unless you've gone in for the complete fixer-upper, it's likely going to need only some minor upgrades. To attract good tenants, find the "low-hanging fruit," easy touch-ups and repairs, to prepare your property for the marketing stage. As you realized when you were doing your research and analysis, there are other rentals in the area that tenants can choose to lease. To make your property competitive, and without sacrificing too much in rental income, you can add little touches to the property to add value and allure.

First, consider curb appeal, a major selling factor for a home. People want to have pride in where they live, even if they are renting. Chipped paint, weeds in the yard, or a missing piece of siding are all easy fixes that make a huge difference in curb appeal. The same goes for cleaning: hire professionals to do a thorough deep clean so that everything is ready to hand over when it's time to sign the contract.

Do minor repairs to the home like replacing lightbulbs and repairing damaged floorboards. These small repairs aren't structural but do contribute to the overall draw of the property. Unless you've already committed to and budgeted for major renovations, this is not the time to do things like a reroof or a complete plumbing overhaul. Although that kind of renovation adds value to the property, this preparation concerns the appeal of the home for renters. And your careful analysis should have pointed out any potential renovation requirements before you got this far.

I think this goes without saying, but you want to make sure that your property is ready to be shown. Simple fixes like pulling weeds or repainting the walls might seem like just adding lipstick, but everything you're doing is aimed at the goal of preparing the property for public inspection.

Advertising

Some people say that the best way to advertise is "everywhere and all the time." While I agree that you need to advertise your property on more than one platform, it's not always about where to advertise but to *whom*. You can throw good money away on wasted advertising if it's targeting the wrong audience.

In my own investing journey, I try to take the least involved path. I work hard at the outset to find good property managers and agents. And once I do, I let them handle the marketing and advertising, with guidelines that I've established, of course.

In my experience, a real estate agent you can trust knows how to advertise your property, and they will do so on a number of platforms to maximize its exposure (and make sure it gets the right kind of exposure).

We've already touched on some of the best channels for advertising—it's where you looked during your analysis of the property you bought. MLS networks, newspapers, and private listings all have their place, and even if you're not using an agent or a property management service to advertise, you can model what they do to attract the same types of tenants.

Prequalifying Tenants

You've probably heard the story of singer David Lee Roth demanding a bowl of M&Ms, (all brown ones removed) in his green room as part of his contract at shows. Rather than being an example of diva demands, this was a very important prequalifier that let Roth's management team know whether the venue's staff had read through the contract carefully. Any brown M&Ms in his candy bowl quickly alerted the band that the venue may have been lax with preparations, potentially endangering them with shoddy stage and electrical work. This prequalifier served as a shortcut to their knowing if it was safe to proceed with the show or if the management needed to go through the contract line by line to ensure everything was as it should be. I encourage a similar prequalifier for tenants as a shortcut way to determine if they will care for your property.

Q: What is the goal when screening tenants?

Let's reestablish ourselves with Neil Hector the Real Estate Investor and the main outcome he was hoping for when going through his options. He was looking at several markets in a couple of states. His number one goal was to eliminate leads, not just to find them. The faster he could churn through the less-than-desirable properties, the quicker he could sift out the best ones.

The process is really no different when you're searching for tenants. Your number one goal should be to screen out and eliminate the bad ones to end up with the good ones. If the economy is expanding and supporting a strong market cycle for rentals, you'll likely be inundated with tenants to choose from. How do you prequalify the promising ones before you make a decision?

One way I create a self-selecting group is by including the phrase "Please include a $20 fee with your application for a credit and background check. The fee will be returned to you if the application is rejected." A $20 refundable fee is a great gauge of how serious your prospective tenants are, and it automatically eliminates those from the pool of tenants who aren't willing to make this small commitment.

Are there other ways to set up these prequalifying tenant screens? Of course. It just depends on the property you're leasing and the criteria you establish. If you're self-managing the property, it helps to prepare an outline of the type of tenant you want to attract. Where do they work? What car do they drive? What do they value? Do they have kids? Are they local? Businesses do this type of profiling all the time to help them identify the customers they want, narrowing down to a very specific niche. If you're working with a property management service, establish guidelines and work with them to identify the types of tenants you'd like.

The Fair Housing Act (1968) prevents you from discriminating against tenants based on race, religion, disability, familial status, national origin, or sex. Check local and state laws before posting any advertising for your property. For more information, go to www.congress.gov/bill/100th-congress/house-bill/1158.

Property Showing

It's been said that a property has to "sell" three times before anybody will sign on the dotted line. First, they have to be sold through the listing. Next, they have to be sold when they do a drive-by. And third, they must be sold when they go through a showing. By the time a tenant has agreed to a showing, either an open house or a private viewing, they've already identified your property as meeting their standards. While this a great time to "sell" your property, it's an even better time to use this face-to-face meeting to discern what type of tenant they might be.

If you are conducting a showing, make sure that you have your antennae up for any warning signs displayed by the potential tenant. Consider this an in-person interview for the position of tenant of your property.

» **Are they late for the showing?** Although it's a small thing, it could be an indicator of a lax view of established rules. Habitually late tenants can sometimes translate into habitually late rent payments.

» **Do they respect the property during the showing?** As they walk through the home, are they careful to respect the place? Do they track in mud or dirt? Are they slamming doors or going off on their own?

» **Do they seem likeable or hostile?** If something in the property surprises them, are they noticeably emotional about it? If something doesn't meet their expectations, are they complaining or displaying annoyance?

In the course of conversation during the viewing, be attuned to their expectations, exactly who will be moving in, why they want to look at your property, and if they are willing and able to abide by the guidelines you established in the prescreening section.

Vetting Your Tenants

Even though they may have passed a credit check and given you a favorable impression during the showing, how can you vet the tenants who show real interest in your property? People often ask me what I screen for. Here are some of my criteria:

What I Look For in Tenants:

»   **They have a reliable source of income.** Do they have a steady employment history with a reliable source of income? Ideally, a tenant will have a gross monthly income that is four times what you're asking for rent. For example, if the rent is $1,000 per month, you'll want a tenant with a gross monthly income of at least $4,000 per month.

»   **They have no prior evictions.** The past is a good indicator of the future, although it's not a predictor. Prior evictions don't automatically eliminate a prospective tenant from the pool, but you will want to have full confidence that the reasons for the prior evictions aren't still lingering.

»   **They pass full background and credit checks.** Ideally, you'll want a tenant with no criminal history and a clean credit history. A poor credit score may indicate problematic financial management, and a criminal record may indicate a more problematic tenant. Neither issue makes for an ideal tenant. Note that federal law prohibits landlords from discriminating against prospective tenants with a criminal history—see the latest requirements on the HUD website (www.hud.gov).

»   **They have positive references from prior landlords.** How a tenant behaved in their previous property is the best indicator of how they'll behave in yours. Problematic prospective tenants are often unwilling to provide references from their current and prior landlords. Long-term tenants with good relationships with their landlords will have no trouble providing the references.

Questions for Tenants:

»   **Why are you looking to move?** Gauge the reason for the tenant's decision to relocate, such as moving to a new city, changing their job, upgrading to a larger home, etc.

»   **Who will be moving in?** Know how many people will be in the home. This is also when you can ask about pets or children, as some landlords don't allow them.

» **How long are you expecting to rent?** Ideally, you want long-term renters, so to avoid wasting your time with a short-term tenant, get this question settled quickly.

» **What is your employment history?** Stable employment is a good sign of a stable tenant. Look for long-term employment in their history.

» **Would your current landlord provide a favorable reference?** You're going to talk to their previous landlords (if applicable), so this is a question that reflects their honesty more than anything else.

» **Do you have character references?** Beyond employment or tenancy references, is there anyone in their life who can account for their character? The willingness to supply character references is a good sign as well.

Questions for Previous Landlords

» **Does the tenant owe you any money?** An outstanding debt can be a major red flag. You can also talk about rent payments and if there were any issues with tardy payments.

» **Would you rent to this tenant again?** The former landlord is eminently qualified to answer this question. If they would be happy to rent to them again, it's a good sign that you'll be happy as well.

» **Were there any major repairs needed during their tenancy?** This doesn't have to be the fault of the tenant. If major repairs were needed, how did the tenant handle it? Were they respectful of the property? Quick to report faults or damage?

The previous list doesn't encompass all the important considerations regarding tenant selection. I've supplied a complete checklist of the questions you should and shouldn't ask when screening prospective tenants in the Digital Assets that are downloadable at **www.clydebankmedia.com/rei-assets.**

Lease Contracts

There's really no such thing as a bullet-proof lease contract. No matter how much time and energy you pour into crafting a good contract, it's not a guarantee of results. But it's important to establish the baseline and expectations in the beginning with your tenant. List all the requirements of your agreement at the outset, and you should have no problems if your tenant agrees to comply with those expectations.

A solid lease contract is for your protection and limits your liability. It's best to work with a lawyer to draft a lease agreement that complies with local regulations and laws. Even if you already have a lease agreement that you like, have a lawyer review it before committing it to a signature. Yes, the cost can be high for a legal review, but that is outweighed by the protection you have with a solid contract in place.

A good lease contract is also protection for your tenant. Assuage the tenant's fears by laying out your own responsibilities. Include such things as the timing of inspections, rent payment dates, notification for repairs, and the process for ending a contract early. They have the contract as a reference for when they can contact you, how they are to fulfill their obligations, and to protect them during the time of their tenancy.

Rather than outline each and every item you should include, I've provided a template that you can download to inform the writing of your contracts. Use this in conjunction with a lawyer to revise for your own needs in your local jurisdiction. I use a very similar lease contract for all my investments.

Contract Terms

Ideally, you want a long-term contract over a period of years for the benefit of your profit projections. But there are a couple of options for the term of your contract, depending on the type of investment that you operate.

» **Month-to-Month:** If you don't have any agreement in place with your tenant, the legal system considers the tenancy a month-to-month agreement in which either party can end the contract once the month is up. Usually either party requires thirty days' notice to end the contract. These can include "handshake" contracts, simply a verbal agreement between landlord and tenant. The tenant is not required to pay a deposit and the landlord can evict, raise the rent, or change the terms with the same thirty-day notice. Normally, a month-to-month agreement is put in place while renewed terms are negotiated, or if the tenant can't agree to a fixed end date for their tenancy. Month-to-month agreements can be short-term or go on for years.

» **Fixed Term**: With a fixed-term lease, the tenant agrees to remain in the property for an agreed-upon period of time. Investors like this lease type because it gives them the option to plan out their investment into the future. Tenants are usually expected to supply a deposit, typically the first and last months' rent, and they agree to forfeit that deposit in the event of damage to the property or breaking the term of the contract.

We talk about different options in terms of trade-offs. If you choose to sign a fixed-term contract, you gain the ability to predict your income over the term of the contract. You know you'll receive X amount each month for the next twelve months. But you lose the ability to change the terms of the lease, raise the rental amount, or terminate the lease without suffering a penalty of some sort.

Policies

While the Fair Housing Act prohibits you from discriminating against tenants, a lease agreement lays out your clear expectations for the property. You can set reasonable policies that you expect the tenant to abide by during their time in your property.

These policies might extend to pets. If you're going to allow pets, prepare a damages clause that the tenant agrees to pay should their pets cause any permanent odors or other damage during their stay. Pets present a risk to your property, and the right policy in your agreement can mitigate or prevent that risk. Another common policy item is smoking. This should be part of your screening process, but for extra protection, include a policy on whether smoking is allowed. Again, a damages clause protects you from incurring high costs for cleaning smoking discoloration and odors.

Establish clear maintenance responsibilities. Who will be maintaining which aspects of your property? Set out what you will manage and what you expect the tenant to manage. Set out a policy that also establishes communication and timelines for major repairs for things like water damage or structural problems. As a guideline, the landlord is generally responsible for keeping the property habitable. All other elements, such as giving notice, the freedom for the tenant to act without your approval, and when it's applicable for you to be notified of concerns or issues, are within your discretion.

One thing I'd like to touch on is the inclusion of a subletting policy for short-term rentals of your property. It's becoming more common for tenants to lease properties and then list them on short-term rental sites like Airbnb and Vrbo. Tenants try to get around this by saying that they are hosting guests, but that's not the case if they're collecting money. Your explicit stance on subletting needs to be established in your lease agreement, usually using terminology like "subletting in the form of collecting money or compensation in any form from houseguests for any length of time is strictly forbidden without express prior written consent from the landlord."

Sites like Airbnb claim to offer insurance for the property, but subletting still exposes you to extra liability. In my opinion, it's not a good idea for landlords to allow subletting in their properties, because the tenants aren't covering that extra liability and it can be difficult to recover lost rent and damages from these big platforms. Some landlords agree to their terms, especially in high-tourism areas, but I'm not convinced the risk is worth it for them. If you want to benefit from a local booming short-term rental market, consider finding a property manager to turn your property into a short-term rental directly, rather than allowing a tenant to do it.

Deposits, Fees, and Renewals

The typical deposit request is equivalent to one month's rent, but there are some exceptions. Most landlords want to collect the first month up front on top of a security deposit equal to one month's rent. But these norms vary, depending on the market. The rule of thumb is to try to collect as large a deposit as possible. If rentals are in high demand, you can request first *and* last months' rent as well as a security deposit, weeding out all but the most serious of tenants. If it's a tough market, lower your deposit requirements to first month's rent and a 50 percent security deposit. You may need to waive the extra deposit altogether to attract tenants. Alternatively, if you feel a tenant presents a higher risk, then you can require a larger security deposit to mitigate your risk.

If you intend to charge late fees, include provision for them in your initial lease agreement, because you can't tack them on at a later date.

Most states don't have explicitly stated limits on late fees, but keep it reasonable; generally it's no more than 5 percent of the monthly rent. Be sure to include a grace period of three to five days before the late fee comes into effect. Some landlords charge differing late fees according to the delay in rent payment; for example, twenty-five dollars for anything less than ten days late and one hundred dollars for rent ten days or more past due. As always, check local and state laws to ensure that your late fee is compliant before you include it in your contract.

There is no hard-and-fast rule about price increases for rent. When the lease is up, it's your opportunity to negotiate a higher rate, if that's justified. It's a contentious issue. Where I live, in Pasadena, the city council met twice in one day recently to discuss passing a law to restrict specific rent increases that could be interpreted as predatory. In India, a rental agreement comes with the expectation that every year the rent increases by 10 percent, as a standard across the whole country. That provision can be negotiated with the landlord, but the expectation of the increase is already there from the beginning.

Chapter Recap

» While your initial analysis demonstrates the potential of your investment, it is your management that realizes that potential.

» Whether you manage the property on your own or hire a professional service depends on your time commitment and participation.

» Most of the work is done up front to prepare and plan for a successful investment.

» Finding the right tenant requires quick elimination and thorough screening.

» Establish guidelines through a solid lease contract to manage expectations with the tenant.

» Secure the help of a lawyer to review any screening or lease contracts you set in place.

| 10 |

Protecting Your Investment

Chapter Overview

> » Protect Your Property with the Right Landlord Insurance
> » Protect Your Income with Rental Insurance
> » Establish a Limited Liability for Personal Protection
> » Outline Your Success with Strong Contracts

People who live in glass houses should take out insurance.

— ANONYMOUS

Insurance companies are experts at assessing risk. They use **actuarial tables** to quantify all manner of risk to determine how much to pay out and how much to charge. For instance, did you know that insurance companies believe that clergy members inherently present more risk than typical office workers? Or that if you were a gold miner working in the Gold Rush, you would get charged four times the premium for life insurance than someone in any other profession?

Protection of private property is a fundamental right protected in a strong democracy.

— JIM RYUN

The cost of an insurance policy depends on the amount of risk that the insurance protects. For example, if you were to run a golf tournament, you might want to include a hole-in-one prize on a specific hole. The risk, although minimal, is that a golfer might make the unlikely hole-in-one shot, and you would have to pay out the prize money as advertised. Most long-shot prizes of this nature are covered by insurance policies. If a spectator throws a half-court shot in an NBA game to try to win a car, there is an insurance policy in the event that they make the shot. If someone tries to shoot a puck through a small hole to win ten thousand dollars at a professional hockey game, then you can bet that the possibility of the payout is insured (see figure 66).

GRAPHIC

fig. 66

PRIZE VALUE	HOLE-IN-ONE INSURANCE COST	COST FOR ADDITIONAL WINNER
$5,000	$101	$10
$10,000	$202	$20
$15,000	$302	$30
$20,000	$403	$40

The cost of hole-in-one insurance for an amateur golf tournament with 144 players.

Insurance protects our investments and assets from risks, particularly from unlikely but catastrophic ones. You've probably heard of people who buy insurance for particular body parts because that's what they use to make money. For instance, the singer Miley Cyrus has insured her tongue for $1 million. Soccer player David Beckham reportedly had his legs insured for $70 million when he was playing professional soccer.

QUESTION

Q: Which is riskier from an insurance perspective: amusement park rides or carnival rides?

Insurance issues aren't always intuitive. You might think that carnival rides are sketchy and poorly maintained, and therefore they would be riskier. But to an insurance company, it's amusement parks that are inherently riskier because they never disassemble their rides. Carnivals are constantly disassembling and reassembling everything, giving the operators more chance to inspect for faults.

Investors often look at their investments through just one lens: how much does it cost me and how much does it make me. They often neglect the unlikely (and yet not uncommon) ways in which you can lose investment returns. You want to protect the asset you bought against unlikely risks, but you also want to know which protection makes sense for you to purchase. It's not always intuitive which risks you will have to insure against, so let me elaborate on the types of insurance you'll need for your asset. You also want to protect the income that you've worked hard to achieve. Vacancies and major repairs can quickly put your income in trouble if there's no protection against these issues. Lastly, if you're going to be doing this long term, it almost always makes sense to have a legal entity to operate your investments.

It's a simple way to shield your personal name and assets from any liability you may be exposed to. If you face lawsuits or injury claims, then the legal entity enables you to separate your own bank account from the returns you make as an investor.

Landlord Insurance

GRAPHIC

fig. 67

The problem with insurance is that you don't think you need it until it's too late. But if you've got it, you'll likely never end up using it—until the day you do. One homeowner had their house and contents insured with the local insurance agent. They came home one day to find deep scratches and marks on the side of their house, and their swing set was missing. As it turned out, a moose had been walking past the house, got its antlers stuck on the swing set, and walked away with it, scraping the side of the house in the process. Because the owner was insured, they were able to put in a claim for the damage and the lost property.

But who would ever think they would have to insure against loss of property from a moose? Nobody could predict it, but that's why we have insurance—for all those moments that we can't predict but that do occasionally happen.

NOTE

I don't claim to be an insurance expert, but I am presenting this information per my own experience. Please seek professional insurance advice for your investment property.

Standard home insurance doesn't cover tenant activities, so you need to get specific landlord insurance for your rental properties.

Liability

You've worked hard to find the right property in the market that you love. You've dedicated hours and hours to analyzing the data and the comparable properties in the area. You've spruced the place up and advertised it. You've been screening the tenants to find right renter, and you've just signed a two-year lease on the property.

But your tenant calls to let you know that a cracked board caused him to slip down the basement stairs. He broke his leg and was out of work for six weeks. Are you liable for his lost wages and medical bills? That's what *liability insurance* covers. Through no fault of your own, your rental property caused the injury of someone on the premises. But because of the home's liability insurance, the lost wages and legal and medical costs are covered by your insurance policy.

This liability insurance applies as long as you can prove that the defect wasn't intentional and the accident wasn't through negligence on your part. It's a valuable addition to landlord insurance because you simply can't control what people do on your property. If there are any aspects of the property that present higher risks (for instance, a pool), then you should secure a larger liability limit to cover it.

Dwelling

A dwelling insurance addition has a lot in common with the homeowner insurance on your own property. Your asset and all your belongings are covered against water, fire, wind, or hail damage. The policy does not cover anything that belongs to the tenant; they have to secure their own insurance for their belongings.

In order to claim anything that you've left on your property for the tenant to use, you need to list it on the lease agreement. That way you have a paper trail for any items that are lost in the event of a calamity. You can also insure for malicious damages like vandalization or theft due to tenant neglect (such as leaving a door unlocked or open). If you have left anything on the site for the maintenance and upkeep of the property (like a lawnmower or gardening equipment) that can also be included on the manifest of insured items under your dwelling insurance. But be aware that anything you keep there simply for storage is usually not included.

Landlord Insurance Extras

While not commonly included with basic landlord insurance policies, here are some items you should consider for your own protection.

» **Burglary:** If your rental home is broken into, you can claim damages to the property through a basic landlord insurance policy. But if you want to recover or make claims for stolen property, you need a burglary clause included in your policy.

» **Vandalism:** This is optional and depends on the area where your property is located. The city of Los Angeles pays $7 million every year just to remove graffiti, not counting the repairs made to vandalized public properties. Vandalism insurance makes sense for a place like Los Angeles where there can be as many as twenty-five thousand tags of graffiti in one community.

» **Rental Construction Protection:** If you need to completely renovate the property and it's rendered uninhabitable, you can protect yourself against the construction risks your asset will incur. This type of insurance usually lasts as long as the unit is vacant and becomes redundant once you have a tenant in place.

» **Building Code Upgrade:** If you have an older property, you could be at risk if the building codes are updated. Your property might need heritage protection or a complete plumbing overhaul, or it might need a new electrical system installed to match current codes. This insurance would help you cover the costs of construction as well as the property itself while you made the necessary changes. Consider this coverage only if your property is at risk by having older systems that could require upgrades in the future.

» **Location-Specific Risks:** Different markets have different risks depending on the location. For instance, a property in Southern California might require earthquake insurance, a consideration that would not be made for a property in Kansas City. On the other hand, Kansas City property owners may want to include tornado clauses in their insurance policies. Be vigilant, because the biggest environmental risks are often (purposely) excluded from typical insurance policies. You will need to request them specifically, and it will cost more. But do consider the benefit of covering against environmental risks that are higher in likelihood due to the location of your home, such as tornados, floods, or earthquakes.

Rental Income Protection

GRAPHIC

fig. 68

It's likely that your property will have some periods of vacancy during the life of your investment. If you've already included that in your income projections, you are doing well. Vacancy rates shift so frequently and because of so many variables that it is often hard to predict. Market cycles, jobs, housing prices, supply of units, and economic factors all affect vacancy rates. In 2018, the state vacancy rate for Alabama was 13.1 percent, a very high number. In California in that same year, the vacancy rate was just 4.5 percent.

Because the vacancy of a single-family property can have a dramatic effect on your returns, you can and should consider rental income protection. Some insurers include this as part of your base insurance policy, and others provide it as an available addition.

One element you can't control is suffering the unexpected loss of a tenant. Maybe through job relocation, injury, or death, you are left with an empty property that isn't collecting rent. Rental income protection can cover those lost rent checks for the next twelve months, if necessary. Some insurance policies allow you to purchase one-, two-, or three-year coverage for both residential and commercial properties.

Rental insurance also covers loss of income if your property suffers damage. You might think it's enough to cover the damage from, say, a flood, but what if that flood damage renders your home uninhabitable for the next six months while it's being fixed? Your dwelling is covered, but you can't collect rent checks while the property is undergoing emergency renovations. This is another situation that rental income protection insures against, protecting the money that you planned on coming in when you undertook the investment.

I would never consider an investment unless I had protection for both the asset and the income I expected to make. I do cover for expected vacancies due to natural tenant turnover (based on the local vacancy rates), but a property becoming uninhabitable for an extended period could lead to significant losses in rental income. It's almost always worth the premium to add a Loss of Rental Income provision to your existing policy.

Limiting Personal Liability with Legal Entities

fig. 69

Twenty million civil lawsuits are filed every year. Of those lawsuits, 60 percent (twelve million) are contract disputes. In 2018, the median cost to fight a contract dispute lawsuit was $54,000. Judgments against the plaintiff were, on average, $35,500 for compensation and $68,000 for punitive damages. In other words, lawsuits are common and can be extremely expensive.

Unfortunately, we live in a society where encountering a lawsuit is all too common. And even if you win, the costs to fight your case can be staggering. But if you lose, you could end up personally responsible, which could cost you your personal assets, including your primary home. The sensible way to protect your assets and your personal wealth is through a legal entity, a shield that keeps a level of separation between your investment activities and your personal assets.

Although I don't personally have a lot of experience with trusts, I'm lumping them into the same category as legal entities that exist for the purpose of creating a separation between you and your investments.

One of the most common legal entities used in real estate investing is the limited liability company (LLC). The LLC can be owned by you alone or by you and one or more others. Beginning investors should consider establishing an LLC because banks won't lend to a business entity until it has a proven track record and established profits. Start building that commercial credit history sooner rather than later.

For more information on setting up and operating LLCs, please see the *LLC QuickStart Guide* from ClydeBank Media.

Legal entities carry more benefits than just liability protection from lawsuits. Establishing a legal entity allows you to avoid being taxed twice for the same investment. You can use legal tax deductions to claim business expenses and anything you've spent in relation to the investment.

The legal entities you can use are localized, often varying from state to state. Many states require that legal entities meet certain criteria to avoid the "piercing of the corporate veil," where shareholders are held personally liable for the corporation's actions or debts. Consult with a lawyer to help you set up a legal entity in a way that makes the most sense for your personal financial and tax situation.

Most LLCs are established in Delaware, Nevada, Wyoming, or Oregon, the states with the most relaxed tax laws. LLCs can be owned by other businesses, aren't required to have annual meetings, offer protection for the owners, and the owners can report the profits and losses on their personal tax returns. LLCs can be very simple to set up and require very little ongoing maintenance. The flexibility and ease of taxation also make the LLC a smart choice for any investor.

Tax matters vary greatly from state to state, so check your local laws. Your state might impose a franchise tax or a capital values tax on LLCs. Sometimes there are exorbitant annual fees that must be paid in order to keep an LLC in good standing. These fees can make having an LLC more expensive than having a sole proprietorship. LLCs also require extra work in the form of maintaining separate records for business and personal dealings. But this separation does come with upsides; not only are you insulated from personal liability, but having your financials conveniently separated can make things simpler at tax time.

Limiting Your Liability

Beyond establishing a legal entity to separate your personal and business activities, there are some simple, straightforward actions you should take to limit your liability throughout the life of your investment.

» **Establish a solid lease agreement**. Set the boundaries early with a contract that lays out the responsibilities of both parties in the deal. A good contract is protection for both the landlord and the lessee.

» **Be selective with your tenants**. Do the work up front to find better tenants. It will pay dividends in the long run with a reduced workload in maintaining the property and the investment.

» **Maintain a good paper trail**. Where possible, try to keep all communication in written form. Written documentation always has the upper hand when settling legal disputes. Did you know that a court of law will include journals and diaries as evidence because they are written down? Your paper trail should include communication with all contractors, professionals, tenants, and property management services. Keep all receipts and reports associated with the property. The act of good record keeping alone will also help you establish credibility with the courts and the banks.

» **Perform regular inspections**. The industry standard is to perform (or have your property manager perform) regular inspections. I recommend one agreed-upon inspection every six months for your first investment. Give adequate notice to your tenant, and let them know what it is you are inspecting for, such as major damage, structural problems, and overall care of the property. Keep the reports of your inspections.

» **Enforce a "no pets" policy**. In some cases, if your tenant owns a pet that causes injury to someone else, you could be liable for the costs. If you knew that the pet had aggressive tendencies and you did nothing about it, such as notifying the other tenants (in a multifamily or multiunit complex), you could be liable. It's very complicated to make a case-by-case assessment for every tenant, so it's a wise option to simply have a blanket "no pets" policy to cover your own liability.

» **Make timely repairs**. If the tenant makes you aware of any problem with the property, have it dealt with in a timely manner. Demonstrate that you have made all attempts possible to have the issue resolved quickly, especially if it could cause injury to the tenant or cause the property to be uninhabitable.

» **Require renters insurance**. Renters insurance is for the tenant's own benefit, and the reason I recommend asking for it is twofold. First, it creates an extra barrier in the event of loss, theft, or damage of the tenant's belongings while they are on your premises. Second, requiring renters insurance is another of those prequalifying indicators I use to screen out tenants before they live in my property. If a tenant isn't willing to get renters insurance, as cheap as it may be, I will have serious reservations about renting to them.

» **Hire only licensed professionals**. This goes without saying, but for all work done on your property, choose to use only licensed professionals. The insurance that they are required to provide safeguards you and your asset, should their work prove faulty or injurious. Never take the risk of hiring an unlicensed professional to do any serious maintenance or renovations.

» **Maintain ethical and legal activities**. Just one fraudulent or illegal activity can make all your insurance and policies null and void. Avoid the temptation to cut corners at the risk of losing your reputation and protection. If you decide to break the law, you're on your own.

Chapter Recap

» Buy landlord insurance to protect your property and everything in it that belongs to you.

» Rental income insurance protects your returns from the loss of a tenant or unforeseen damage that costs you rent.

» Create a separation between your investment assets and your personal assets by setting up a legal entity.

» Make smart choices to limit your liability and protect the investment you've worked hard to secure.

| 11 |
Adding Value

Chapter Overview
- » Control Your Returns by Adding Value to Your Investment
- » Make Smart Renovations that Contribute to Your Bottom Line
- » Secure Stronger Returns with Additions
- » Refinance Your Property to Validate Your Work

Not adding value is the same as taking it away.

– SETH GODIN

My progression in investing has given me the opportunity to be a mentor to others. I'm still a real estate investor primarily. I still get emails every single day from agents with leads for my next potential investment or pitches from wholesalers for deals they've found for me. I am still looking through markets and identifying the properties that suit my standards. But I'm delighted that I also get to teach others to do what I've done and continue to do. This book is an obvious by-product of my desire to help others invest and make their own secondary or replacement income using the lessons I've learned along the way. I also have several hundred thousand online students who've participated in my courses, watched my lectures on all aspects of real estate investing, and begun putting their newly acquired knowledge into practice.

Occasionally, I step away from the screen and help people in person with their investment goals. These clients come to me to guide them toward making smarter choices about where they buy, what they buy, and what they should do with the property once they have it, as well as how to structure their investments with their business partners with full alignment of incentives. I want to frame this entire chapter around two of my real-life clients—both, coincidentally, in the Los Angeles area, both looking to buy a residential property with the potential to add value.

In part I, we covered the three investment strategies: core, opportunistic, and value-added.

We have Claire, buying a property in Silver Lake, a nice neighborhood that's undergone a huge transformation in the last decade. For those who don't know the area, Silver Lake is a large community about halfway between downtown LA and the Hollywood sign in Griffith Park. The improving neighborhood has drawn Claire to find some older properties that are performing well under what the market shows her that she could be making. Rental prices in Silver Lake have seen tremendous growth in the last five years, and she has the potential to make a solid steady income with the right property.

One challenge in Los Angeles is that the traditional fix and flip model isn't working very well. For investors who want to make very simple façade improvements, maybe a splash of paint here, a touch of lawn maintenance there, they will find that the margins are razor thin to make any profit in resale. In order to make serious headway in adding value, you have to find an older property with lots of renovation requirements. If you consider the investment strategy scale, the closer your property is to the core side (basically a new home with no potential to add value), the harder it will be to make a profit with a short-term investment play like a quick flip. In the current Los Angeles market, flip investors need to find more creative ways to add value, given the higher prices they must pay to acquire the properties.

Claire already has a couple of investment properties under her belt, and she feels confident that she can replicate the success she's had with this new Silver Lake investment. The reason she's consulting with me is that she's from Denver and the Los Angeles market is both frightening and alluring at the same time because she's never tried it out. Her potential, especially in the lucrative Silver Lake market, is high, but the risk profile is also high. She wants to double-check every move before she makes it, because failure can be costly.

And then we have my other client, Jorge. He's a proud Angeleno, a local who's lived in the LA area his whole life. He's never felt the need to venture outside of his hometown to make investments, and he's pretty familiar with the landscape. Jorge isn't looking to make a simple flip, however. He's identified some remarkable potential to add value to properties in the Glendale area. Glendale is a sprawling community, almost a city unto itself, with a dynamic that you won't find anywhere else in LA. Just like Claire's Silver Lake, Glendale is remarkably different from what it was like just ten years ago. It used to be a neighborhood where you *had* to live just to be able to afford to live in the LA area. It was neither desirable nor attractive as a community. Now, it's the place where you *want* to live, full of great dining, shopping, and a friendly atmosphere. It has been listed as one of the safest cities in the United States. Jorge's been watching this change closely over the past few years, and he's located some properties with high return potential. But Jorge's not interested in the traditional flip model, trying to cut as many costs as possible just to squeak an extra half percentage point on the resale. Jorge wants to try something more ambitious and force a high revaluation by adding more floor space to the property. Additions on a property are certainly further up the value-added scale (see chapter 3), much closer to opportunistic than a traditional rental model, but the rewards can be high. Jorge approached me because his past investment experience has been almost entirely with simpler value-added properties, and he's heard about the possibility of adding more floor space as a viable model from other investors in his circle.

With these two examples, you will learn what it takes to add value to your property, a feature of real estate investing that sets it apart from every other type of investment. Adding value to a property isn't something that occurs to investors as a secondary thought. By the time you've identified and purchased a property, you already know the potential that the property has and the work that it will take to realize that potential. Although the scale is quite broad, I find that this scenario is where most investors end up. It just depends on the risk profile that you're willing to accept, and as you'll soon see, the range is quite wide within this value-added model of investment. Most property deals where you can add value won't get as involved as the two case studies we're about to review. In fact, a typical value-added investment allows for some initial cash flow while you improve the operating efficiency and acquire higher rents and greater occupancy with your improvements. But because of the unique Los Angeles market, we're looking at more complex examples, though the principles remain the same.

The Advanced Fix and Flip Property Analyzer shows you what you can expect to spend, some of the assumptions you can make about the property, and what your returns might be. Download it by going to **www.clydebankmedia.com/rei-assets.**

Renovations

No matter what type of investment you are making, purchasing a home with the potential to add value means purchasing it at well below the market value price in the area. For example, if a typical three-bedroom home in good condition is worth $400,000 in a certain neighborhood and can be rented for $2,200 per month, a similar three-bedroom home that costs $300,000, in need of moderate renovations and currently sitting vacant, may have some potential to have value added to bring it up to the level of other homes in the area and start earning you a solid rental income.

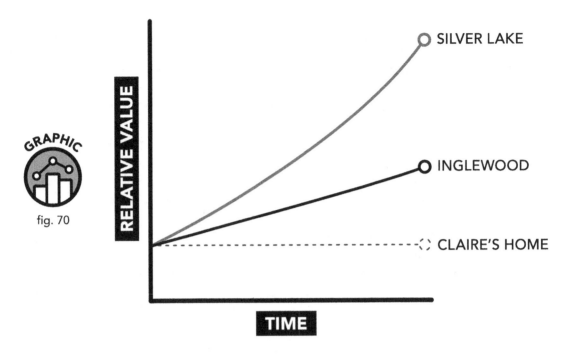

GRAPHIC

fig. 70

In figure 70, you can see the difference in potential for the same house in two different neighborhoods. If Claire had bought the same property that she has now in another neighborhood, like Inglewood, there would be potential to bring up the value, but to a lesser extent than there would be in Silver Lake. The home itself isn't in serious need of major structural repairs and renovations. But given that property in the Silver Lake community has improved dramatically in value, the perceived gap (and therefore the appeal) is significantly less in her home in Silver Lake than if that same house was in Inglewood. Make sense?

So, what did I advise Claire to do? First of all, I'm impressed with her analysis of the area, considering she doesn't live there. She's identified a profitable market with the potential to make serious returns on her investment. She's been able to locate and purchase a modest two-bedroom home in Silver Lake well under the expected market value. But because it's so undervalued, there is a lot of work to be done to bring it up to where she wants it. Claire's goal isn't to sell the home once she's added value, but to capitalize on the possibility of greater rental returns.

QUOTE

Art is never finished, only abandoned.

– LEONARDO DA VINCI

When you have a property like Claire's, it can be overwhelming at first to consider the tasks ahead. Each room you walk through offers potential for improvement, and the work is never done. Like in the da Vinci quote, the only way to finish the improvements is to walk away from them, because there is always something more that could be done. It helps to create a priority list for the intended work. Because nobody's budget is unlimited, the priority list helps you set aside money toward the best renovations before you blow it on unnecessary work.

Here is how I advised Claire to prioritize her limited budget and the work she could get done:

>> **Safety**: These are the renovations that have to be done in order to keep the home safe and habitable. They must be done immediately and first. This includes addressing things like structural defects, mold, asbestos, infestations, water damage, leaks, and exposed wiring.

>> **Must-Have Amenities**: In order to attract top-paying tenants and to remain competitive, you need to include the amenities that everyone else in the area has. Look to the top-selling and highest-priced rents in comparable homes for those marketable must-have amenity ideas.

>> **Extra Amenities**: These are things that not every home has, but that offer a nice touch. It only makes sense to add these extras if the market can support it and if they are something tenants would be willing to pay for. For example, it's nice to have a backyard pool but nobody in Duluth, Minnesota, will pay an extra three hundred dollars per month in rent to have one.

The priority for Claire's work, then, is as follows (figure 71):

fig. 71

SAFETY WORK	
Foundation – earthquake retrofitting	New cement
Garage	New rafters, new door
Living room	Ceiling – water damage
Systems	Replace cooling system

MUST-HAVE AMENITIES	
Kitchen	New applications, cabinets/counters, flooring
Bathroom	Shower, vanity, flooring, tiling
Bedrooms	Carpet, closets
Walls	Plasterboard, paint
Backyard	Landscaping
Exterior	Siding, paint, porch

EXTRA AMENITIES	
Garden shed	Build from scratch
Interior	New windows
Tech upgrades	Smart home devices, wired speakers
Second floor	Balcony

With the work laid out like this, Claire can see at a glance what she can afford do and the order in which she needs to do it. There will be no compromise on the safety renovations—fixing the water damage to the living room ceiling, replacing the wonky garage door, and installing a new cooling unit to make the home habitable during the hot LA summers. After that, she can add the amenities that every other home in Silver Lake offers, like modern kitchens and bathrooms, landscaped yards, and a nice clean exterior that looks welcoming and fits in with the neighborhood aesthetic. If there's room in the budget after all that, she'd love to consider adding a garden shed in the backyard, and the windows are old and tired and could use an upgrade. A lot of people like the addition of smart home devices. And the overall appeal of the home would be improved if she could include a small balcony outside of the master bedroom, overlooking the street.

This is simplified for the sake of this book, but I would also advise Claire to keep an eye on the life expectancy of some of the other components of the house, namely the roof, the HVAC unit, the hot water heater, and the concrete or masonry in the home. Since she would like to do all these renovations without tenants living there, it might make sense to include repairs on something like the roof, which has a life span of twenty-five years. If the roof is twenty or more years old with obvious leaks during the rainy season, it would be better to do it now rather than evict or inconvenience established tenants later. A newer roof can also be a selling feature when it's time to sell the property in a few years' time.

Rental Property Renovations

One key factor in renovating is whether you are going to sell the property immediately afterward and use the added value as equity in the home, or whether you want to hold the home and use it as a rental property. If you plan on renting, there are some important considerations to factor into your decision.

Access the Advanced Rental Income Property Analyzer spreadsheet in your Digital Assets at **www.clydebankmedia.com/rei-assets.** You can play around with the numbers on this spreadsheet built specifically for the scenario in which renovations will interrupt your rental returns.

First, the financing means that you'll hold an amortized loan, so debt servicing will affect the returns you can expect. The longer it takes to renovate, the longer it will be until you have rent checks covering the debt service costs for the loan.

You'll likely want to know the expected rental returns on the property as well as the vacancy rates in the area. For a frame of reference, a vacancy rate of 7.7 percent equates to four weeks out of the year when your property won't collect any rent checks. Therefore, if you estimate that your renovations will take four months to complete, count on not receiving rent for five months to account for the vacancy contingency.

The rental growth rate accounts for how much you expect the rent to grow each year. Generally, the longer you hold the property, the more rent you can charge. Also, a repair allowance for the year is typically included, but if you've just completed major renovations you might be able to assume smaller allowances for the new features you've just added to the property. You are guaranteed not to have a zero in that category; there has to be some allowance for things to go wrong. Finally, we talked about the "cost versus time" trade-off for managing your property. If you choose to use a property manager, they will charge a percentage of rent collected, so that expense must also factor into your final cost assumptions.

Additions

While many of Jorge's calculations will be similar to Claire's, his goal for his addition is a quick sale to capitalize on the improved market value of the home.

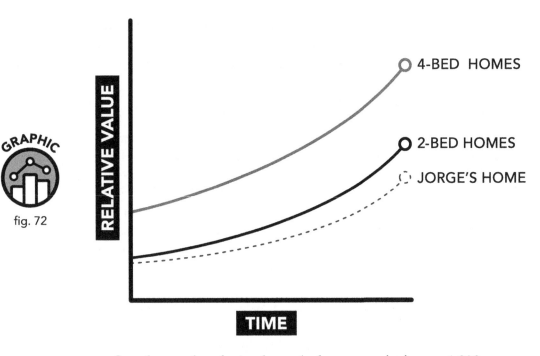

fig. 72

Jorge has purchased a simple two-bedroom, two-bathroom, 1,800-square-foot home in Glendale for $700,000 on a large lot with room for an extension. In figure 72, you can see the potential value gap between Jorge's home and the other options in the neighborhood. There is a tight margin of difference between the value of his home now and that of other two-bedroom homes in the area. Rather than focus on the difference in anticipated returns between his investment and the average two-bedroom home, Jorge would do better to focus on the huge leap in value that differentiates a two-bedroom from a four-bedroom. If it makes financial sense, he can hire a contractor and double the size of the home, adding an additional 1,800 square feet and creating a four-bedroom, four-bath home to greatly increase the value of his investment.

To give you an idea of the potential returns on this investment, Jorge projects that the value of the property will be $1.4 million after he completes his addition. Since his original investment was $700,000, that's an incredible value gain of another $700,000! Jorge has determined that the average cost to do work like this amounts to $275 per square foot, so he factors in a construction cost of $495,000 for the finished product. With an extra $25,000 for contingency costs (most commonly due to delays in construction), his returns would easily be $180,000 for the twelve to eighteen months it would take to complete the project.

What changed for Jorge? Not a lot, really, when you compare Claire's investment to his. He still has to evaluate the major repairs he needs to include, starting with a priority list of work to help plan and budget the money he has to invest. His renovations are major, so his priority list will not be the typical Safety/Must-Haves/Extra Amenities. His first priority, in order to realize the potential profit he has in the home, will be to focus entirely on the additional floor space he wants to add. Only when that is complete can he look at other work like flooring, kitchen cabinets, and bathroom repairs, should the time and budget allow for it.

A major consideration when adding value with additions is the extra time and costs included in this type of work. Planning, permits, architectural and engineering work, and surveys all take time. Use the downloadable spreadsheet included in your Digital Assets to account for timing of the renovations.

fig. 73

RENOVATIONS	COST ($)	DURATION
Permitting/Approvals	$6,500	9 months
Preconstruction (e.g., third-party A&E)	$ 9,500	2 months
Total construction (est. to be $32,000)	$469,000	5 months
Months needed to sell	$4,500	2 months

You'll notice in figure 73 that the spreadsheet has some considerations that you can play with. With additions, the time you need to factor in will be for the permitting and approvals stage, as well as the preconstruction phase in which reports and surveys need to be submitted. In some markets, Los Angeles in particular, these can eat into your time dramatically. Because Jorge's goal is to flip the home once he's done the work, he has elected to have an interest-only loan, so his debt servicing costs are lower. But time will continue to eat into his profits as he goes through the tedious process of permitting and approvals.

The other major concern that I worked on with Jorge was the increased construction risk for an addition. What he is doing isn't just "putting lipstick on a pig," as some investors call minor façade upgrades. This is a major overhaul that requires precision and time to complete. I counseled Jorge to increase the projected construction costs as well as the time, just in case things went south during the work. Any number of factors can cause delays and costs, such as weather, labor strikes, material damage, or unexpected work needed on the property. Better to account for it in the beginning than to have your profit margin overrun with an unforeseen three-month delay.

Revaluing and Refinancing

I advised both Claire and Jorge to seek out an assessment and refinancing for the property. Jorge needed it because he was going back to market with his home once the addition was done. But Claire needed the refinanced loan because the increased value allowed her more equity to borrow from. Just like in the BRRR(R) investment model, she was able to pay off her initial loan and construction costs, secure a new loan against the improved value of the home, and walk away with a significant chunk of change for her next investment project.

In Claire's case, she looks at the comparable rents in the area to help calculate what she can achieve with her renovations. I helped with her assessment and was able to demonstrate that, with her improvements, she could earn an extra four to six hundred dollars per month in rent from her new and improved home. On top of that, I showed her how holding on to the property for five years with just 65 percent of the purchase and construction costs leveraged with debt would allow her to achieve a 2.25x cash multiple on her initial investment. But with her refinanced home, she was able to walk away with an extra $45,000 in cash, which will go a long way in her Denver market if she chooses to invest it there. Great work, Claire!

For Jorge, we worked out the costs of time and money for the addition. In the end, the addition work went smoothly, which can be rare in the construction world. Permitting and approvals did take around nine months, which is fairly normal in the LA area for major projects. The city council rejected his original plans twice, delaying his expected start date. The problem was that Jorge was using an inexperienced architect to save money, and thus the plans ended up needing more revisions. Jorge was also asked to provide new environmental studies on the property. Thankfully, his estimates had anticipated those delays. While Jorge budgeted for an eighteen-month project, he was idealistically hoping for a twelve-month turnaround. The delays in approving the plans and the required environmental studies cost him several months due to his own error in choosing the wrong architect. Those delays ate into his profits on two fronts: he incurred the extra expense for the environmental studies and increased interest expense on his debt load. But, ultimately, the return on his sale of the property was quite close to his projections. It actually took less time than anticipated for the property to sell, and because of this Jorge was able to recoup some of the costs lost in the permitting stage. He was able to achieve a tidy 1.8x cash multiple on his initial investment, with an eighteen-month turnaround on the whole project. Fantastic job, Jorge!

Chapter Recap

» Adding value to a property isn't a rushed decision. It's an outcome planned before you ever make the investment.

» Adding value means a measure of risk. However, the greater the risk, the greater the returns at the end.

» The goal of adding value is to improve a property after purchasing it below market value level.

» Renovation costs need to be prioritized to maximize the budget you have.

» Addition costs are more opportunistic and require an element of time as well as money to calculate.

» Revaluing and refinancing the home allows you to recoup costs quickly and walk away with liquid capital for the next investment.

| 12 |
Planning Your Exit

Chapter Overview
- » Know Your Goals When Planning Your Sale
- » Effective Tips for Listing Your Property on the Market
- » Evaluating Your Performance After the Sale
- » Planning Your Next Investment

Great is the art of beginning, but greater is the art of ending.
— HENRY WADSWORTH LONGFELLOW

While I'm no fanboy, I do prefer the Android smartphone. I just happen to think it works for me, but I have no dog in the fight between Android and iOS products. Some people, however, really throw their weight behind one or the other, claiming they own the superior product and the other phone system is worthless junk. I remember one YouTube video from 2008 when the first iPhone was released. It was a news report about people lining up for hours and even days to get their hands on the first iPhone ever. The report showed one woman who had planned on buying $100,000 worth of iPhones only to sell them on eBay. She went to the front of the line and paid the kid waiting there eight hundred dollars for his spot in line. But when the doors opened, she was not allowed to buy more than one phone, as AT&T had restrictions on their limited supply. That kid walked away with a free phone from someone who never needed to pay for the spot in the first place.

It's really no different these days. People still line the block or pre-order right at midnight to upgrade from their perfectly functional phone to the latest and greatest release. Their phone works just fine, but they insist on buying the next one. Sometimes it doesn't make sense to upgrade. But sometimes it does.

And this is true when you think about your property investment. You have a good property with a trustworthy and loyal tenant. They pay their rent on time, and the property has done well for you over the years. You've been able to achieve the income you wanted, and everything is working in your favor. The market has seen significant improvement and has steadily provided more equity for you in the years that you've held your property. So why would you ever think about selling it? What are the good reasons for considering an exit from your perfectly functional (and profitable) investment? When does it make sense to want to sell?

Cast your mind back (or simply flip the pages) to chapter 1, when you set goals before you ever invested. You had a mixture of short-term and long-term goals. Maybe the short-term goal was to own a successful rental property within twelve months. Maybe the long-term goal was to operate a rental and sell it after five years to realize the appreciation in the property. Those goals help you determine when you're likely to sell.

Some investors set goals to create a retirement fund. They sell the property because they're cashing in and using the profits for their next venture or as a nest egg for their sunset years. You might think it would make sense to continue holding the property, but remember that active management can become a full-time job in itself.

Some investors need to exit their investment for the cash. Their goals were to make X amount of money, and with the condition of the market it makes sense to cash in their profits and earn some liquidity with their assets, especially if there has been a major market run-up in value. For some, the market cycle is about to hit a downturn, and owning a rental property in a market with significant risk of job loss in the future doesn't make sense. Remember, we talked about how smart investors choose more cash-based investments leading up to and during a recession, so they don't lose out on the equity they've built.

But for most investors, it's time to upgrade to a better-performing investment. Most investors use their property much like a steppingstone, a way to raise more capital in order to afford a better-performing asset that they couldn't afford beforehand. Maybe they want to buy several units, or they want to upgrade to a property that offers higher rental returns each month. Maybe they simply want to move their capital from a lower-quality property into a higher-quality one. Most investors are on the hunt for their next investment, and sometimes you need to think about your exit because it's time to trade up to something better.

I think now is a good time to talk about the 1031 tax deferment scheme, a favorite tool for many high-net-worth investors and institutional investment companies. Basically, a 1031 tax-deferred exchange allows you to delay the payment of capital gains tax, at both the federal and state levels, that you would normally have to pay from the proceeds of the sale of your property. Effectively, you get an interest-free loan from the IRS to help you purchase more property than you would otherwise be able to.

As you can imagine, saving that tax lets you use the equity toward the purchase of your next property, allowing you to buy even better property than if you had to pay the taxes. A 1031 allows you to defer that tax onto the next property you buy. There are some stipulations you must abide by in order to take advantage of this scheme, including some changes made to the laws in 2004 and 2017. You must use the profits from your first sale within six months on the purchase of another income-producing property. Specifically, you need to identify your next purchase within 45 days of the sale and acquire the new property within 135 days of identifying it. You must use the proceeds of the sale in a "like-kind" purchase, meaning that you must make another investment in the same vein as your first investment. For instance, you could sell a commercial building and use a 1031 to buy raw undeveloped land. Or you could exchange a single-family rental for an apartment unit. But the definition is generally broad, and practically any real property that can be put to productive use will qualify.

This is a fantastic way to extend the profits you'll make for the purpose of achieving greater rents in higher-performing properties. Please consult with your legal and financial advisors to help you navigate the laws and apply this tax deferment to the exit of your next property.

No matter the reason, you're going to need to prepare your home (and tenant) for the eventual sale. And once you've finally sold it, you're still not done with that investment. After the exit is a great time to think and evaluate the performance of your property. How did it do? Could I have achieved more? What lessons did I learn? What are the final numbers on my investment? In the beginning of this whole process, you were predicting and assuming a whole lot of numbers to calculate your investment. Now, you get to evaluate and analyze your performance using real numbers, all so that you can do better next time.

Putting It on the Market

Why don't we check in with our favorite investor, Neil Hector the Real Estate Investor? He's five years older (and hopefully wiser) now, with a home that he's been operating in Las Vegas as a solid rental property. Neil's investment plan was always to use this first property to gain experience, but now he wants to play in the big leagues. In his social circle, he's been exposed to some very promising properties. He's developed a reputation as an investor and, as such, agents and other investors have been including him in some potential deals in the city. Maybe it's time for our fearless hero to think about selling his property and putting it back on the market. It's been a good ride for Neil, but now seems like the perfect time to think about trading up to make some serious money, with the goal of quitting his full-time job in the near future.

What does Neil have to think about? Although the checklist could be very long, it boils down to just two elements: price and appearance. There is a lot outside of his control that Neil can't change, but he can change the price point of his property and the way it looks to the next buyer. We'll be looking at one example, but the principles that we talk about here apply to every type of property, from rentals to fix and flips to condos, and commercial properties as well. Whether you're doing this on your own or using an agent, you can still take the same actions when it's time to put your property on the market.

Pricing the Property

Although investing can easily be regarded as a science, just inputting data and interpreting hard facts, I love that there's an element of psychology to it as well. This is never more evident than when it comes time to sell your property. You have to contend with the personal thoughts and emotions that get in the way of accurately pricing it, as well as learning how to use the psychology of the buyer to your advantage.

It's very tempting for a newbie investor to set a price point based on nothing other than "I think it should be worth this much." But the market doesn't respond to what you think. It's a mixture of objective and subjective factors. What's the right price for your property? In the end, the right price is the one that the buyer and seller agree on. It's not a hard science, and not really all that elegant, but that's just part of the investment process.

Seasonality

One of the ways Neil can improve his chances is to use the seasonality of the market. Although every market is unique, there are definite peaks and valleys of demand during the year. In many locations around the United States, sales in the peak season can easily double, or in some cases triple, the sales volume of low seasons. In other words, this isn't just an interesting note, it's something that Neil should plan around, taking advantage of the increased attention properties will get. In the United States, the data shows that May, June, July, and August typically have the highest volume of home sales (figure 74). If Neil wishes to capitalize on this trend, then he'll have to seize that four-month window of opportunity. Better yet, he should drill down his analysis to focus specifically on trends in his target market.

fig. 74

US – 2019 EXISTING HOME SALES MONTHLY VOLUME NORMALIZED TO MONTHLY AVERAGE

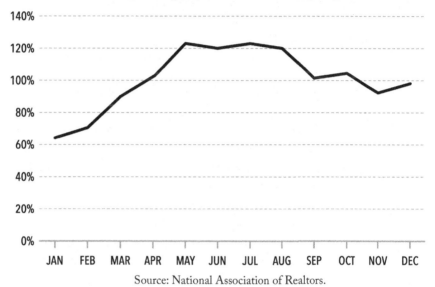

Source: National Association of Realtors.

One of the best books that you (probably) haven't read yet is Robert Cialdini's *Influence: The Psychology of Persuasion*. In it, Cialdini talks about the six factors that influence people to make decisions. One of those factors is scarcity. If we think an opportunity will be unavailable soon, or we perceive that an item is rare, we're influenced to want it more. Neil can use this to his advantage by introducing some good old-fashioned Fear of Missing Out, or FOMO. Maybe Neil can have the agent mention that there are other offers on the table or that there are other parties interested in the property. Or Neil could create scarcity by framing his property as unique. "This is the only four-bedroom home with a pool in this school district, that's listed right now" could set his property apart as unique and scarce, and therefore more desirable to buyers.

Our investment hero wants to set a reasonable price on his property, but he knows that there are two issues he wants to avoid. If the price is too high, then he risks the home losing appeal as people balk at the steep figure. This would cause it to sit stagnant on the market for a few months and then he would be forced to drop the price. Dropped prices tend to trigger a negative response in buyers, who think that something must be wrong with the property. As happens all too often, if Neil begins with too high a price, the final figure will often be lower than he could have otherwise achieved. The other issue is that he could price it too low. Neil likes the thought of sparking a bidding war by setting a low price point, but that only works if it's a seller's market. How does that saying go? Be careful what you wish for? If you set a low price, hoping for a bidding war, you might actually sell the property at that low price.

Neil asks his agent to look around at comparable properties (commonly called "comps"), both to help him set the price point and to justify his decision. As he gathers property data from the last few months, he is also looking at the amenities of those homes. If he can ensure that his property offers better amenities than those of the comps, then he can set the price a little higher.

One trick that works with the psychology of buyers is to allow them a win. If Neil were a real client of mine, I would advise him to settle on a price based on the comps and amenities around him, and then increase it just a little bit. Let's say Neil settles on a price of $500,000 for his home, based on his analysis. If it's a buyer's market, I would advise an asking price of $520,000, with the intention of agreeing to drop the price to $500,000. Neil would get the price he wants for his home, and the new buyer would feel like they'd won in the negotiations. That cushion helps you land the deal you want to make. After all, it's hard to beat a bargain, even with big purchases in real estate.

I think a lot of investors tend to get too fixated on the price they want and give no thought to the timing of the sale. Do you really want to achieve that target price even if it takes you two years to sell? Or would it be worth it to you to take 5 or 10 percent less on the sale if you could exit the investment earlier? If you want to trade up to a better property, the timing is really going to matter, because the faster you sell and buy again, the sooner you'll realize those larger rental returns. The trade-off to sell quicker can be worth it in the right scenario.

Staging

We've been looking at the scenario where you sell a rental property, most likely to another landlord who will maintain that rental and keep the tenant. What should you do when you're selling a flip or a renovated property with no tenant? Although some of the same principles apply for setting the price point, the other factor to be considered is the staging of the property.

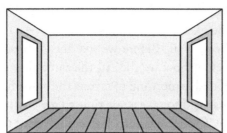

Which of these two rooms looks more appealing?

A few years ago, the world of staging was relatively unknown, except to a few investors. It's now grown into an entire supporting industry in the real estate investment world. Essentially, staging involves setting up a (usually) vacant property in a way that looks professional, clean, and inviting. A staging company will use their own high-quality furnishings to professionally stage the property to look as appealing as possible, either just for a photo shoot or for a period of weeks to account for showings.

If you have a short-term fix and flip, you'll typically hold an interest-only loan. The timing needs to be tight, and in order to sell for the maximum profit, staging the home might be a good idea. It offers buyers the chance to picture how the property could look rather than showing them sterile empty rooms. The cost to hire a staging company is generally less than the cost of another month or two on the interest of the debt, so it often makes good financial sense to stage a property.

MY TAKE

The only time I would advise against a staged property is during a busy market. If the inventory is low and homes are selling quickly, staging a home is an expense that may not pay off. But if you're in a down season and you really are pressed to sell quickly, that's when a staged property makes a difference in the sales price and expediency.

Performance Review

Neil Hector the Real Estate Investor has been learning over the last few years. He's taken his experience, his lessons, and his risk tolerance up a notch higher with this first investment. The sale of the home went very well, and he's been quite pleased with the whole experience. In fact, it's given him a bug, an itch to keep going on to the next project. He could really see himself doing this long term, executing on more than one property, maybe moving into small units, or even a couple of locations outside the city. The sky is the limit for Neil, and he's keen to get started.

But hold on there, Neil. Before we get ahead of ourselves, let's take a moment to look back at how we did. In the same way that NFL teams all come together on Monday morning to review the game film, even if they had a huge win, investors need to take some time to review their investment after it's all said and done. Our protagonist has worked hard to achieve some tidy profits, but do they match up to what he projected in the beginning? And since Neil wants to seriously consider doing this long-term, is there anything he could improve before he begins the process again? It's review time.

Internal Rate of Return

We've already spent some time discussing how to calculate the IRR, so we won't rehash it here. This is the time to evaluate the timing (or efficiency) of Neil's returns. Remember from chapter 6 that Neil's original plan was to hold on to this property for ten years. But since he's identified some potentially lucrative properties coming up for sale, he's sold his property earlier than he initially projected. Has that hurt his investment? Or did his investment still perform pretty well? What we want to do is calculate the interest rate as if Neil had loaned the money out and collected interest on that loan for the period of the investment.

A dollar today is worth more than a dollar tomorrow.

In his analysis, the property he bought had a projected IRR of 6.6 percent and that was based on the net rent he would collect as well as the profits from the sale he anticipated after ten years.

As you can see in figure 76, in Neil's projection, his actual IRR before factoring in financing was higher than he anticipated, but not by much. The price he would have sold it for in another five years, although higher, would not have made the whole endeavor more efficient. The projections he made didn't account for rental price increases, but with higher rental returns year after year, he would still be better off selling at a lower amount earlier than waiting a further five years. Remember, however, that he did not factor in financing in his initial projections, nor did he account for the closing costs during the purchase and the sale. Looking at his actual results after factoring in financing, we can see that Neil performed well overall with a 12.5 percent IRR. However, if we look more closely, we see that he had luck on his side. Notice that he was barely cash flow positive in years two to four and was even cash flow negative in year one! He was only able to achieve his 12.5 percent IRR because he was able to sell his investment for $475,000 in year five. Even after the 6 percent closing costs, the gains he got from the sale more than offset the poor cash flow returns during his hold.

GRAPHIC

fig. 76

	IRR	DAY 1 1/1/20	YEAR 1 1/1/21	YEAR 2 1/1/22	YEAR 3 1/1/23	YEAR 4 1/1/24	YEAR 5 1/1/25
Projection (no financing)	6.6%	−350,000	12,000	12,000	12,000	12,000	12,000
Actual (if no financing)	8.0%	−355,329	12,010	12,409	12,818	13,237	460,167
Actual (60% financing)	12.5%	−142,132	−204	195	605	1,023	254,721

	IRR	YEAR 6 1/1/26	YEAR 7 1/1/27	YEAR 8 1/1/28	YEAR 9 1/1/29	YEAR 10 1/1/30	Total Cash Flow
Projection (no financing)	6.6%	12,000	12,000	12,000	12,000	512,000	$620,000
Actual (if no financing)	8.0%	-	-	-	-	-	$510,641
Actual (60% financing)	12.5%	-	-	-	-	-	$256,340

What can Neil learn from this analysis? Although a lower selling price earlier can be just as good for Neil as a higher selling price down the road, he has to be careful with financing. Ultimately, his luck allowed him to trade up to a higher-quality investment property earlier, but it could have gone the other way under different market conditions. For his next analysis, Neil resolves to carefully consider financing to make sure he has a solid handle on the actual cash flows he'll get, so that his returns do not have to rely on a great exit. He also knows that holding an investment longer is not always better. That's good to know, Neil thinks. Maybe the next investment can be for a much shorter term, like two or three years, and he can trade up again for higher-quality properties until he finds one he can be happy with owning for life. But he had better factor in financing correctly or he could be looking at another cash-flow-negative investment.

Cash Multiple

Although it's easy to see the magnitude of his investment, Neil sits down to work out the net profits he made from his property by using the cash multiple analysis.

Originally, Neil had projected a cash multiple of 1.77x for his investment (before financing), assuming he would hold the property and collect rent ($12,000) for ten years and then sell at a price of $500,000 (figure 76). When he made his projections, he had neglected to factor in financing. Uncertain whether the financing helped to offset his shorter hold period, our anxious investor gathers his cash flow figures to see how he actually did from a cash multiple perspective.

Neil's actual investment results are as shown in figure 77:

fig. 77

	Cash Multiple	Investment	YEAR 1	YEAR 2	YEAR 3	YEAR 4	YEAR 5	Total Cash Flow
Actual (if without financing)	1.44	$355,329	12,010	12,409	12,818	13,237	460,167	$510,641
Actual (with financing)	1.80	$142,132	-204	195	604	1,023	254,721	$256,339

Without financing, the total cash flow from his five years of holding the rental would have been $510,641—all of the net rents from years one to five plus the profits from the sale at the end of year five. This total, divided by his initial investment, which would be $355,329 if he invested all cash, would be his cash multiple. This figure is 1.44 (assuming he invested all cash), which would be quite a bit lower than his projected 1.77x, but that is to be expected given that he exited in year five rather than year ten.

To calculate his real performance, however, we have to look at his figures after accounting for his financing. With financing, the total cash flow he got was $256,339, which is the sum of the net rents from years one to five after debt service plus the profits from the sale at the end of year five after paying back the remaining principal on the loan. This total, $256,339 divided by his initial investment, which is $142,132 (about a 40 percent down payment) turns out to be exactly 1.80x, which is nearly identical to the projected 1.77x cash multiple from his original 10-year, cash-only projection.

Neil ended up doing as well as he expected, though he didn't get there the same way and had some luck on his side. For every dollar he invested, he got back $1.80 as a return. And with a higher IRR, that cash multiple is a great result for his first investment property. He thought that he had earned less because he pulled out sooner, but this performance review is teaching him some valuable lessons. As it turns out, early sales can sometimes make sense, in both the timing and the efficiency of returns. A longer term doesn't necessarily translate into better performance, and that will certainly inform Neil as he goes forward into the next investment. However, he does need to take much more care with projecting his cash flows so as to avoid relying on a big exit in order to have a great return. He anticipates better returns sooner and certainly intends to allot more attention to building stronger investment cash flows. The prospect of quitting his job is realistic and much closer than he thought. This is quite exciting!

Chapter Recap

» Revisit your goals from before you invested to determine the best time to exit.

» Upgrading to a better-performing investment is usually the best reason to sell your property.

» Pricing the home is both subjective and objective. Market prices are an agreement between buyer and seller, not an exact science.

» Use comparable prices to justify and set the price of your home. Incorporate a cushion to allow the buyer to feel like they're getting a deal.

» Sales are seasonal, with volume doubling in certain periods.

» Price and timing of the sale both matter to your exit strategy.

» After the sale, review the performance to learn what to improve for the next investment.

PART IV

EXPANDING YOUR PORTFOLIO

| 13 |
Multifamily Real Estate

Chapter Overview
» The Steppingstone from Residential to Commercial Investing
» How to Add Value to Multifamily Properties
» Unique Multifamily Financials
» Should You Hire a Live-In Manager?

If you're ready to see what's next as an investor, I have news for you. The natural next step from residential investing doesn't have to be a leap into the unknown. Multifamily properties are technically included in the commercial investment asset category, but they have more in common with the residential properties you already know and love. The same principles we covered in the first three-fourths of this book apply now to how you find, assess, and operate a multifamily property.

Any property with five or more units is considered commercial, even if it's a residential dwelling.

URBANIZATION OF THE US POPULATION

fig. 78

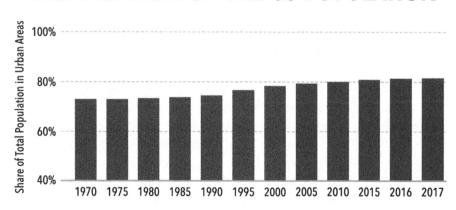

The slow and steady urbanization of the US population.

So, if you know it all by now, what else do I need to say about multifamily properties? With experience in residential investments, it's an easy transition into this asset. Here are just a few of the considerations you should be aware of before you look at this very appealing investment opportunity.

Four out of five Americans live in an urban center. We have slowly been moving away from rural areas to the city (see figure 78). Trends like this can be explained with the rise of 18- and 24-hour cities, big metropolitan centers with multiple industries supported in one location. There are more jobs and opportunities in these centers, and the trends show people moving to take advantage of what they offer. Couple that with the rise of millennials, a demographic that the news can't report on fast enough. This generation is coming of age and making decisions that affect homeownership rates throughout the country. Millennials are waiting longer to get married (seven years later than the national average in 1970) and waiting to have children as well (increased birth rates in women over thirty-five and a 15 percent decline in birthrates among women in their twenties). In the mentality of a millennial, if you aren't getting married and having kids, what's the point of a huge expenditure like a house? Rising house prices have pushed many millennials to postpone their first home purchase, putting more renters into the market. Though renting and living in the city isn't the first choice of millennials, the lifestyle and opportunities offered there are hard to pass up.

The trend toward urbanization is good news for multifamily property investors. As a result of this trend, multifamily investments have become quite popular, especially among older and institutional investors. Moreover, multifamily has become one of the top-performing assets among all real estate investments, at least since 2008. The rush of investors has driven the prices up and the cap rates (a commercial real estate metric defined in chapter 14) down. Traditionally, multifamily units would sell at 7-8 percent cap rates, but high premiums to get in on the trend have pushed down cap rates in some markets, like Los Angeles and New York, to sub 4 percent levels. That means you're going to pay at least twenty-five times the net operating income (another commercial real estate metric defined in detail in chapter 14; it is essentially what the property earns, less expenses) to buy a multifamily property in a hot market. This is not the case everywhere, mind you, but I see the trend moving this way, across the board, in the future.

What makes the multifamily so attractive, besides the fact that more people move to the city and need them? It's a stable investment with strong performance records. People looking for wealth preservation and stable, dependable returns seek out this investment strategy, and they are willing to pay those high premiums to get it. It's not the highest return on investment out there, but it's a solid choice for the long-term investor looking for predictable cash flow.

I've included real estate case studies in my course as part of the free Digital Assets. Follow along with these case studies to get a real sense of how investors are using real estate assets to make solid returns in today's market.

Value-Added Strategies

By now, you should understand that most real estate investments fall somewhere on the value-added spectrum of strategies. Even if you're just making minor repairs and cosmetic changes, you still want to add value to a property in any way you can. In the last chapter, I made it a point to clarify that all decisions to add value to a commercial property are to serve the highest and best use for that property. All decisions to add value in residential property are to serve the tenant's desires for their dwelling. Multifamily property falls somewhere in the middle. It is a commercial asset, so you want to increase the profitability. But at the same time, the tenants want better amenities in their dwelling.

There are three main ways to identify properties in which you have the potential to improve the value. These are different from the residential metrics that you already know about. Let's cover some of the unique opportunities found in the multifamily category.

Finding Below-Market Rentals

You've located a multifamily property, but after you analyze the rents, something isn't adding up. Neighboring properties are collecting much higher rents from their tenants. The reason for this shortfall in rent collected is usually related to one of the following three areas: maintenance, marketing, or management.

Poor rental returns are usually a symptom of low occupancy rates and cheap rents. Maybe the vacancies are higher than average for the market. Maybe tenants are defaulting more often in this property. Let's assume that you're looking at a good location with the potential to attract top tenants and charge top rents. The first step in recovering the property's lost potential is usually to raise the level of all maintenance. Replacing the carpets, painting the units, installing better security systems, and upgrading technology can positively distinguish the property from others in the area. It's amazing how the simple addition of modern public amenities can make a property more attractive. Think like a potential tenant. How would you decide between two different properties where both had units that were similar in square footage and design, but one offered a private pool and a laundry room? The extra features of that second property might be worth a nominal increase in rent.

Another thing that can be responsible for less-than-adequate rental income is the marketing of the facility. How the multifamily property is perceived by the market affects the kinds of tenants that choose to live there, subsequently affecting the rent you can charge. Marketing upgrades can be as simple as adding a professional website for the property that highlights the amenities.

New York's Lincoln Square has just opened a thirty-three-story multifamily apartment building. It is equipped with luxury amenities and overlooks the river. Prices start at $1.3 million per unit. But in order to take advantage of tax breaks and increase their development size, the owners decided to include lower-income rental units in the same building. Controversially, they built a separate entrance for these rental properties. People started referring to the second entrance as the "poor door," and entering through the poor door was a noticeably different experience than walking into the grand lobby of the "rich" side of the building. Although ninety thousand people applied to live in the building, the financial "apartheid" likely damaged their marketing/PR efforts and thereby lowered possible returns.

Finding Repurposed Conversions

In a growing market, older buildings are often repurposed for their highest and best use as a multifamily property. Throughout the world you can find old factories, breweries, or even office spaces converted into multifamily properties. It's less common as a strategy for adding value, but when done right, it can create good returns on the initial investment. Furthermore, this type of conversion is not found only in big cities, although that's most common. In England, large country manors are regularly converted into apartment buildings.

When repurposed conversions are used to accommodate the demand for more units in a market with a low supply, a certain expertise and risk tolerance are required. The permitting, construction, and leasing of these repurposed units all take time and experience to do properly. There will be a long period of time from the construction to the leasing, which will delay your income stream and eat into your funds. Also, you won't have the wind in your sails when you take over the ship. You will have to lease the property from a starting point of zero occupancy. It will take some time to start making a return on the investment.

New York City building inspectors shut down two single-story condos that had been repurposed into nine different micro-units. In some places, the ceiling was four-and-a-half feet high, and residents were being charged up to six hundred dollars a month for rent. Both landlords were fined $140,000 for illegal building practices, and the whole building was closed.

Reducing Expenses

When we calculate the *net operating income (NOI)* metric in commercial real estate, we have to factor in the operating costs of the property. The higher the costs, the lower the NOI. And because multifamily properties operate off a cap rate valuation, if you have a low NOI, the value of the property is lower. But if you can increase the efficiency of the property and reduce the expenses needed to operate it, then you can increase the NOI and thereby increase the cap rate valuation.

Many investors use a consultant to help identify these inefficiencies. Maybe you need to replace older appliances that draw too much power. You could renegotiate with expensive contractors for maintenance or management services. You could install new systems to automate the property, such as security doors and keycards to replace on-site security staff.

In order to identify properties where you can add value by cutting costs, you will need to study the financials carefully when considering the purchase. It takes some experience to identify the lack of cost control or the poor management that raises running costs. Strict cost control and better accountability must start on day one to maintain the rental returns throughout the life of your investment.

Multifamily Financials

You understand residential investment financials. You understand commercial investment financials. What are the unique characteristics of the multifamily property that you should know about before you undertake an investment like this? This is especially applicable if you're making the transition from residential to multifamily opportunities, as there are some key differences you need to analyze.

Rule of 72

In the investing world, we always want to find a way to create an apples-to-apples comparison between two different properties. With multifamily units, you have several tenants in one building, and the age and operation of each building are totally different. You will often find comparing one multifamily to another is not an apples-to-apples comparison. It's more like apples-to-snorkels. There's no easy way to look at both properties objectively and make an informed decision.

But you can see how long it will take to double your money in what's called the *Rule of 72*. You may have come across this formula in other scenarios, as it's a pretty common metric, but here's how you apply it to a real estate deal. Before anything, you must calculate the cash-on-cash return (or the yield) of a property. It's a simple formula that shows you the percentage you make on an investment (figure 79).

fig. 79

$$YIELD = \frac{ANNUAL\ CASH\ INCOME}{TOTAL\ CASH\ INVESTMENT}$$

The advantage in real estate investing is that you aren't totaling the purchase price, just the money you put into the property. Let's say that you have a property worth $1 million and you make $100,000 a year in rental income; that's a 10 percent yield on that property. But if you've leveraged that purchase price with debt, you have a larger yield on the money you invested, less the debt service costs. Let's say that you financed 70 percent of that same property, so you only invested $300,000 and, less the debt service costs, you make $60,000 a year in rental income.

Annual Cash Income / Total Cash Investment = Cash-on-Cash Return
$60,000 / $300,000 = 20% Yield

fig. 80

$$\frac{72}{CASH\text{-}ON\text{-}CASH\ RETURN} = YEARS\ TO\ DOUBLE$$

In the financial world, the Rule of 72 uses an interest rate to determine how long an investment takes to double your money, but for multifamily properties, we're going to use the yield we just calculated.

Investing in this multifamily property will see you double your money in just over three-and-a-half years. This simplified metric allows you to look at how effective each investment will be for you. Take several different properties with different tenants, units, and rental returns, and the Rule of 72 makes it an easy apples-to-apples comparison of how quickly each investment doubles your money.

Rent Roll

If you're new to multifamily properties, this may be the first time you've needed to think about multiple rental payments coming from the same property. The rent roll is a document that shows you all the pertinent information about the income collected for that building. This is where you'll uncover the true value of the property, so it's important to understand how the rent roll works.

On the document, you'll find listed the space rented out, the names of the lessees, the start and end dates of the leases, the rental incomes collected, and the amounts paid and balances due for each unit. The rent roll is a quick visualization tool, allowing you to identify your rate of occupancy, your risk for vacancies, and your current leasing rates (figure 81).

GRAPHIC

fig. 81

Unit Name	Unit Type	Tenant Name	Lease Start	Term	Move-in Date	Lease Expiration	Security Deposit	Rent
101	Studio	Linley, Thomas	3/1/13	12	3/3/13	2/28/14	$850.00	$850.00
102	3br	Millhouse, Kinsey	12/1/00	12	12/1/00	11/30/01	$1,200.00	$1,200.00
103	2br	Marlowe, Philip	2/1/11	12	2/1/11	1/31/12	$1,050.00	$1,050.00
104	2br	Spade, Sam	7/1/99	MTM	7/1/99	6/30/00	$1,200.00	$1,100.00
105	3br	Alleyn, Roderick	6/1/13	12	6/1/13	5/31/14	$1,200.00	$1,200.00
106	3br	Maigret, Jules	2/1/11	12	2/1/11	1/31/12	$1,200.00	$1,200.00
107	Studio	Wimsey, Peter	2/1/00	12	2/1/00	1/31/01	$850.00	$850.00
108	3br	Marple, Jane	6/1/13	12	6/1/13	5/31/14	$1,200.00	$1,200.00
109	2br	Poirot, Hercule	2/1/12	6	2/1/13	7/31/13	$1,050.00	$1,050.00
110	2br	Holmes, Sherlock	9/1/12	MTM	9/1/12	8/31/13	$1,050.00	$1,050.00

Unit Name	Last Increase	Concession	Parking	Other	Amount Paid	Balance Due
101	–	$0.00	$50.00	$0.00	$850.00	$0.00
102	12/1/13	$0.00	$50.00	$0.00	$600.00	$600.00
103	2/1/13	$0.00	$50.00	$0.00	$1,050.00	$0.00
104	7/1/12	$0.00	$0.00	$25.00	$1,200.00	$0.00
105	–	$0.00	$50.00	$0.00	$800.00	$400.00
106	2/1/13	$0.00	$0.00	$25.00	$1,200.00	$0.00
107	–	$0.00	$50.00	$0.00	$0.00	$1,700.00
108	–	$0.00	$50.00	$25.00	$700.00	$500.00
109	2/1/13	$0.00	$0.00	$33.00	$1,050.00	$0.00
110	–	$0.00	$50.00	$25.00	$1,000.00	$50.00

An example of a rent roll for a small apartment building, including lease dates, extra income, balance owing, and terms for units. For large multifamily properties, there can be several hundred items in one rent roll.

From the perspective of a buyer, analyzing a rent roll can help in identifying risks. For example, if the lease dates all end in December or January (a time when people are less likely to move), that could present a leasing risk if tenants choose not to renew their lease. It can also help identify the rental rates and how they compare against the market values in comparable properties. If all the lease dates are recent, that could present a risk for occupancy and high turnover, as there's no sign that the property has longevity among the tenants. If many of the tenants have balances owing, then you'll want to know why. Maybe they aren't paying their rent due to garbage collection issues or poor management. Identification of these risks can present opportunities for improving cash flow and the value of the property.

Tax Benefits for Multifamily Properties

Governments like to incentivize the purchase and management of large multifamily properties. You need to know what benefits investors may qualify for when operating this type of investment asset. In some cases, the tax benefits you earn can make the difference between a property that loses money and one that provides a healthy cash flow.

Check with an accountant in your local area to determine what local, state, and federal tax benefits apply to you. Be sure to select an accountant who is experienced in real estate, because special tax considerations apply, such as a "cost segregation" study whereby you could potentially shorten the depreciation time of some capital expenses to improve short-term cash flow.

» **Interest**: In most places in the world, the interest you pay on your real estate debt (or a portion of it) is tax-deductible.

» **Depreciation**: Depreciation costs can offset any taxes you might otherwise have to pay when you report the income on that property. With large accelerated depreciation, you can potentially have negative income but positive cash flow in the early years of an investment.

» **Travel**: If you hold a property that is not your primary residence, you can deduct any travel costs incurred when visiting that property, even if it's long-distance.

» **Repairs**: You can deduct any necessary repairs to the property, as long as they are justified and receipted.

» **Personnel**: The operating costs to hire employees or independent contractors can be included as a deduction.

» **Management**: Even if you self-manage, you can deduct costs like the home office and phone expenses you use for management of the investment.

» **Legal and Professional Services**: If they are related to the daily operations of the property, legal and professional services can be tax-deductible as well.

Property Management

In a residential investment situation, you have the option to choose to self-manage your properties, especially if the cost of professional management services makes the margins too thin. That's just not the case with a multifamily property. With dozens of tenants, leasing arrangements, maintenance, upkeep, rent collection, and an entire building to oversee, in my opinion it doesn't make logistical or financial sense to self-manage a multifamily property. Although you might save 5 or 10 percent on management fees, the time trade-off is too valuable for a long-term investor to consider.

The quality of property management has a profound influence on the returns you will make. With multifamilies, the pros of reduced time on-site and outsourcing issues to professionals almost always outweigh the cons of the management fees and the energy you spend to hire the right manager.

If you want to keep your involvement to just collecting rent and keeping the property at maximum occupancy, spend the time to find the right management service. This allows you to consider properties in out-of-state locations and frees you up for more productive activities.

Frankly, any good property manager will likely have the resources and experience that you lack. Their incentive is geared toward keeping the ship afloat, maintaining the course that you set. If you have vacancies to fill, provide incentives for your property manager to actively look for tenants. This aligns their interests with your own.

One of the challenges of hiring a property management service is that many of them are so large that it may be difficult to get to a point of feeling that they have your best interests at heart. Large firms might present a good front and solid numbers, but will they really seek to make your property stand out from the crowd? Take a stroll down the street to look at competing multifamily properties. You may find that they are managed by the same large firm you are considering hiring. In this case, you have to ask, "Whose side will the management firm really be on?" Because if they have a tenant looking for a place to live, the management firm will still get paid regardless of whether that tenant chooses your property or the one down the road also managed by that firm. Bottom line: try to find out who is managing the properties of your closest competition before making your selection of a property management firm.

You might also find that your property requires full-time staffing. As we've discussed previously, this can be a tax-deductible expense for the operation of your asset, but be sure to consider what you need. The rule of thumb is that for every one hundred tenants, you need two employees: one to handle all the leasing and management of the property and another to handle the maintenance and repairs on-site. Property managers are often running from one fire to the next, so make sure that you don't leave your property understaffed.

Live-In Management

If you are hesitant to hire a big firm to manage your property, you can hire a live-in property manager. When you have a manager that lives in the community, they tend to have a vested interest in maintaining it. They are known by the tenants, and that bond helps build trust between management and renter. A live-in manager is on call for any emergencies that pop up, while a larger management firm might take longer to respond to the concerns of your tenants. It can be a marketing feature for your property as well, to have someone on-site and able to provide tenants with more immediate attention.

There is really no hard-and-fast rule for deciding whether to hire a live-in manager. You pay them a salary or stipend to live there, but the trade-off is that they take up occupancy of one of your units. If you have ten units, a live-in manager will remove 10 percent of your potential profits right off the bat. And that doesn't include the salary you pay for their services. Generally, it doesn't make financial sense to hire a live-in property manager unless you have twenty-five or thirty units. You have to compare the cost of the salary and free housing against the cost of hiring a traditional property management service.

If you have a smaller multifamily unit, one option is to negotiate a reduced rent or provide a subsidy as part of their compensation. Free rent doesn't look good on the rent roll, so a stipend allows you to maintain the integrity of that rent roll for the future sale of the property. You also want to ensure that it's not free rent if your property manager is not full-time. Otherwise, the deductions you claim at tax time for the operating costs are outweighed by the loss of income from their unit. If it doesn't make financial sense to have a manager for just one property, you can always consider buying more in the same area and having one live-in manager float between them.

Chapter Recap

» Multifamily properties are the natural next step up from residential investments.

» Multifamily properties are considered commercial investments but have a lot of principles in common with residential properties.

» Value-added strategies involve improving the management, reducing operating expenses, and upgrading the amenities of the facility.

» The repurposing of older buildings into multifamily units in busy markets can provide a good return on your investment.

» Multifamily investments come with multiple units and thus multiple tenants, reflected in a rent roll.

» The Rule of 72 is a formula to quickly and roughly estimate the length of time it will take to double your investment. It is a key measure in making an apples-to-apples comparison between two multifamily properties.

» The optimal property management firm is both competent and incentivized to aggressively pursue your best interests.

» Live-in property managers can work if you have enough occupied units to mitigate the reduction in financial returns.

| 14 |
Commercial Real Estate

Chapter Overview
» How to Level Up from Residential to Commercial Real Estate
» Learning Key Commercial Real Estate Distinctions
» Analyzing the Finances of Commercial Properties
» Adapting to New Risks

Always have something to look forward to.

– DAVID BECKHAM

If you've made it to this section, congratulations. This is where you learn what's next and what's possible in the world of real estate investments. Mind you, this is *not* for beginners. What you are about to read applies to experienced investors with some degree of comfort with typical residential investments. After a few years of working with rental properties, securing tenants, collecting rent, and investing in the residential market, you need to know what it looks like to start investing in commercial real estate. Most investors don't leap straight in to commercial properties. They choose to invest indirectly through syndications, or they operate a successful multifamily property before making the leap to the big leagues.

I believe this is a very exciting time for commercial real estate investors. Not even five years ago, investors didn't have the same level of access to investing opportunities that exist today. If you were a brand-new investor, you'd have a very slim chance of any kind of exposure to commercial real estate. But with crowdfunding platforms and indirect investing options, even the most inexperienced investor can test the waters of commercial real estate. These platforms don't involve full control of the asset like you would expect in residential real estate, but I believe it is still a valuable teaching tool to use sites like Fundrise, CrowdStreet, RealCrowd, and RealtyShares, among dozens of others, to gain unprecedented experience without the capital you would have needed a decade ago.

But even with these crowdfunding options, when the barriers to entry for the beginner commercial real estate investor are lower than ever, the learning curve can still be steep. While many of the intricacies of commercial real estate investing are beyond the scope of this book, my hope is that I can, at the very least, help you understand certain fundamental concepts. I want to pull back the curtain to show you the possibilities. After residential property, commercial property represents the next target for real estate investment opportunities. Although it requires a significant amount of capital to start, the rewards are that much higher compared to traditional residential real estate. Commercial investment isn't the first step for a real estate investor, but it can certainly be a next step for those who are ready to see what else is out there beyond the horizon of homes, units, condos, and apartments.

In the spirit of full disclosure, in addition to investing in residential properties, I personally invest in commercial real estate, primarily through private syndications and crowdfunding platforms such as Fundrise. I continue to give my portfolio exposure to multifamily projects in the American heartland—Midwest states that I believe will see higher long-term performance than the pricey and volatile coastal markets.

There is no doubt that as we start to get into the finer details of the differences between residential and commercial investing, you will realize that commercial is more complicated and more costly. The sheer number of potential asset classes alone could take up an entire book. The cost can be prohibitively high as well, with many properties costing hundreds of millions or even billions of dollars. But the stable returns and other positive elements create alluring potential for the ambitious investor. What we are going to explore in this chapter is just a taste, a sampler of commercial real estate, but I hope it inspires you to consider commercial investing as a long-term goal in your career as a real estate investor.

Key Differences in Commercial Real Estate

Many of the topics we already discussed, such as analysis, key metrics, and day-to-day operations, apply specifically to residential property. The tenants and properties in commercial real estate operate in such different ways that they require a fresh look.

Conceptually, many of the ideas we already talked about in previous chapters are familiar to most investors. You understand the concept of flipping a home. You understand what it means to rent out a property to a tenant. You understand renovating a property in order to collect more rent or a higher selling price. These are pretty basic concepts that are easy to grasp. The category of residential real estate is fairly accessible to us because we are all renters and homeowners. We also see the many house-flipping, real-estate-themed television shows that augment our firsthand knowledge. Commercial real estate is more complex and not as easy to grasp. Maybe because we don't deal with it daily the way we do residential property.

Purpose of Use

Residential properties are meant for dwellings. Commercial properties are designed to produce a profit.

A residential property with more than four units is considered a commercial property. An investor with a fourplex owns residential property, whereas an investor with a five-unit apartment building owns commercial property.

This distinction of purpose is the key difference. Because commercial property is designed around profit and not people, the key phrase that will come up again and again with commercial investors is "highest and best use." We touched on this concept earlier, but it's really one of the core concepts of commercial real estate. In the residential investment world, you can make the property look more appealing, you can include more amenities, and you can modernize it. That's all for the benefit of the people living in it. That makes residential real estate somewhat subjective. If someone likes it (and is willing to pay for it), then it makes sense to include it in the property. Commercial real estate has a very different underlying concept, which is based on discovering the best way for the property to generate profit.

Within the highest-and-best-use decision framework, the investor may choose to keep the property as it is, tear it down and build something new, or repurpose the use of it. Let's say you've invested in a parking garage that gives you residual income from the parking fees you collect. But let's imagine that over time, the population of your city doesn't need to drive as much as they do now. Maybe the mass transit infrastructure has improved in your area, making it convenient to leave the car at home. Maybe the rise of self-driving vehicles diminishes commuters' need to park where they work, allowing them to park off-site. Maybe job losses reduce the number of people who need your garage. Would the most profitable use be to tear down the parking garage and build an office building in its place? Possibly. These things are what you need to factor in when making a commercial real estate investment.

Many people remember dining at Pizza Hut, a treat for the whole family. But those days are gone for some, with the closure of hundreds of stores all over the country. The model of a sit-in pizza restaurant no longer makes sense in today's environment; Pizza Hut reports that just 10 percent of their sales come from dine-in customers.

fig. 82

Source: www.reddit.com/r/FormerPizzaHuts/

What makes the Pizza Hut situation unique is their distinct building shape. The roof with its cap makes it instantly recognizable—a marketing strategy in the early days. From an investor's perspective, the Pizza Hut story is a perfect way to understand the concept of highest and best use. It no longer made financial sense to operate dine-in restaurants, so Pizza Hut closed stores to focus on deliveries and pickup. You'll see remnants of their past in repurposed restaurants all over the country. Former Pizza Hut buildings are now being used as Chinese restaurants, diners, daycare centers, municipal buildings, used car lot offices, dental practices, and even churches. There's a website (usedtobeapizzahut.blogspot.com) and a subreddit (reddit.com/r/FormerPizzaHuts) dedicated to spotting old Pizza Hut buildings.

Assets and Classes

Commercial property has a simple grading system that applies to all asset types, such as retail, industrial, and hotels. The system, which is not definitive or objective, is based on the overall characteristics and quality of the property. It's a great way to gauge a property's relative competitive position and how it holds up against similar properties in the market. It factors in the rent you can collect, the age of the property, value appreciation over time, and amenities.

Although the grading system is universal, there is no standard description of what an A, B, or C grade means. Brokers and investors typically use comparable properties to assign a grade. Buyers will argue the grade down ("I think this is a B+"), and sellers will tend to skew it higher ("I think it's closer to an A-"). Listing brokers will often research properties with similar amenities and age to create a set for comparison. The rating is often a dialogue between buyers and sellers, who agree to a grade based on how the property compares against other options in the market.

But it's a good starting point, nonetheless. It's tempting to think that A-graded properties are better than B-graded properties. Investors have discovered that the grade of a property is no guarantee of the income it will generate. A-grade properties often slip into B-grade status over time, gradually losing rental income along the way. Another important note is that you can have a Grade A property located in a Grade B market, and that location may effectively lower the grade. You have to factor in both the performance of the current market and the amenities that the property offers.

MY TAKE

When evaluating your commercial properties using this grading system (or any other means), I want you to think in terms of trade-offs. What do you receive and what are the inherent risks involved with each class of property?

GRAPHIC

fig. 83

» **Class A:** These are the top-tier properties in premium locations. You'll find that these properties are usually very new, with modern designs and materials. They come with high-end finishes, technology, systems, and amenities. You could call these "trophy" properties; they achieve the highest rents and better-quality tenants, and they tend to have the lowest vacancy rates. But they are also pretty expensive because of those factors. We'll discuss the metric shortly, but Class A properties also have very low capitalization, or "cap" rates, and low yields. These investments tend to offer stable returns and good cash flow over longer periods of time.

» **Class B**: Class B properties are the middle-tier investments. The locations are not as highly trafficked or as visible as those of Class A. Some are former Class A properties that have aged out of that top-tier class. They're "middle of the market" properties with good construction and design, good finishes, adequate technology and amenities. Class B properties are generally a little older and less useful than Class A investments. There will usually be some upgrade potential, but they're not unusable in their current condition. With some restorative work, investors can achieve higher rents and attract a reputable tenant base. Vacancies remain low to moderate in this class. Moderate cap rates and yields typify this riskier investment, and there is potential for good returns with more work and operational effort.

» **Class C**: There is no doubt about what's considered a Class C property. They are at the lowest tier, in the worst locations, and they are generally almost obsolete in function. In terms of construction, technology, and amenities, they are the worst option in their current state. They don't command good rent. They almost always require upgrades and renovations. The tenants they attract are typically poor and short term. Vacancies are felt keenly in these properties with very high cap rates. They have the highest yields and the best returns available in the market, but that expected return is a trade-off for accepting higher market, construction, and financial risks.

In terms of purpose of use, if a property is Class A, then it is usually already achieving its highest and best use, while Class C properties almost always require a complete overhaul to bring them up to market standards. Chasing better returns with lower-grade properties means accepting that trade-off of a higher risk profile. What level of risk are you willing to accept? Do you prefer long-term sustainable and stable income? Or would you like to take on more risk in order to make a huge return on selling the investment after major renovations?

fig. 84

WAREHOUSE EXAMPLES BY CLASS			
	CLASS A	CLASS B	CLASS C
Year built	2017	2001	1970
Ceiling height	50'	30'	20'
Location	2 minutes off major exit from 3 regional major highways, near heart of major city.	5 minutes off major exit from major highway, in major city.	20 minutes off exit from major highway, in suburb or outskirts of major city.
Loading docks	30	12	6
Additional amenities	Temperature and humidity controlled, food grade, LEED Platinum, inventory management system, large office, 250 covered parking spaces, robot automation ready.	LEED Silver, moderate office, 120 parking spaces.	No office, 80 parking spaces.

A comparison of properties of a particular asset type (warehouses) using grades.

COMMERCIAL REAL ESTATE INVESTMENTS

fig. 85

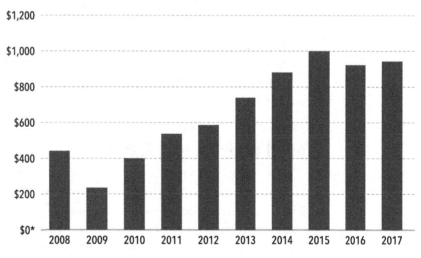

*Amount in Billions USD

The worldwide growth of the commercial real estate investment market.

Deal Sizes

In most markets, residential properties are a few hundred thousand dollars, some approaching a million dollars or more. But commercial properties are on a scale of their own, often in the millions and billions.

Generally, the deal size and the returns depend on the state of the property. Some properties for sale are finished products; they are already built and well-employed. They have tenants, most of which are leased in for long periods. Returns on investment usually run between 4 and 8 percent each year. Examples are a newly built office building with several companies renting out space, or a new strip mall with an anchor retail store already locked in place. For core investments like these in the commercial sector, you're looking at figures starting at $5 million.

Acquiring an older property, however, could involve some rehab work, upgrading old systems and materials to attract better tenants or achieve a higher purpose. Returns fall in the 10–20 percent range with a moderate level of risk to undertake. These deals can start at around $5 million, and the level of investment depends on the amount of work done to the property. An investment like this can be flipped or become a long-term asset with consistent income.

As for Class C properties, the easiest way to make better returns is to tear down the old building, making way for a complete rebuild. Construction costs can end up being higher than expected, and the timing longer; the risk of delays and overruns often factor into this type of work. After construction, investors can sell the finished product or lease it out for higher rent. The typical return is at least 20 percent on these types of investments.

Select Metrics and Ratios

We have spent a lot of time talking about metrics and finances in this book. In order not to overwhelm you with further information, I will be as brief as I can here and just showcase some of the major differences that matter for commercial real estate investors. Some terms and concepts are universal, while others will apply to just one market or asset type. For instance, the way you measure the return for a hotel is very different than how you measure returns for an industrial research and development facility located outside the city limits.

Gross Rent Multiplier

As a quick back-of-the-envelope tool, you can't pass up the *gross rent multiplier* (GRM) for assessing the returns of a specific investment property. The GRM is a rule-of-thumb guide that screens the potential properties you're analyzing to see if they are under- or overpriced.

fig. 86

$$\text{GROSS RENT MULTIPLIER} = \frac{\text{PURCHASE PRICE}}{\text{ANNUAL GROSS RENTS}}$$

The reason this tool is used only as an estimate is because the formula doesn't account for the expenses of the property. So you can't include the utilities, the insurance costs, or the taxes you pay after collecting rent. That final GRM number shows the number of years it would take to pay off the property if you only collected 100 percent rent and had no expenses. Let's look at an example.

Neil Hector the Real Estate Investor (yes, he's looking at commercial property now) has been interested in a property in town that's been on the market for a while. He doesn't want to devote too much time to his evaluation of this one property, because his investor friends have told him that he needs to look at a minimum of one hundred potential properties before he can expect to find one solid lead. The purchase price for the small warehouse is $1.4 million. Is that price too high? Because the warehouse has been on the market for nine months, Neil thinks it might be. He calculates the GRM to see how the purchase price compares to the rent the property collects. The current tenant, with a shipping/storage business, is paying $8,000 a month in rent.

Purchase Price / Gross Annual Rent = GRM
$1,400,000 / ($8,000 x 12) = 14.58 GRM

The lower the GRM, the lower the price versus the rental income. So 14.58 seems very high, especially considering that some of the other properties he's been looking at score around 10. In this case, either the purchase price is too high or the rent is too low. In order to make this investment comparable to other properties, he'd have to acquire the property for less than a million dollars or increase the rent by almost 50 percent to over $11,500 a month. It looks like this isn't the right price, so our (future) commercial investor discards it and keeps looking.

Net Operating Income

Unless they purchase a property in pristine condition, most investors will take some action to improve the value of their property. The goal is always to bring it as close as possible to its highest and best use. By using the net operating income (NOI) metric, you can measure the potential value that a property can achieve (figure 87). The analysis takes into account all the potential income from all sources as well as the complete expenses of the *property*, not the *investment*; you are not accounting for any debt service costs, depreciation, or leasing costs. This is one of the primary ways to measure the value of a commercial property.

NET OPERATING INCOME FORMULA

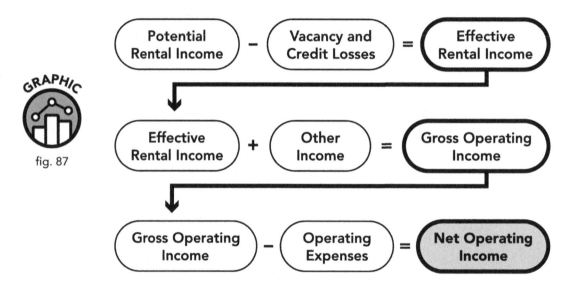

fig. 87

Potential rental income is assuming 100 percent occupancy with the best tenants at the best negotiated prices for that asset class. You can use comparable or historical data to calculate the losses and vacancies.

Neil Hector's been busy. After a lot of looking around, he's identified a warehouse that looks more promising as an investment. In order to figure out the value of the property and whether it's where he wants it to be, he makes some calculations of the net operating income (figure 88).

At 100 percent occupancy, the property should earn $1 million in rental income. Vacancies are pretty low for this Class A property, just 5 percent, so the rental income is reduced by only $50,000. There is paid parking on-site that earns an extra $60,000 a year, making up the extra income section.

Potential Rental Income	$1,000,000
Vacancy and Credit Losses	($50,000)
Effective Rental Income	$950,000
Other Income	$60,000
Gross Operating Income	$1,010,000
Operating Expenses	($400,000)
Net Operating Income	$610,000

An example of the NOI for a warehouse with paid parking that offers additional income ("other income").

Operating costs for the year are roughly $400,000, so after deducting that expense from the total, Neil has figured out that this warehouse has an NOI of $610,000. A rough estimate of the operating expense ratio (operating expense divided by income) for this property is over 39 percent, which seems a little high. After some research, Neil discovers that other warehouses in the same market average a 33 percent operating expense ratio. This tells him that the warehouse is not operating very efficiently. Perhaps some improvements could reduce costs and increase profits. Even if Neil cannot improve the market rents, lowering the operating expenses will help make him more money.

Neil's calculations show around $50,000 per month coming in as income after the operational expenses are accounted for. That NOI figure helps him calculate whether he can cover the other costs in this investment. Taxes, debt service costs, and any commissions paid to agents and brokers for leasing the property should be covered by his NOI. Our fearless investor is one step closer to determining the value of his intended investment, but in order to obtain a precise estimate he's going to require another evaluation tool.

Capitalization Rates

Above all else, this is the key metric for determining the value of a property. If you are familiar with the financial world, you may have come across the term "return on assets." Capitalization rates, or *cap rates*, are similar in nature, but they are very specific to real estate investments. The formula for the cap rate is simple, but I've found that it's a concept not easy for my students to grasp intuitively.

$$\text{CAP RATE} = \frac{\text{NET OPERATING INCOME}}{\text{CURRENT MARKET VALUE OF ASSET}}$$

How do we apply this to Neil's warehouse in our previous example? He has calculated an NOI of $610,000, but how can he use this formula to help determine the value of the property?

Asking Price: $9.5 million
NOI: $610,000
$610,000 / $9,500,000 = 0.064, or 6.4%

The cap rate for this property is 6.4 percent; the asking price is roughly fifteen times what the property can earn in a year.

fig. 90

3% – 6% **5% – 9%** **8% – 12%**

Rough cap rates for the classes of commercial properties in Neil's Las Vegas market.

On its own, the cap rate doesn't tell Neil that much, so he needs to look at the market and the current rates for different classes. In his area, a 6 percent cap rate indicates a Class A or Class B property, depending on the amenities and age of the facility (figure 90). Neil's prospective property has exceptional modern office space with some high-tech amenities in place for automation and robotics. Since it is most comparable to other Class A properties, this property is also graded as Class A. The value of the property gives him an advantage: the potential to attract better clients and earn more rent. The newer facility costs Neil less money than what he would have to pay in other markets for comparable properties.

There are many more metrics and ways to calculate income and investments than I could reasonably present here. If you want more information on metrics, I suggest learning about the following:

- Capital stack
- Revenue items
- Contingency reserves
- Operating expenses
- Ratio utility billing systems (RUBS)

Financing

The main difference between residential and commercial loans (other than the magnitude) is the terms of the loans. Commercial financing tends to be in shorter terms. Let's say you take out a typical thirty-year mortgage on a residential loan. After thirty years of consistent repayments, the loan is fully paid off with that final payment in the thirtieth year, both the interest and principal portions. Some commercial loans are different in that you'll have a loan term that is shorter than the amortization period—for example, a five-year loan with a twenty-year amortization schedule. That means that after five years, even if you made all of your payments in full and on time, you will not have paid off the entirety of your loan. The remainder of the balance will become due. At that point, you will either pay off the balance in cash (perhaps from your sale of the property) or you will roll the debt over into a new loan. This structure represents but one way that commercial loans differ from standard residential mortgages. A common structure, especially for construction and rehab projects, is the interest-only loan. You pay only the interest over the five-year period, and when the term is up, you must repay the entire balance of the principal, which, again, may be facilitated through the sale of the property or by restructuring or rerouting the debt.

The first option for a commercial loan is the construction loan, which typically has a term of one or two years. It's often a loan of 75 to 80 percent of the value of the property, and it must be paid when the building has been declared "stabilized," or when it reaches 90 percent occupancy. Loan monies are drawn from the bank incrementally, in tandem with the completion of specific construction milestones; for instance, 5 percent completion may give you access to 5 percent of the funds, and so on.

Once the construction phase is complete and units are leased, a commercial investor will take out what's called a permanent loan. The permanent loan is there to pay off the construction loan costs once the building has reached 90 percent occupancy. It's a long-term (sometimes 40 years) fully amortized loan. I want you to remember this loan because when we talk about risk, you'll see how this type of loan introduces a new risk that residential investors never have to think about.

When Neil, our residential-turned-commercial investor hero, determines the costs for his loan, he needs to consider the same metrics he used for his residential investments: loan-to-cost, loan-to-value, and the debt service coverage ratio. These metrics are all familiar to Neil (a welcome respite from commercial real estate's seemingly alien metrics), so he's fully prepared for lenders to evaluate his investment proposal and secure the loan he needs to purchase his carefully selected warehouse property.

Finding Deals

Unlike with residential real estate, in the world of commercial real estate it takes more finesse to source the deals that are up and coming. It's not just an MLS network or an agent contact that helps you locate your next potential deal. Yes, some deals can be found through the traditional platforms, but others require a little more initiative and creativity. I'd like to teach you how to source the best commercial deals before they even formally come to market. It's a world of land and zoning maps, understanding the sentiment and atmosphere of a city, and analyzing the approved projects already in motion.

City Planning and Development

A city planning commission is responsible for overseeing the work of preserving a community and making sure that it's economically viable in the years to come. City planning involves zoning and rezoning of areas that are set aside to be used as commercial properties. This can have a major impact on the commercial investments available to you now and in the future. But these types of changes don't happen overnight. Council meetings, surveys, environmental concerns, public concerns, and traffic concerns have to be addressed before any changes are made. As an investor, keep your eye on zoning changes, as they represent significant opportunities for you to find a good deal.

More than anything, the commercial investor is interested in municipal *density*. Every city in the world must face the challenge of a shortage of affordable housing. As the population tends to relocate into cities, the only way to increase the available housing options is to increase the approved population density of certain pockets of the city. Keep an eye on where your city will increase the density zoning, creating opportunities to add value to existing properties. A former fourplex in an increased density zone might have a better use as an apartment complex.

The following are some considerations when developing the commercial properties in a city:

» Preservation of the features of the city
» Historical preservation for tourism and future generations
» Environmental concerns
» Anticipating the economic needs of the city before they arise
» Meeting health, convenience, and security needs

While it's not the most riveting or entertaining forum, you should be attending your local city planning commission meetings to gain an understanding of the general sentiment of the community. Many of these meetings are offered online as well, so you can attend the sessions for markets outside of your area. In particular, pay attention to the reasons given for development approvals and rejections. This gives you a greater understanding of what the key values and considerations are in a community. Let's say that you have access to a new transit system plan for your area.

fig. 91

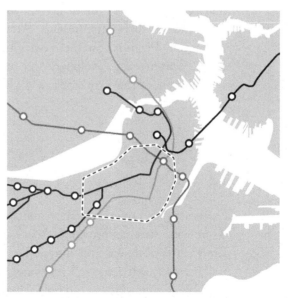

City planning for public transportation upgrades. Property values are expected to increase inside the highlighted dashed area.

With a transit map like the one in figure 91, you can see areas where a city's next development will be focused. Look for land and property in these areas as having high potential for a rapid increase in value. As an investor, you will win because you are investing where the values will rise, not where they have already risen.

Employment Trends

Job growth is a huge factor in increased value. We saw this earlier in the book when Neil was considering different markets for his initial investment. Las Vegas has a population of approximately 650,000 and Reno has just 250,000. And yet, because of the major job opportunities in Reno, its real estate is significantly higher in value than that of Las Vegas, even though it's a much smaller place.

In early 2017, Amazon released a list of twenty North American cities that it identified as potential locations for its second headquarters. Why did it do this? For one thing, Amazon knew what it was offering. With a new headquarters, it could potentially bring fifty thousand jobs into one community. With that kind of draw, cities faced immense pressure to offer better incentives and tax breaks to entice Amazon to select them.

And that's exactly what these cities did. For example, North Carolina introduced a new bill that offered incentives for any company that invested at least $4 billion into the economy and provided at least five thousand new jobs. In the end, Amazon selected a site just north of Arlington, Virginia, for their two-million-square-foot campus dubbed HQ2. Commercial developers and investors swarmed the area once it was announced that Amazon's new HQ2 would house tens of thousands of new employees.

A rising tide lifts all boats.

–JOHN F. KENNEDY

Increased job growth impacts multiple commercial real estate sectors. More jobs mean more retail space, increased demand for industrial sites, better shipping and storage facilities, and more hotels to account for increased activity—and that's not all. Even land itself can become a valuable commercial asset to hold when you know that the area is soon to be flush with new jobs.

Commercial Real Estate Risks

Given the scope and size of most commercial real estate investments, they generally present greater risk than their traditional residential counterparts. Let's look at some of the more potent risks you could face as a commercial real estate investor.

Debt Risk

As we have discussed, the financing you take on with a commercial entity will be different in structure and timing. Using debt to leverage your investment can be a smart play, but with commercial properties, it can quickly turn into an overleveraged investment. If you lose tenants, the risk is that you won't have enough rent to cover the debt you've incurred.

The other risk is with the term of loans, a shorter length than you'd get in a conventional mortgage. If you lock in a good rate for your mortgage, you can shield yourself against rate increases over time. But with a commercial debt, you don't have that luxury. After each five-year term, you have to cover the debt with a new loan, sometimes at a higher rate. When the loan matures, you have no guarantee of a new loan if the market is in a downturn. The higher loan-to-value ratio created by a recession market may prevent banks from lending you enough money to cover the debt shortfall. This was a very common problem leading up to 2008's housing crisis. Building projects that had started when the economy was in the middle of the bubble had their loan terms come due during the recession. Because the value of the property had significantly diminished (in extreme cases, up to 50 percent), the banks were unwilling to loan out money because the loan-to-value ratio had plummeted to the point where developers had to declare bankruptcy rather than continue with the project.

Cap Rate Risk

The capitalization rate of the property has more impact on your investment than any other metric. If the cap rate percentages move just slightly, this can have a substantial impact on the value of your asset.

Let's say that you have a property with a net operating income of $100,000, and the cap rate drops from 16 percent to 12 percent. That $1.6 million property you own just turned into a $1.2 million property, a huge swing from a small shift in the cap rate. The problem is that the cap rate is dependent on many variables, such as the ten-year Treasury bond rate, economic swings in the area, and increased debt amounts in the market.

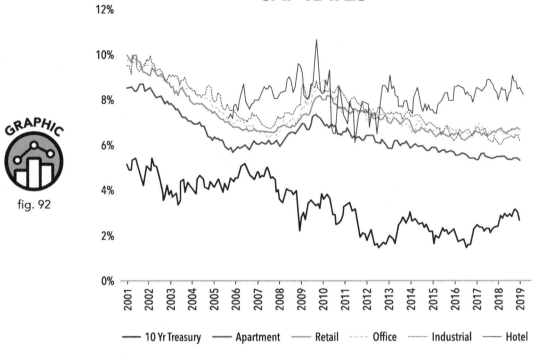

CAP RATES

GRAPHIC

fig. 92

— 10 Yr Treasury   — Apartment   — Retail   ---- Office   ········ Industrial   — Hotel

Cap rate trends over time with the 10-year Treasury rate as a guide.

Are cap rates swinging up or down? Take this risk into consideration as you plan, securing yourself against the worst-case scenario with an exit strategy that covers this risk.

Tenant Risk

Typically, a commercial property will have more than one tenant. In an office building, you might have several companies as tenants. How reliable are those tenants and how good is their stability and credit state? Will they be able to continue paying you rent? Tenants in fluctuating industries or start-up companies are riskier, due to the uncertainty of their future livelihood. On the other hand, a tenant like Best Buy or Walmart is a good bet, with low risk and a high stability factor.

If you have only one tenant, then you can easily go from 100 percent leased to 100 percent vacant. As with any investment, the way to mitigate tenant risk is to diversify. If possible, select tenants that span a number of industries and economies. Select a mix of large and small businesses. Diversifying in this way may mean that you will not always have 100 percent occupancy, but it also means that the loss of just one tenant won't affect your bottom line as much. As with so many things in real estate investing, there's a trade-off to consider.

If you purchased a property with an existing tenant, it's likely that you paid a premium for the length of their remaining term. If they had another three years on the lease, for instance, then you had three years of certain income. Investors like that certainty, and they pay more for a property that includes longer lease terms.

But the rollover from one lease term to the next presents a risk. You could lose the tenant altogether or the tenant could negotiate cheaper rent. It's part of your job as an investor to work with the tenants before you make the purchase and to plan ahead if lease terms are just about complete.

Leasing Risk

You have no control over whether you will be able lease your property or not. Maybe the property you own is not as good as the other properties in your area. Maybe you have an agent that's not very good, and after spending time and money they haven't been able to help you secure any tenants for the property. Or maybe the potential tenants looking at your facility can get better incentives and tenant improvement allowances from other places (it's a common amenity for owners to offer the tenant some allowances to make improvements to suit their business).

If you can't compete with what other properties offer, then you face the risk of vacancy. There are ways to mitigate leasing risk. Good buildings have been left vacant for months simply because the owners did not have enough capital on hand to offer the tenants the customizations they needed to make. Plan ahead with your financing so that you don't depend entirely on collecting rent for liquid capital. Keep enough in reserve, all the more so if you know that leasing risk is a high possibility in your market. Typically, commercial properties can take up to a year to find a new lessee. Negotiations and customizations take time, so be prepared for your vacant lease to remain vacant longer than you hoped.

Construction Risk

As with residential properties, whenever you have a commercial property that requires some work, you will inevitably encounter some level of construction risk. The scale of commercial construction risk is much higher than that of most residentials. You could face cost overruns that amount to hundreds of thousands of dollars. You could face delays that hinder your attempts to secure tenants. You could encounter unexpected issues like an environmental concern that has to be surveyed and resolved before you can continue.

In Toronto, one condo's construction was delayed because of severely cold weather. The harsh winter kept construction crews from working outside, and equipment could not be operated due to risk of malfunction in the cold. Although construction crews attempted to account for cold-weather delays, the owners of the seventy-six-floor condo unit claimed they had 50 percent more cold-weather days than they had planned for. In one wintry cold spell, crane operators were delayed five days because the temperature never climbed above safe levels. Although construction companies do strive to make up time by working through the weekend, these delays end up being a fact of life in cold-weather climates.

Cold-weather delays are just the tip of the iceberg. There are many reasons for construction delays and simply no way to predict them all. This is why commercial projects attract higher returns from their riskier profiles.

Chapter Recap

» Commercial real estate investments are not for beginner investors, but you should know what's available if you want to achieve the next level of investment returns.

» The scale of commercial investments prohibits many investors from pursuing these assets, but crowdfunding measures can provide experience and access to even the most inexperienced investor.

» All commercial property is designed to make a profit.

» The principle of highest and best use determines the potential returns you stand to make from a commercial property.

» Different analysis metrics are required to understand the health and viability of commercial investments.

» Significant risks come with commercial investments, usually greater and more pronounced risks than with a residential property.

| 15 |
Working with Partners

Alone we can do so little. Together we can do so much.

— HELEN KELLER

Nikola Tesla immigrated to the United States from his home country of present-day Croatia in 1884 with just a few cents to his name. But he had an idea. He was convinced that the electric model of direct current (DC) was inefficient, expensive, and dangerous. You couldn't send electricity long distances, and power plants were required every mile or so just to power the homes around them. Tesla was steadfastly confident that a new model of electric current, alternating current (AC), was the way of the future. And with his innovative idea for an AC motor, he could create electricity and send it thousands of miles down cables. He just needed someone to believe in him.

At first, Tesla approached his hero, the inventor Thomas Edison. Edison hired Tesla to work in his company, using Tesla's engineering skills to improve the DC motors he was running. Tesla tried again and again to talk to Edison about AC electricity, but Edison's name and reputation were tied to the direct current model. Tesla resigned and started his own laboratory to work on his AC motor. He still needed help, however, to see his ideas come to pass.

Tesla was eventually approached by George Westinghouse, a brilliant engineer and inventor himself, who saw the genius of Tesla's designs and offered to buy all his AC patents on the spot. He even threw in a licensing deal in which he would pay two dollars and fifty cents for each horsepower generated by AC motors. If that licensing contract hadn't been ripped up by Tesla later in life, it would have earned him trillions in residual income. Westinghouse and Tesla made an exceptional partnership. Together, they worked hard to demonstrate that AC current was the superior choice for electricity. Edison felt so threatened by their teamwork that he launched a vicious smear campaign that involved electrocuting live animals in front of crowds in an attempt to discredit their efforts. Edison even helped design a new means of capital punishment, the electric chair, but suggested that they use Tesla and Westinghouse's AC current to power it—a snide attempt by Edison to further portray AC power as dangerous and crude. In the end, however, the Tesla and Westinghouse duo won over the world with a fantastic display of AC power at the World's Fair in Chicago in 1893 (the same fair that introduced the Ferris wheel and Cracker Jack). Alternating current became the world's choice for electricity, and Edison's DC model faded into obscurity.

I tell this story to introduce a point. What if you were presented with an unimaginably good opportunity, but you didn't have the means to capture it? Tesla saw the incredible opportunity that alternating current would provide to the world, but he couldn't do it alone. Only after partnering with George Westinghouse was he finally able to take advantage of the potential returns. Most of this book has been covering what it means to be a solo investor, but I want to show you the power of working with other investors.

Working with others means the ability to pool your capital and your skills, split the work, and invest in larger properties or more properties than you could on your own. Do it right and you can reap tremendous rewards that would be unattainable to a solo investor. Do it wrong, however, and you'll face serious downsides. You could end up feeling used or let down or cheated. Some partners claim unfair compensation for the sweat equity they poured into the property. This can ruin relationships and future partnerships if not treated in the correct way. In this chapter, I want to show you how to invest with others in a safe, synergistic manner that improves everybody's results.

Why You Should Invest with Partners

You'll find that, in the top echelons of real estate investors, almost all of them invest in groups or with partners. Why is it that investors with millions and millions in personal capital still want to take the risk of investing with other people? We talked about the risk factors of investing. Introducing someone else into a deal can present serious risks, and yet time and again, the wealthiest investors choose to work with someone else rather than on their own for the majority of their deals. Why?

Pooling Resources

As a single investor, you are limited by your time, your money, and your experience. There is a limit to the number of investments you can pursue, the money you can put into them, and the knowledge you need to work those investments. But when you partner with others, you immediately throw their money, time, and knowledge into the mix.

Neil Hector the Real Estate Investor (yes, we're back to visit him again) has gained some experience and had some huge wins in the last fifteen years of his investment portfolio. It's time to start looking at bigger opportunities. But the problem is that although he's got $500,000 in available capital, he's still looking at the same market, sorting through the same ads, churning through the same basic returns that he's always seen. With time, Neil has developed a thicker skin regarding risk, and he'd like to check out some investments tilted toward the opportunistic end of the spectrum. One idea that he's had in the back of his mind is investing in some land and building his own multifamily property. The population in Las Vegas is aging, and Neil has the foresight to see a greater need for retirement homes and assisted living centers to cater to that growing portion of the population. There is one problem, though. Actually, several problems. Neil doesn't have nearly enough capital to start a project like that, and with his lack of experience, finding a lender that will help finance the investment will be difficult.

But Neil's experience has also put him in contact with several other investors in the Las Vegas area. He has been having lunch every week with two of his good buddies, John Mender the Financial Lender and Eric Trist the Venture Capitalist. Neil floats the idea of his latest opportunity and brings up the possibility of the three of them doing some work together. Neil has the experience with real estate in Las Vegas, and Eric and John both have contacts with reputable developers and architects. Eric even has investments in an architectural firm that has recently won some awards for their designs. Together, they have millions in capital, and John's and Eric's prestige should allow the trio of investors to secure a meeting with any lender in the tri-county area. This could become a reality for Neil!

One of the side benefits of working with others is the extra set of eyes that look over your investments. Better analysis always leads to better returns. An extra partner or two to look over the deal can help identify areas of risk and reward that might go unnoticed by the solo investor.

Dividing Tasks

I've found that when two or more partners work together, they each bring skills to the table that can complement the others' skills quite well. One person's natural ability to work with people makes them an excellent negotiator and manager for the contractors working on the project. Another has the handyman skills needed to walk through a property and know exactly what needs to be done to maximize the potential returns on that investment.

In my investment journey, I work with other investors to maximize my reach and potential returns. My own skill of analysis makes me the ideal candidate to do all the evaluating needed to identify the most profitable deals before we make an investment. My partners who are more well versed in development, design, leasing, and sales will own other tasks they're better suited for.

Partners can also divide up the jobs that need to be done on the investment. Some tasks are labor-intensive and take a lot of work to get right. Others can be done behind the scenes and require less time. Having partners allows you to divide up the work so that the complicated tasks don't all fall to one person but get spread out over the partnership.

Mitigating Risk

One of the highlights of working with others is the ability to spread around your risk. What do I mean by that? Let me show you.

fig. 93

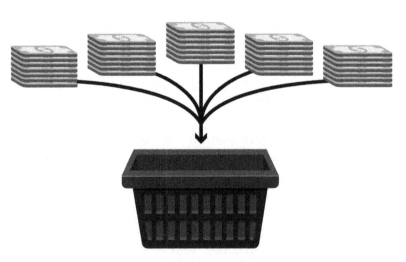

Your capital available for investing and your one investment opportunity.

The money depicted in figure 93 represents all the capital you have for your investment. As a solo investor, your capital will go into this one basket, which represents the property in which you make your investment. Even with the most careful analysis and operations, everything can still go south. What if the worst-case scenario happens and disaster befalls your investment?

fig. 94

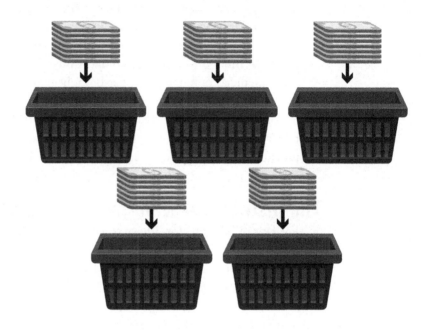

But look what happens when you invest with partners (see figure 94), taking that same capital and spreading it out over several different properties. The total amount of your investment is the same, but your capital is spread evenly over several properties, lowering the risk with each individual investment. Even if one or two properties catastrophically collapse, you aren't financially ruined.

Expanding Investment Range

For a month, Neil Hector has been meeting with John and Eric, his investing partners, hashing out the details of their large development plan to build a state-of-the-art senior care facility. But in their meetings, Eric and John have talked about some warehouses they've been looking at, and they've asked Neil to go over the financials of the property. Neil went into this partnership without any explicit intentions beyond working on the senior care facility, but John's and Eric's ideas and networks have exposed him to more opportunities than he otherwise would have had.

That's the power of investing with others. The range of your investments widens exponentially as you add more partners to your group. It is rare to find single investors looking at commercial properties, because it's so unlikely for a single investor to find a deal they could afford. But because working with partners provides greater purchasing power, there is greater access to a wider variety of deals. Neil's investing opportunities have grown since he's been working with John and Eric. The "Investor Avengers," as they've come to be known, are much more powerful as a group than they ever were on their own. John and Eric's investing exposure had been limited to more traditional things like stocks, businesses, and other financial products. Neil has brought them into a new world of real estate investing, while he benefits from their greater capital and network opportunities. On their own, they were reasonably successful, but since they've joined forces, they've been able to look at investments with greater potential returns than they had seen in the past.

The Distribution Waterfall Framework

For fans of Neil Hector, I have some good news and some bad news. The bad news is that Neil's uncle has passed away. Neil found out that he has inherited the entire estate. He flies to Portland to deal with the house and collect his uncle's belongings. The good news? In the midst of cleaning, Neil happens upon a unique thumb drive, which he opens up on his laptop. On the thumb drive he discovers that his uncle has some Bitcoin stashed away. At the going rate, Neil's find is worth close to $700,000! Wow. Now, what is Neil to do with this newfound stash of cash? After he calms down from the initial shock and begins to think logically and long term, Neil decides to give Eric and John a call to suggest they go forward with the plan Neil's been dreaming about for a long time—he's going to make a big investment in commercial real estate.

Neil, Eric, and John agree. Their partnership makes sense, and the selected project shows promise for great returns. There is, however, one more obstacle to overcome before they can all sign on the dotted line: how to divvy up the proceeds. The project is going to require a total of $10 million in equity. Neil offers $500,000 of his newfound wealth to invest, which is just 5 percent of the total needed. But that's where Eric and John fill the void. They each contribute $4.75 million, making up the other 95 percent needed for the investment.

This property has been Neil's baby from the beginning. He found it, he studied it, and he believes he knows how to run it. He knows how to make it profitable for all parties involved. He's only funding 5 percent of the investment, but he'll be doing most of the operations work once they take possession. When that first rent check comes in, how will the three partners fairly split the money, so that everyone feels compensated appropriately for what they put in? How do you measure invested capital against invested time and energy?

One of the most common ways to break up the payments in a fair way is to use the distribution waterfall. It's a way of equitably assigning the profits and cash inflow in a way that accounts for the work and capital each investor contributes to the investment. This can be a complicated concept, so I'm going to lay out a simplified version. Let's begin by envisioning a test case in which each investor contributes an identical amount of labor but differing amounts of capital (figure 95).

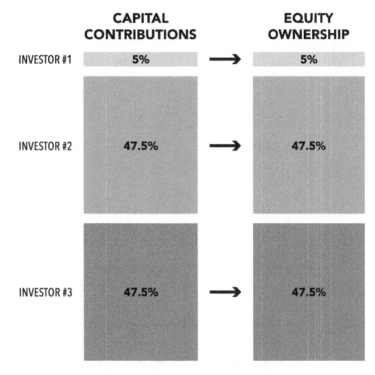

fig. 95

Assuming equal amounts of work, each investor should get the proportion of the investment they put in.

If the trio invested in a property that was truly passive, requiring no work at all, they would simply split the profit distributions according to what they invested. If Neil invests 5 percent, he only gets 5 percent of the profit distributions, including profits from rent and from appreciation in property value at exit. That's fair, right? The problem is that investors rarely put in the same amount of work. Much more common is a partnership where one partner does most of the work while the others simply contribute capital. Neil's not putting in a lot of money, but he's going to end up doing almost all of the work. For a while, acquiring and optimizing this property is going to be Neil's full-time job. Now, take a look at figure 96.

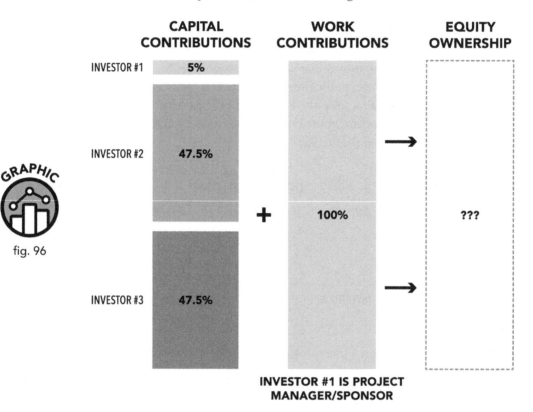

GRAPHIC

fig. 96

When the work done is unevenly distributed, how do we determine a fair distribution of the payments?

Given the enormous work contribution of Investor #1, it doesn't make sense for him to be forever relegated to receiving only 5 percent of the proceeds. But how do we incorporate the contribution of his blood, sweat, and tears? Before we get into the mechanics of the distribution waterfall, let's clarify some terms.

» **Sponsor:** Typically, in a partnership, the sponsor does all the work while the others write checks. The sponsor may also be known as the general partner, or GP. Normally, the sponsor puts in 1–10 percent of the total capital needed. In our case, this is Neil. He's contributing the majority of the time and energy needed to run the project but supplying just 5 percent of the capital.

» **Preferred Return**: Before the trio decides how to divide up the money, they need to identify the minimum return they are willing to accept on their invested capital. This is called the preferred return. In other words, this is the lowest total amount of profit that all three investors are willing to tolerate from this investment, given what they know about its risks and opportunities. Until the investment does better than this preferred return rate, the distributions will remain strictly proportional to the capital outlay of each investor—5 percent of all returns will go to Neil and 47.5 percent each to Eric and John. Depending on the nature of the investment, the market, the market cycle, and the parties involved, the preferred return rate will generally fall in the 6–12 percent range. Less risky investments in less risky markets by experienced and proven sponsors will have lower preferred returns. Riskier investments in riskier markets by less experienced and unproven sponsors will have higher preferred returns.

» **Carried Interest**: We are using the word "interest," but this is not related to debt service costs. Carried interest, sometimes referred to as "promoted interest," is the return that is above and beyond the return they get from their capital investment—and this is the portion of the profits given to the sponsor for their sweat equity. In other words, this is incentive money. It's an extra portion paid to the investors who put in the work and show proven results for their efforts. It's kind of like a performance measure for the sponsor. If Neil's efforts lead to an investment that returns more than the preferred return rate, he receives a bonus amount, the carried interest.

Incentives and Interests

How does a distribution waterfall give everyone an incentive and a payout equal to what they put in? To answer that, imagine a waterfall flowing over a cliff. The water spills over into a pool, which gradually fills up. Once that water reaches the top, a new waterfall spills over the edge into a new pool down below. Each pool has to be filled before the water spills over into the next pool. John and Eric, by virtue of contributing 95 percent of the investment capital, are sitting by the first pool, sucking up the majority of the water (the returns) that spills over from the source (the main waterfall, the investment). Where is Neil in this scenario? He has his straw in the second pool (one down from Eric and John). Neil will only get little sips until he can get more water flowing from the source to overload the first pool and create a greater flow to the second pool, his pool. In the investing world, those pools are known as "hurdles."

The first hurdle is the preferred return, or the initial minimum return that investors demand from the property. If it's a shallow pool—a lower preferred return—then it will be easier to fill up.

Once the project begins demonstrating better performance than the preferred rate, new measures kick in to pay each investor.

These new performance measures will affect the payments to John and Eric, but they won't be upset because their pool is already full and overflowing. They're getting more than they would have had they invested elsewhere. They're happy. But Neil is hungry. The more efficiently the property runs, the more money the sponsor gets. This is Neil's incentive to work hard. These "pools" and "hurdles" are also known as tiers of investment (I know; there are a lot of terms). With each tier that is surpassed, a new payment structure is established. Let's explore some of the payment structures commonly found in tiered waterfall compensation setups.

There are other hurdles that can be written into deals, such as the targeting of specific IRR and cash multiple goals. You may recall that we learned about those metrics and others in chapter 6.

For the sake of brevity (and your sanity), I'm only going to cover the most basic two-tiered distribution waterfall structure here in the *QuickStart Guide*, but I have a thorough explanation of three- and four-tiered waterfall structures in my course, which you can access at **www.clydebankmedia.com/rei-assets**.

Two-Tiered Distribution Waterfalls

The simplest waterfall is a two-tiered structure. In this case, there is one initial hurdle that the investment performance must meet before triggering the carried interest payouts for the project sponsor in the deal.

Although the tiers drastically affect the returns for the sponsor, the payouts also change for the other parties involved in the deal.

To see how this works, let's dig deeper into the property deal being pursued by Neil and his Investor Avengers:

The property will cost $50 million, thus Neil will have control over an investment that's worth one hundred times the initial capital he's put in (talk about leverage!). This is the benefit of a partnership in action, opening access to a deal that's much bigger than one could otherwise afford.

The preferred return on this $50 million property is 10 percent, because that's how much Eric and John expect to make from their best alternative investment options. As long as the property is returning less than 10 percent, the proceeds are distributed according to the percentage invested in the property.

Neil – $500,000 (5% of the total investment)
Eric/John – $9.5 million (95% of the total investment)

So long as the investment is bringing in less than the 10 percent preferred rate, all proceeds are split evenly according to capital allocation. For every dollar returned, Eric and John each take 47.5 cents and Neil gets a nickel. If the total return never exceeds this 10 percent hurdle, then Neil will never see the carried interest from the project—why should he expect to get a bonus if the project did not even meet the minimum return hurdle?

This is where the tiered structure incentivizes Neil to operate the investment well. Once the investment return exceeds 10 percent, the distribution of the returns above and beyond the 10 percent changes. The Investor Avengers agreed to a 70/30 split after that hurdle was passed. For every dollar that comes back *after the preferred return is met*, Neil takes a 30 percent bonus in carried interest. The remaining 70 percent is divided according to their initial investment's gain (5 percent to Neil and 47.5 percent each to Eric and John). Notice that Neil still gets his share of the returns from his initial investment as an investor, but only Neil takes part in the carried interest as the project sponsor.

To visualize this payout structure (and how each partner fares during the deal), take a look at the spreadsheet shown in figure 97. You will see how the payouts change after the preferred rate is met. For the sake of simplicity, let's imagine that the preferred return hurdle is equal to the investment returning $100,000 in monthly cash flow. If the returns are less than that, Neil gets just 5 percent of the money coming in. But if he knuckles down and works hard, his compensation just goes up and up.

PARTNER RETURNS BEFORE AND AFTER PREFERRED RATE				
	Initial Investment	For Returns < $100,000/mo	For Returns > $100,000/mo	
		Preferred Return	30% Carry Interest	70% Rest of Returns
Neil	5.0%	5.0%	100%	5.0%
Eric	47.5%	47.5%	0%	47.5%
John	47.5%	47.5%	0%	47.5%

GRAPHIC

fig. 97

SCENARIO 1		
	Initial Investment	$80,000/mo Return
		Total Return to Each
Neil	5.0%	$4,000/mo
Eric	47.5%	$38,000/mo
John	47.5%	$38,000/mo

SCENARIO 2				
	Initial Investment	$150,000/mo Return		
		First $100K	$15K (30% of $50K)	$35K (70% of $50K)	Total Return to Each
Neil	5.0%	$5,000/mo	$15,000/mo	$1,750/mo	$21,750/mo
Eric	47.5%	$47,500/mo	$0/mo	$16,625/mo	$64,125/mo
John	47.5%	$47,500/mo	$0/mo	$16,625/mo	$64,125/mo

A simplified two-tiered waterfall with Neil as the sponsor partner of the deal.

Neil is clearly going to make much more money if he can improve the bottom line of the investment's returns. Per the two scenarios illustrated in figure 97, if the property makes, let's say, only $80,000 per month, then Neil takes just $4,000 per month of that incoming cash. But if he bumps up the monthly income to $150,000 by filling vacancies and increasing the rent, he pockets 30 percent of those additional returns of $50,000 per month, in addition to his 5 percent on the remaining 70 percent of additional returns. His total take would grow to $21,750 per month.

The amounts and percentages of the tiers all relate to the experience of the investor, the returns the investors could make otherwise, and the level of difficulty in the investment. If the investment had a very high preferred rate of 25 percent, the sponsor would probably not be able to reach the hurdles and would therefore not see any significant returns from their work. On the other hand, if the hurdles were too low, the other investors would feel that they were not adequately capturing the investment's potential and that the sponsor lacked adequate incentive to boost returns. As long as everyone is satisfied that they have their interests and experience covered in the waterfall payout structure, each member will be happy with the returns measured out according to what they contribute, whether time, capital, or sweat equity.

Chapter Recap

» Investing with partners has more upsides than downsides, so long as you do it right.

» Each partner contributes more than just money; they bring experience, capital, and skills to the investment project.

» Even though partner contributions are different, there are ways to equalize the payments made to compensate for each partner's contributions.

» The distribution waterfall incentivizes each partner and provides fair compensation throughout the life of the investment.

Conclusion

Congratulations on taking your first step as a real estate investor. The concepts you have learned in this book will provide a smoother path forward for your investing endeavors. Though we have covered a great deal on this topic, you have many lessons ahead of you and hopefully a great many successes as well. And even if you encounter a few failures along the way, I hope you will take them in stride, as a natural part of the process.

The point of this book is to introduce you to real estate investing, to give you an in-depth *first* look at a concept that most people only understand at a superficial level. I have endeavored to strip away the myths and misguided information that surround this topic, so that I might offer you the unfiltered truth. We have explored some new concepts, new ideas, and new strategies, all of which will undoubtedly lead to new possibilities and new questions.

And the first question is usually "Now what?"

My advice is to begin with what you can do right now. Look for investments that are compatible with your current level of risk tolerance, skills, and resources. If you do not have the capital or the means to explore direct investing, start investing in real estate through REITs or crowd investing platforms, where you can get started with a few hundred dollars. There are many ways to succeed in real estate. Some will focus exclusively on single-family home rentals, and others will focus on fix and flips, multifamily, or commercial plays. You don't need ten hammers to drive down one nail. You just need to find one good strategy to follow. Your very first investment should lead to the next, and so on. Minimize the cost of your early mistakes by starting small and conservatively building up to bigger and better investment opportunities.

I also advise looking down the road to see what investments you'd like to make in the future. Would you be interested in a multifamily property? Does commercial investing appeal to you? What are your personal investment goals? Are you aiming for a particular net worth target? Do you want to turn dilapidated properties into marketable Class B real estate? Your personal goals and your vision for yourself as a real estate investor will help you decide what types of investments you should pursue. For example, if you'd like to invest in a small multifamily property, I advise looking at duplexes, triplexes and fourplexes to get a sense of the rents and property values. If you're interested in commercial properties that require more capital, then you will want to become an expert on raising capital for that market. You will also fare better if you can find partners to invest with you.

The investor you are today will be radically different from the investor you will be in five, ten, or twenty-five years' time. You will likely find that your risk tolerance evolves as you learn more about the rewards and dangers associated with various investments. Your resource pool, network, and working knowledge will surely grow and open the door to a broader pool of opportunities. I recommend establishing ambitious but attainable goals for yourself, goals that are appropriate for where you are right now. And then, chart a course toward where you would like to see yourself in the future. For example, if your goal is to collect rents from a total of one thousand tenants, then your plan of action will involve acquiring a multitude of rental properties, and adding an apartment complex or two to your portfolio may help you reach your goal faster.

For more help in your journey, don't forget to check out the course I've put together for beginner investors. This bonus is just for you, the reader, to give you a resource that goes beyond the scope of this book. Visit www.clydebankmedia.com/rei-assets.

Finally, I would like to stress the importance of taking action. Your commitment to read this book, take the course, and otherwise further your study is commendable, but it is your willingness to take action that will ultimately define your success. And I want to push you toward action. The information in this book and in my course is meant to be used, not shelved. Thousands of my students began their journey in real estate investing using the principles I teach, but only because they took the first step. I encourage you to do the same. And do it today.

The door is now open; I hope you'll step through it, and I look forward to seeing you on the other side.

REMEMBER TO DOWNLOAD YOUR FREE DIGITAL ASSETS!

 **Advanced Rental Income Analyzer**

 Advanced Fix & Flip Property Analyzer

 Due Diligence Checklist

 Wholesaling Deal Analyzer

TWO WAYS TO ACCESS YOUR FREE DIGITAL ASSETS

Use the camera app on your mobile phone to scan the QR code or visit the link below and instantly access your digital assets.

 SCAN ME

or

www.clydebankmedia.com/rei-assets

VISIT URL

Appendix I

Tools

I've assembled an entire catalog of tools and spreadsheets to use for analysis and calculations. Visit **www.clydebankmedia.com/rei-assets**.

Analysis Tools

Here is a list of online real estate resources and tools I've gathered over the years through my own study or as recommended by my students and colleagues.

Property Value Research
» PropertyShark.com
» Zillow.com
» Trulia.com
» Redfin.com
» Realtor.com
» Homesnap.com
» DealMachine.com
» Propstream.com (not free but powerful)

Rental Rates Research
» Zillow.com
» Rentometer.com
» Zumper.com
» RENTCafe.com
» RentJungle.com
» Onerent.co

Market Data and Research
» Zillow Research
» Mashvisor.com
» Federal Reserve Bank of St. Louis Economic Research (fred.stlouisfed.org)

- » General Neighborhood Research
  - AreaVibes.com
  - NeighborhoodScout.com
  - Neighborhoods.com
  - Niche.com
  - WalkScore.com

- » Crime Research
  - FBI's Uniform Crime Reporting Statistics (https://www.fbi.gov/services/cjis/ucr)
  - SpotCrime.com
  - CityProtect.com

- » Natural Disasters Research
  - FEMA.gov

- » School Research
  - GreatSchools.org
  - Niche.com
  - NeighborhoodScout.com
  - National Center for Education Statistics (nces.ed.gov)

General Online Real Estate Resources
- » BiggerPockets.com
- » ConnectedInvestors.com
- » ActiveRain.com
- » Mashvisor.com
- » HousingWire.com
- » Realtor.com

Foreclosures, REOs, Short Sales, Auctions, etc.
- » Hubzu.com
- » Foreclosure.com
- » RealtyTrac.com
- » ForeclosureListings.com
- » Xome.com
- » RealtyBid.com
- » BankForeclosuresSale.com
- » WilliamsAuction.com
- » Auction.com
- » HomePath.com by Fannie Mae

- » HudHomeStore.com (HUD foreclosures)
- » FDIC.gov/buying/owned/

Fix and Flip Information
- » Rehabvaluator.com
- » FHA 203(k) Renovation Loans
- » FlippingJunkie.com
- » InvestFourMore.com
- » ThisOldHouse.com
- » FundThatFlip.com

Finding Contractors
- » Angie's List (angieslist.com)
- » Houzz.com
- » HomeAdvisor.com
- » Thumbtack.com
- » Porch.com
- » National Association of Home Builders (nahb.org)

Property Management Apps
- » Tellus
- » Stessa
- » RentTrack
- » AppFolio
- » Buildium
- » ApartRental

Tenant Prospecting
- » RentMarketplace.com
- » MyRental.com
- » RentPrep.com
- » Experian.com
- » MySmartMove.com
- » Zumper.com
- » E-renter.com

Commercial Real Estate
- » LoopNet.com
- » Reonomy.com
- » RealMassive.com
- » Spacelist.co

- » Brevitas.com
- » CommercialCafe.com
- » QuantumListing.com
- » Biproxi.com
- » Commercial Real Estate Exchange (crexi.com)
- » OfficeSpace.com
- » Commercial Brokers Association (commercialmls.com)
- » Ten-X.com
- » TotalCommercial.com
- » Imbrex.io
- » Catylist.com
- » Truss.co
- » CityFeet.com
- » Digsy (getDigsy.com)
- » 42Floors.com
- » Rofo.com
- » SquareFoot.com
- » TheBrokerList.com

Popular Real Estate Podcasts

- » The Real Estate Guys
- » The Flip Empire
- » Real Estate News for Investors with Kathy Fettke
- » Flipping Junkie
- » Apartment Building Investing with Michael Blank
- » Creating Wealth with Jason Hartman
- » Best Real Estate Investing Advice Ever with Joe Fairless
- » Wheelbarrow Profits: Multifamily Real Estate Investment
- » BiggerPockets
- » Old Capital

Crowd Investing Platforms

- » Fundrise
- » CrowdStreet
- » RealtyMogul
- » Yieldstreet
- » Equity Multiple
- » Rich Uncles
- » PeerStreet
- » iFunding

- » Patch of Land
- » Prodigy Network
- » RealtyShares
- » RealCrowd
- » Fund That Flip

These previously mentioned sites are those I prefer for performing analysis here in the United States. My students, from 179 different countries, have recommended favorite sites in their respective markets.

Real Estate Sites for Canada

- » Realtor.ca
- » Rew.ca
- » Remax.ca
- » Craigslist.ca

Real Estate Sites for the UK

- » Rightmove.co.uk
- » Zoopla.co.uk

Real Estate Sites for Latin America

- » Zapimoveis.com.br
- » Vivareal.com.br
- » Pisofincasa.com

Real Estate Sites for the UAE

- » Dubizzle.com
- » PropertyFinder.ae

Real Estate Sites for India

- » IndiaProperty.com
- » 99acres.com
- » Housing.com
- » Magicbricks.com

Real Estate Sites for China

- » Fang.com
- » Dichan.com
- » Juwai.com

Real Estate Sites for South Africa

» PrivateProperty.co.za

» Property24.com

Other Real Estate Markets

» Realtor.com/international

» EuropeanProperty.com

» Suumo.jp

Calculators

Everybody seems to offer some version of a mortgage calculator. Here are some of my online favorites. I've also included an amortization schedule calculator as a downloadable resource for you.

» MortgageCalculator.org

» Zillow.com/mortgage-calculator (This is convenient when using Zillow for your back-of-the-envelope analysis. It also includes current interest rates for accurate calculations.)

» usbank.com/home-loans/mortgage/mortgage-calculators

Appendix II
Rental Property Analysis Case Study

I'd like to show you what it looks like to analyze a rental property from start to finish. In order to do that, I've chosen a specific market to focus on, Las Vegas. Although everything I do in this illustration is focused on Las Vegas, you can simply substitute your own selected market and perform the analysis in tandem with me.

One of the tools I've included as a bonus with this book is a *Back-of-the-Envelope Rental Analyzer* spreadsheet. You can download your copy at **www.clydebankmedia.com/rei-assets**. I suggest filling in the spreadsheet as you go through this case study to get a feeling for how the BOE (back-of-the-envelope) analysis works.

Throughout the book, we followed the exploits of a fictional hero, Neil Hector the Real Estate Investor. Since Vegas is his backyard, let's continue walking alongside him on his journey to find the perfect rental investment property.

Neil has done his homework. He's been looking all over Vegas, taking weekend drives and visiting parts of his city he never knew existed. During the course of his extensive research, he's come across an interesting part of town that looks appealing, just west of the downtown core. The amenities are great, transit options are good. It offers shopping, dining, and a friendly environment for kids. But is it the right location for an investment?

A good way to evaluate a property, Neil recalls, is to compare one property against others in the area. He wants to know, were he to invest in a property here, what competing properties would look like. How much rent is being charged? How long does it take to fill vacancies? What are recent sales figures? How many properties are on the market at any given time? Using a site like Zillow.com., Neil has access to a world of information without driving anywhere. Using his back-of-the-envelope spreadsheet, Neil begins to pull together data on some other properties in the area to get a sense of what's available. For comparison, he needs to look at three different elements: the properties for sale right now, recent sales figures for homes sold, and the rental figures of other properties. Neil narrows his search to include only listings by agents (he doesn't want the distorted owners' selling prices, which can be overpriced and skew his results) and he sets filters for number of bedrooms, days on the market, and square footage. He wants everything to be compared on an apples-to-apples basis (figure 98).

GRAPHIC

fig. 98

	LISTED FOR SALE					
	Property #1	Property #2	Property #3	Property #4	Property #5	Avg. of Listed
Address	217 Nunca St.	5204 Longridge Ave.	6116 Evergreen Ave.	6548 Bourbon Way	5400 Del Monte	-
Include? (1=yes, 0=no)	0	1	0	1	1	-
S.F.	1391	1364	1208	1308	1428	1367
# of Rooms	4	3	3	3	3	3
# of Baths	2	2	2	2	2	2
Lot Size	7840	7405	6969	6098	6534	6679
Year Built	1968	1961	1960	1963	1965	1963
Days on Zillow	3	10	5	20	24	18
Listing Price	$165,000	$148,000	$179,999	$149,900	$149,600	$149,167
$/S.F.	$119	$109	$149	$115	$105	$109.29
Date Last Sold	Jul 12	Oct 10	Mar 13	Jul 12	Sep 07	-
Last Sold Price	$87,000	$78,250	$40,000	$67,000	$89,000	$78,083
Last Sold $/S.F.	$44	$40	$20	$34	$45	$33
Curb Appeal (1=worst, 5=best)	3.5	3	1.5	1.5	1	1.8
Fixtures	4	2.5	1.5	1.5	1	1.7
Work Needed (1=least, 5=most)	2	3.5	4.5	4	1	2.8

Different properties are currently for sale in the area; for illustrative purposes we are showing only a handful of properties, but in practice it is beneficial to have more options to evaluate.

Some of the information is easy to find, like the square footage and when the property last sold. Some of it is subjective and based on Neil's assessment of the pictures in the listing. At the bottom of the spreadsheet in figure 98, we see that Neil has had to make some assumptions about the property. For example, if the curb appeal isn't so hot and wouldn't be attractive to renters, then Neil assigns it a 2. If the fixtures in the home look relatively new and usable, then he might assign a 3.5 or a 4 in that category. All of this data collection will provide him with an average for properties in the area, so he knows how his property compares.

Look at 217 Nunca Street, which is Property 1 in the spreadsheet. It's a four-bedroom, two-bath, 1,391-square-foot home that's listed for sale at $165,000. Using the listing on Zillow, Neil inputs the lot size (7,840 square feet), the year it was built (1968), and when it was last sold (July of 2012). Going by the pictures accompanying the Zillow listing, the front yard looks clean and well-maintained, but it's nothing special. It won't need a lot of work. Neil gives it a 3.5 for curb appeal. The interior looks great, with new fixtures in the kitchen, bathrooms, and bedrooms. He assigns the fixtures a 4. Making the property appealing to renters won't require a lot of money, maybe just a coat of paint, some landscaping work, and minor repairs throughout. He assigns a 2 in the "work needed" category.

Neil pulls out several examples and fills in the rest of the spreadsheet. As he begins to gain a sense of what the typical house in the area looks like, he spots some outliers within his data set, specifically Property 1 and Property 3. Property 1 (217 Nunca Street) is slightly larger, with four bedrooms, and the other houses all have three bedrooms. Property 3 (6116 Evergreen Avenue) is a smaller home (smaller than average) but the asking price (and price per square foot) is remarkably high. The property would also need a significant amount of work, compared to other properties in the area. This could be a case where the owner is delusional and wants to ask for more than the house is worth. In the field just below the address, Neil assigns a "0" to both Property 1 and Property 3, which removes them from consideration.

On the right-hand side in the "Avg. of Listed" column, the spreadsheet tallies up each cell and creates an average for the neighborhood. In this area, the average home has 1,367 square feet of living space, is currently listed for less than $150,000, doesn't offer a lot of curb appeal, and requires a moderate level of work before being put on the market.

The next step is to select properties that have sold (again, by agent) in the last thirty days. If there isn't enough data, you can always extend the timing to sixty or ninety days, because the market isn't going to change that much within a three-month period.

	RECENTLY SOLD						
	Comp #1	Comp #2	Comp #3	Comp #4	Comp #5	Avg. of Recently Sold	Avg. of Listed
Address	6340 Bristol Way	6320 Garwood Ave.	5621 Idle Ave.	6317 Bannock Way	200 Newcomer St.	-	-
Include? (1=yes, 0=no)	1	0	1	1	1	-	-
S.F.	1274	1453	1250	1208	1365	1274	1367
# of Rooms	3	3	3	3	3	3	3
# of Baths	2	1.75	2	1.75	2	1.9	2
Lot Size	6098	6098	5662	6534	9148	6861	6679
Year Built	1961	1963	1955	1961	1976	1963	1963
Date Last Sold	Mar 16	Mar 16	Mar 16	Mar 16	Feb 16	-	-
Last Sold Price	$137,000	$120,000	$129,000	$129,000	$155,000	$137,500	$149,167
Last Sold $/S.F.	$108	$83	$103	$107	$114	$108	$109
Curb Appeal (1=worst, 5=best)	2	3	4	3	5	3.5	1.8
Fixtures	4.5	3	5	5	3	4.4	1.7
Work Needed (1=least, 5=most)	2	5	1	1.5	2	1.6	2.8

GRAPHIC

fig. 99

	Avg. of Recently Sold	Avg. of Listed	Listed/Sold
S.F.	1274	1367	107%
# of Rooms	3	3	100%
# of Baths	1.9	2	103%
Lot Size	6861	6679	97%
Year Built	1963	1963	-
Date Last Sold	-	-	-
Last Sold Price	$137,500	$149,167	108%
Last Sold $/S.F.	$108	$109	101%
Curb Appeal (1=worst, 5=best)	3.5	1.8	Listed properties are uglier and older
Fixtures	4.4	1.7	
Work Needed (1=least, 5=most)	1.6	2.8	Needs more work

Five different properties that have sold within the last thirty days. Although for illustrative purposes we show only five comparable properties here, the more you can find the better your analysis will be.

Neil chooses five properties that have recently sold and fills in the same data as in the previous step (figure 99). You can, for instance, see that Property 1, 6340 Bristol Way, a 1,274-square-foot home, sold for $137,000 and had three bedrooms, two bathrooms, and a lot size of 6,098 square feet. Again, Neil spots the outliers quite easily. As he calculates the data for Property 2, he notices that it needs a lot of work. The previous owners, it seems, tried to start renovations, but abandoned them halfway through and sold the place "as is." This could skew results, so Neil sets Property 2 at "0" (below the address) to exclude it from the analysis.

On the right-hand side again, under "Avg. of Recently Sold," the spreadsheet does the work and tallies up the average for all the properties he's selected for comparison. It also conveniently brings down the averages from the previous step, so Neil has a side-by-side comparison of the homes for sale right now and the homes that have already sold. On average, asking prices are $149,000, but homes are selling for almost $12,000 less at the final sale. That's an 8 percent difference, but in such a small sample size it's tough to determine whether that average differential will accurately reflect the broader market average. Neil can also see that the average home sold had three bedrooms, 1,274 square feet, moderate curb appeal, and functioning fixtures. But the homes that were sold in the past three months are nicer than what's advertised right now. Current listings, on average, are uglier on the outside, older, and need a lot more work. Neil notes that this means there could be room for discounts on the purchase price.

In the last step, Neil uses the same source to find properties that are advertising for tenants right now. This will give him a good sense of the competition, if he goes ahead with the investment.

Please note that if there aren't enough properties to analyze, you can always expand the map to widen the search area, as long as you remain in the same general vicinity.

RENTAL COMPS							
	Comp #1	Comp #2	Comp #3	Comp #4	Comp #5	Avg. Rental Comps	Avg. of Listed
Address	1053 Neil Armstrong Cir.	5124 Lytton Ave.	7910 Palace Monaco Ave.	3601 Sanwood St.	8117 Redskin Cir.	-	-
Include? (1=yes, 0=no)	1	1	1	1	1	-	-
S.F.	1214	1314	1423	1345	1374	1334	1367
# of Rooms	3	3	3	3	3	3	3
# of Baths	2	2	2	2.5	2	2.1	2
Lot Size	5662	7752	3920	2613	3920	4773	6679
Asking Rent	$1,150	$1,000	$1,200	$1,100	$1,099	$1,110	-
Curb Appeal (1=worst, 5=best)	3	1.5	4	3	3.5	3	1.8
Fixtures	3	2.5	4	4	4.5	3.6	1.7
Work Needed (1=least, 5=most)	1.5	2.5	1	1	1	1.4	2.8

GRAPHIC

fig.100

Properties in the area that are currently advertising for renters. Again, the larger the pool of good data, the better.

Neil finds properties that are looking for renters, and again he can draw an average by inputting several elements into his spreadsheet. It looks like average rentals are collecting $1,110 a month in a 1334-square-foot home with three bedrooms and two bathrooms. The data from the listed properties have been brought down to show a side-by-side comparison (figure 100).

What are the assumptions that Neil collects from this simple analysis? First, he determines that he could reasonably expect rent somewhere between $1,000 and $1,200 per month. The property might need some work to achieve that level of rent, because these properties tend to look a little nicer than what's for sale right now.

The Analysis

Neil has a sample size sufficient to show what this market looks like for rental properties. His selections give him a good understanding of the options right now and how they compare to neighboring properties. But in order to complete his analysis, he must select one potential property that really catches his eye.

Q: Go back to figure 98 and look at the properties listed there for sale. Which one stands out to you?

"Wow, these are some pitiful options," thinks Neil as he looks at the properties. These homes are old, they feel tired and gloomy, and they don't seem to offer any appeal. Except one. The first property, 217 Nunca Street, seems promising. Even though he excluded it from the averages, it looks pretty good compared to the rest. It offers an extra bedroom, the lot size is bigger, and it wouldn't require much work to be ready for renters.

Let me summarize what Neil has input here in the figure 101 spreadsheet, along with the results that were returned. First, he set the proposed rental income at $1,200, which could be quite conservative given that he'll be offering an extra bedroom compared to other houses in the market, and the whole property is in a relatively nice condition. He's allowed for $2,500 in renovations to attract top-quality tenants. He has a goal to sell the property after seven years for $220,000, which allows for reasonable growth in the Las Vegas market. Neil wants to invest 20 percent of the purchase price and finance the rest, so to purchase the property his costs would be $34,000.

How well does Neil expect this investment to perform? For one thing, he's expecting an internal rate of return of 24.8 percent, because he's using debt to help finance the project, which is well above the target he set out to find. The yield looks promising and the cash multiple tells him that for every dollar he invests, he'll make $2.82 back. But is it the best property he could choose as an investment? To compare, let's look at another property on his list, Property 2 at 5204 Longridge Avenue (figure 102).

GRAPHIC

fig.101

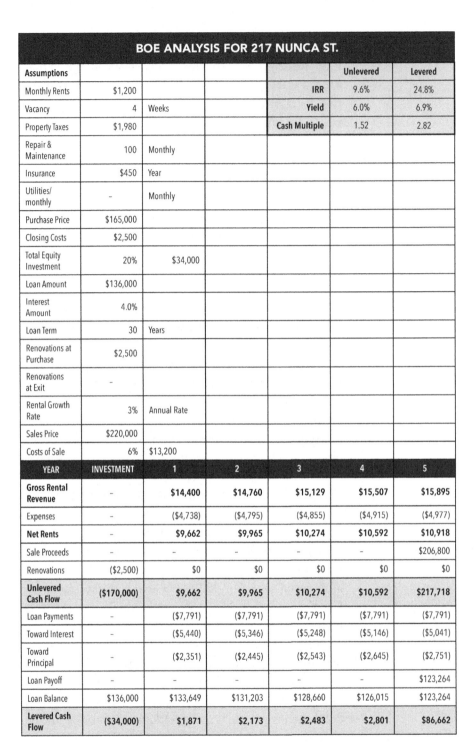

BOE ANALYSIS FOR 217 NUNCA ST.						
Assumptions					**Unlevered**	**Levered**
Monthly Rents	$1,200			**IRR**	9.6%	24.8%
Vacancy	4	Weeks		**Yield**	6.0%	6.9%
Property Taxes	$1,980			**Cash Multiple**	1.52	2.82
Repair & Maintenance	100	Monthly				
Insurance	$450	Year				
Utilities/ monthly	–	Monthly				
Purchase Price	$165,000					
Closing Costs	$2,500					
Total Equity Investment	20%	$34,000				
Loan Amount	$136,000					
Interest Amount	4.0%					
Loan Term	30	Years				
Renovations at Purchase	$2,500					
Renovations at Exit	–					
Rental Growth Rate	3%	Annual Rate				
Sales Price	$220,000					
Costs of Sale	6%	$13,200				
YEAR	**INVESTMENT**	**1**	**2**	**3**	**4**	**5**
Gross Rental Revenue	–	$14,400	$14,760	$15,129	$15,507	$15,895
Expenses	–	($4,738)	($4,795)	($4,855)	($4,915)	($4,977)
Net Rents	–	$9,662	$9,965	$10,274	$10,592	$10,918
Sale Proceeds	–	–	–	–	–	$206,800
Renovations	($2,500)	$0	$0	$0	$0	$0
Unlevered Cash Flow	**($170,000)**	$9,662	$9,965	$10,274	$10,592	$217,718
Loan Payments	–	($7,791)	($7,791)	($7,791)	($7,791)	($7,791)
Toward Interest	–	($5,440)	($5,346)	($5,248)	($5,146)	($5,041)
Toward Principal	–	($2,351)	($2,445)	($2,543)	($2,645)	($2,751)
Loan Payoff	–	–	–	–	–	$123,264
Loan Balance	$136,000	$133,649	$131,203	$128,660	$126,015	$123,264
Levered Cash Flow	**($34,000)**	$1,871	$2,173	$2,483	$2,801	$86,662

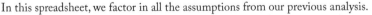

In this spreadsheet, we factor in all the assumptions from our previous analysis.

BOE ANALYSIS FOR 5204 LONGRIDGE AVE.						
Assumptions					**Unlevered**	**Levered**
Monthly Rents	$1,100			**IRR**	9.7%	24.8%
Vacancy	4	Weeks		**Yield**	5.6%	4.8%
Property Taxes	$1,764			**Cash Multiple**	1.53	2.89
Repair & Maintenance	100	Monthly				
Insurance	$450	Year				
Utilities/ monthly	–	Monthly				
Purchase Price	$148,000					
Closing Costs	$2,500					
Total Equity Investment	20%	$33,100				
Loan Amount	$132,400					
Interest Amount	4.0%					
Loan Term	30	Years				
Renovations at Purchase	$15,000					
Renovations at Exit	–					
Rental Growth Rate	3%	Annual Rate				
Sales Price	$220,000					
Costs of Sale	6%	$13,200				

YEAR	INVESTMENT	1	2	3	4	5
Gross Rental Revenue	–	**$13,200**	**$13,530**	**$13,868**	**$14,215**	**$14,570**
Expenses	–	($4,429)	($4,485)	($4,542)	($4,600)	($4,659)
Net Rents	–	**$8,771**	**$9,045**	**$9,327**	**$9,615**	**$9,911**
Sale Proceeds	–	–	–	–	–	$206,800
Renovations	($15,000)	$0	$0	$0	$0	$0
Unlevered Cash Flow	**($165,500)**	**$8,771**	**$9,045**	**$9,327**	**$9,615**	**$216,711**
Loan Payments	–	($7,585)	($7,585)	($7,585)	($7,585)	($7,585)
Toward Interest	–	($5,296)	($5,204)	($5,109)	($5,010)	($4,907)
Toward Principal	–	($2,289)	($2,381)	($2,476)	($2,575)	($2,678)
Loan Payoff	–	–	–	–	–	$120,001
Loan Balance	$132,400	$130,111	$127,730	$125,254	$122,679	$120,001
Levered Cash Flow	**($33,100)**	**$1,185**	**$1,460**	**$1,742**	**$2,030**	**$89,125**

GRAPHIC

fig.102

Here are the key assumptions that have changed in this calculation: the property is slightly smaller and is less marketable than the Nunca Street home. He could conservatively estimate $1,100 rent, but that might be high. It will take a lot more work to get this property ready for tenants, so he has allowed for $15,000 for major repairs. He plans on selling and hopes to get $220,000 for the property in seven years. Look at the difference in the returns. The IRR is similar at 24.8 percent, the yield is less appealing at 4.8 percent, and his cash multiple is nearly identical at 2.89. The projected returns are slightly worse, and with all the extra risks he'll assume in renovating this house, it is looking less attractive than the Nunca Street property.

In a matter of minutes, Neil could work out the projected returns he'd make from a rental in this area. He's also got a good indication of where he could make some improvements. For instance, if he is able to attract some good tenants at Nunca Street and collect $1,300 in rent, then his cash multiple will increase to 3x. Maybe the market will do well, and he can sell the home for $240,000 in seven years. In that event, his cash multiple will go up to nearly 3.55, giving him $3.55 back for every dollar he invests. By playing with his assumptions, Neil can develop some very clear expectations (and ambitious hopes) with regard to how well his investment can perform in this area.

GET YOUR NEXT
QuickStart Guide™
FOR FREE

Leave us a quick video testimonial on our website and we will give you a **FREE *QuickStart Guide*** of your choice!

RECORD TESTIMONIAL   **SUBMIT TO OUR WEBSITE**   **GET A FREE BOOK**

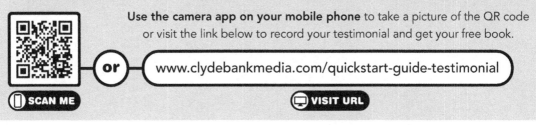

About the Author

SYMON HE, MBA

Symon He, MBA, is an author, best-selling online business and real estate investing course instructor, licensed real estate investor, and consultant based in Los Angeles. His training courses in real estate investing, deal structuring, and financial modeling have reached over 300,000 students in nearly 180 countries. His real estate investing expertise has been cited in numerous prominent media outlets including the *Wall Street Journal*, *Reuters*, *Forbes*, *CNBC*, and Skift. He has previously partnered with prominent finance companies such as RichDad.com.

Mr. He's consulting services help private real estate investors make smart acquisitions and profitably structure their deals. Previous to this line of work, he was the head of marketing analytics at the Panda Restaurant Group. Before that, he worked as a manager in the global M&A unit for Ingram Micro, a Fortune 80 company. Going even further back in his professional career, he worked on commercial real estate acquisitions at a private equity real estate fund, covering a wide range of asset classes across the western United States. Symon received degrees in computer engineering (magna cum laude) and economics (summa cum laude) from UC Irvine and received his MBA from Stanford University.

Symon is a cofounder of LearnBNB, a boutique consultancy and education blog that specializes in the home-sharing economy. Connect with Symon at www.learnbnb.com, explore the world of real estate investing on his blog at symonhe.com, or find Symon on LinkedIn.

About ClydeBank Media

We create simplified educational tools that allow our customers to successfully learn new skills in order to navigate this constantly changing world.

The success of ClydeBank Media's value-driven approach starts with beginner-friendly high-quality information. We work with subject matter experts who are leaders in their fields. These experts are supported by our team of professional researchers, writers, and educators.

Our team at ClydeBank Media works with these industry leaders to break down their wealth of knowledge, their wisdom, and their years of experience into small and concise building blocks. We piece together these building blocks to create a clearly defined learning path that a beginner can follow for successful mastery.

At ClydeBank Media, we see a new world of possibility. Simplified learning doesn't have to be bound by four walls; instead, it's driven by you.

Your World. Simplified.™

Glossary

Actuarial Tables
Spreadsheets of tables used to determine the probability of risk. Insurance companies input data points to assess the likelihood of risk and calculate insurance policy premiums from the results.

Amenities
The features of a location or building that make it appealing.

Amortization
The scheduled paying down of a loan over a period of time. A fully amortized loan schedule calculates the repayments to incorporate both the principal and interest payments to be repaid by the maturity date of the loan.

Anchor
A large, well-known retail store that draws in lots of consumer traffic, such as Walmart or Best Buy. Smaller stores situate themselves near these popular locations in the hope of skimming off some business for themselves.

Appreciation
The increase in the value of an asset over time.

Asset Class
A group of investments that behave in a similar fashion in the marketplace. There can be several types of investments within an asset class, but they all generally respond the same way to market conditions.

Balloon Payment
The final payment due at the end of a loan that is much larger than the scheduled repayments, common in short-term loans or commercial loans.

Capitalization (Cap) Rates
A real-estate-specific measurement for comparing two investments. The metric is the ratio of the net operating income and the initial cost to purchase the property.

Capital
The value of money and possessions used to produce wealth. In the real estate world, capital is money, raised through debt or provided by the investor.

Case-Shiller Home Price Index
A widely accepted method for measuring trends in the real estate market through the purchase and resale prices of single-family homes in nine major divisions in the United States. Through repeat sales, the index measures the price increases and decreases of these homes, standardized to the number 100 in January 2000.

Cash Multiple
A simple metric that calculates the cash going in and coming out of an investment. Cash flow is divided by the cash invested to determine the multiple, equating to the return an investor can expect for each dollar invested.

Commercial Real Estate
Real estate with the sole purpose of creating a profit, as opposed to creating a domicile for a tenant. Residential buildings with five or more units are classified as commercial property.

Commodity
A financial term that describes a tangible material that can be bought and sold and that holds inherent value.

Condotel

A condo hotel, also known as a condotel, operates as vacation rental properties. Individual units in the building are serviced by a reception desk and hotel management but can be owned by investors for primary use or to be rented out as hotel rooms, operated by the management of the building.

Contingency

Creating provisions, either as plans or in a contract, for a future event that is liable to happen but is not expected.

Density

Cities and counties place restrictions on the allowable uses of a defined parcel of land. Zoning laws measure floor space or housing units per land unit, which dictates the number of properties built in that area. As population goes up, zoning laws increase the allowable density, raising the number of units that can be built on that land.

Discount Rate

The interest rate investors use to determine the present value of the future returns they expect to receive with a conservative investment.

Diversification

An investment strategy to manage risk by mixing the types of investments in one's portfolio.

Economic Cycle

The standard, measurable cyclical movement of the market on a macro scale across the entire country.

Entitlements

Rights to develop raw land as granted by the governing entity, such as zoning, permits, road approval, utilities, and landscaping.

Equities

Shares held in the part ownership of a company.

Equity

The dollar amount of an investment that one would expect to receive if the asset was sold and all debts were paid off.

Federal Housing Administration

A U.S. federal government agency designed to protect housing standards and stabilize the mortgage market by providing home financing.

Financing

The process of securing funding for an investment.

Gentrification

The renovation and rebuilding of a deteriorated neighborhood, usually attracting higher-income residents.

Global Financial Crisis

The term for the 2007-08 housing bubble collapse that caused a global recession.

Gross Rent Multiplier

A "quick and dirty" metric to compare rental returns within a given market. The formula is the market value divided by the gross income for the year.

Hard Money Loan

A debt financed through a private lender outside of traditional banks or credit unions.

Homeowners Association (HOA)

A community-led organization that dictates and enforces regulations about that community. It can be based on a suburb, a condominium, or a planned development.

Inflation

The general increase in the price of goods and the decrease in buying power of a unit of currency over time.

Interest

A fee incurred by a debtor for the right to borrow money, paid over the life of the loan.

Internal Rate of Return

An analysis measurement that determines how efficient an investment is at making returns, excluding factors like inflation and external risks.

Last-mile zone

The stage of delivery from a facility or distribution center to the end user of the goods.

Leverage

The use of debt to finance the purchase of a property, thus increasing the potential returns from that investment.

Liability Insurance

The portion of an insurance policy that protects the holder of the policy against claims, payouts, and legal costs incurred if the property causes injury or harm.

Liquidity

The state of being capable of quickly turning an investment into cash.

Market

A specific system in which one commodity (in this case, real estate) can be bought or sold. Can also refer to a specific location, e.g., the Las Vegas market.

Market Cycles

The natural flow of real estate market conditions between recognizable states of recession, recovery, expansion, and hypersupply. See also *Economic Cycles.*

Multiple Listing Service (MLS)

A network of active listings accessible by licensed real estate agents. Public listing services sourcing data from the MLS often have limited information available.

Negative Leverage

The state in which the cost of borrowing money for an investment is more than the expected returns on that investment.

Net Migration

The flow of a population into a defined area, calculated as the number of people moving into the area less the number of people moving out.

Net Operating Costs

All costs involved in the maintenance and management of a property.

Net Operating Income (NOI)

The income generated by a property after all operational expenses are deducted.

Net Present Value

The calculation of the expected returns of an investment, translated into present-day dollar values, to determine an investment's viability.

Net Rental Yield

An evaluative metric using the annual rents divided by the property value of an investment, determined as a percentage.

Passive Income

Money that is paid to someone regardless of their involvement in the investment.

Permit

Approval for any work to be done to a property, given by the governing body overseeing the area.

Pocket Listing

A property for sale that is not publicly listed on any forums or websites.

Principal

The sum of money borrowed for an investment upon which the interest is calculated.

Private Mortgage Insurance (PMI)

An insurance policy that is designed to protect the lender in the event the borrower does not continue making scheduled repayments on a mortgage. PMI is required when the down payment amount is less than the agreed-upon percent value of the home, often set at 20 percent.

Property Manager

A professional person or service that oversees the daily operations of a property including tenants, maintenance, and marketing.

Refinance

A reevaluation performed by a lender to determine the new value of a property, often resulting in issuance of a loan at a lower interest rate according to the new value.

REIT

Real Estate Investment Trusts (REITs) are companies that operate real estate assets and allow investors to indirectly own a portion of those assets, often within a portfolio of several properties.

Residential Real Estate

Real estate with the sole purpose of housing tenants. Residential buildings with more than five units are not included in this category. See *Commercial Real Estate*.

Returns

The cash flow that is due to the investor from an investment, in the form of monthly rent or as a lump sum after the sale of the investment.

ROI (Return on Investment)

A measure used to determine the money an investor can expect to receive in proportion to the capital invested in a property, expressed in the form of a percentage.

Rule of 72

A simple, back-of-the-envelope calculation to determine the length of time (in years) an investment will take to double in value.

Seasoning Period

The length of time a borrower must hold a loan before the lender will consider a refinancing of the investment.

Secondary Property

A property one owns that is not their primary residence, often used for investment purposes.

Subprime Mortgage

A mortgage issued to borrowers who do not meet the required credit score minimum to qualify for a conventional mortgage.

Tenant

The person or business that occupies a property that is rented from the owner of the property.

Term

The length of time until a loan is fully repaid or due back to the lender.

Vacancy

A property that is unoccupied or without a paying tenant.

Zoning Map

A map determined by a municipal council to show the districts of a region and the approved use of those districts.

References

Aksenov, Pavel. 2013. BBC. September 26. https://www.bbc.com/news/world-europe-24280831.

Altman, Josh. 2015. *It's Your Move: My Million Dollar Method for Taking Risks with Confidence and Succeeding at Work and Life.* HarperOne.

Armstrong, James. 2015. *Global News.* March 10. https://globalnews.ca/news/1874635/harsh-winter-leading-to-delays-on-construction-sites/.

ATTOM. 2019. *ATTOM Data Solutions.* June 6. https://www.attomdata.com/news/market-trends/flipping/q1-2019-home-flipping-report/.

Aziz, Remon Fayek. 2013. "Ranking of delay factors in construction projects after Egyptian revolution." *Alexandria Engineering Journal* (52)3: 387-406.

Coleman, Andre. 2019. *Pasadena Weekly.* November 7. https://pasadenaweekly.com/pasadena-adopts-states-tenant-protection-act-in-special-midnight-meeting/.

Elliott, Josh K. 2019. *Global News.* August 21. https://globalnews.ca/news/5788050/condo-illegal-micro-apartments-new-york-city/.

Garfield, Leanna. 2016. *Business Insider.* October 10. https://www.businessinsider.com/americas-first-shopping-mall-is-now-micro-apartments-2016-10.

Licea, Melkorka. 2016. *New York Post.* January 17. https://nypost.com/2016/01/17/poor-door-tenants-reveal-luxury-towers-financial-apartheid/.

Liker, Jeffrey K. 2003. *The Toyota Way: 14 Management Principles from the World's Greatest Manufacturer.* McGraw-Hill Education.

Mendelson, Aaron. 2015. *Southern Californica Public Radio.* September 10. https://www.scpr.org/news/2015/09/10/54285/la-scrubs-away-30-million-square-feet-of-graffiti/.

Muntean, Pete. 2020. *WUSA9.* January 1. Accessed January 2020. https://www.wusa9.com/article/news/local/amazon-hq2-groundbreaking-2020-plans/65-5a572835-f71a-4f6b-b2a8-515c2e192ca8.

Penrose, James F. 1994. "Inventing Electrocution." *Invention & Technology*, Spring: Volume 9.

Purdy, Chase. 2017. *Quartz.* April 25. https://qz.com/965779/mcdonalds-isnt-really-a-fast-food-chain-its-a-brilliant-30-billion-real-estate-company/.

Romano, Jay. 2001. *The New York Times.* September 9. nytimes.com/2001/09/09/realestate/avoiding-pitfalls-in-buying-raw-land.html.

This American Life. 2008. Episode 355: *The Giant Pool of Money.* New York, May 9.

Index

Notes

EXPLORE MORE BEST-SELLING
QuickStart Guides®

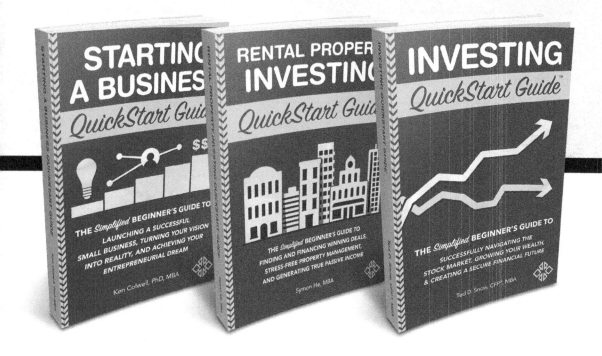

TO EXPLORE ALL TITLES, VISIT:

www.clydebankmedia.com/shop

CLYDEBANK MEDIA

QuickStart Guides™

PROUDLY SUPPORT ONE TREE PLANTED

One Tree Planted is a 501(c)(3) a non-profit organization focused on global reforestation. With millions of trees planted every year, ClydeBank Media is proud to support One Tree Planted as a reforestation partner.

Every dollar donated plants one tree and every tree makes a difference!

Learn more at www.clydebankmedia.com/charitable-giving or make a contribution at onetreeplanted.org

Made in the USA
Columbia, SC
20 January 2022

54517255R00174